Contributions to Economics

The series *Contributions to Economics* provides an outlet for innovative research in all areas of economics. Books published in the series are primarily monographs and multiple author works that present new research results on a clearly defined topic, but contributed volumes and conference proceedings are also considered. All books are published in print and ebook and disseminated and promoted globally. The series and the volumes published in it are indexed by Scopus and ISI (selected volumes).

More information about this series at https://link.springer.com/bookseries/1262

Bernadette Andreosso-O'Callaghan • Serge Rey •
Robert Taylor
Editors

Sustainable Development in Asia

Socio-economic, Financial, and Economic Perspectives

Springer

Editors
Bernadette Andreosso-O'Callaghan
Department of Economics, Kemmy Business School
University of Limerick
Limerick, Ireland

Ruhr Universität Bochum
Bochum, Germany

Serge Rey
Social Sciences and Humanities College
University of Pau and Pays de l'Adour, E2S UPPA
Pau Cedex, France

Robert Taylor
School of East Asian Studies
University of Sheffield
Sheffield, UK

ISSN 1431-1933 ISSN 2197-7178 (electronic)
Contributions to Economics
ISBN 978-3-030-94678-4 ISBN 978-3-030-94679-1 (eBook)
https://doi.org/10.1007/978-3-030-94679-1

This Springer imprint is published by the registered company Springer Nature Switzerland AG
The registered company address is: Gewerbestrasse 11, 6330 Cham, Switzerland

Acknowledgements

Many thanks are due to Technological University Dublin (TUDublin) for hosting the 25th Euro-Asia International Research Seminar in May 2021, which, for the first time ever, was reduced to being an online event. In particular, we are most grateful to Dr Lucia Morales (TUDublin) for her unbounded enthusiasm and efficiency in organizing the event and in particular all technical aspects. We are very grateful to Professor Jacques Jaussaud and to all his team at the Université de Pau et des Pays de l'Adour (France) for their continuous support. Finally, we would like to thank all the authors for their participation in this project.

Contents

Contributors

Bruno Amman Department of Management, Université Toulouse 3 Paul Sabatier, Toulouse, France

Bernadette Andreosso-O'Callaghan Department of Economics, Kemmy Business School, University of Limerick, Limerick, Ireland
Ruhr Universität Bochum, Bochum, Germany

Marion Besse Kedge Business School of Bordeaux, Talence, France

Long Bui Thanh Department of Accounting, School of Economics and Law, Tra Vinh University, Tra Vinh, Vietnam

Emmanuelle Cargnello-Charles Institut d'Administration des Entreprises – Université de Pau et des Pays de l'Adour (Laboratoire de Recherche en Gestion (LiREM), Pau, France

Isabelle Franchistéguy-Couloume Laboratoire de Recherche en Gestion (LiREM), Université de Pau et des Pays de l'Adour (UPPA), Pau, France

Shiho Futagami Graduate School of International Social Sciences, Yokohama National University, Yokohama, Japan

Madi Intesar College of Business, Technological University Dublin, Dublin, Ireland

Jacques Jaussaud Department of Management Sciences, Transitions Energétiques et Environnementales (TREE, UMR CNRS 6031), Université de Pau et des Pays de l'Adour (UPPA), Pau, France

Cuiling Jiang Kedge Business School, Bordeaux, France

Erja Kettunen Turku School of Economics, University of Turku, Turku, Finland

Julien Martine Japanese Language and Civilization, Centre de Recherche sur les Civilisations Orientales (CRCAO), University of Paris, Paris, France

Shuji Mizoguchi Yokohama National University, Yokohama, Japan

Lucia Morales School of Accounting, Finance and Economics, Faculty of Business, Technological University Dublin, Dublin, Ireland

Hiroyuki Nakamura Department of Management, Yokohama National University, Yokohama, Japan

Serge Rey Faculty of Law, Economics and Management, University of Pau (Université de Pau et des Pays de l'Adour – UPPA), Pau, France

Yan Tan Business School of Yulin Normal University, Yulin, China

Robert Taylor University of Sheffield, Sheffield, UK

Utai Uprasen Department of Economics, Pukyong National University, Busan, South Korea

Yang Yang College of ASEAN Studies, Guangxi University for Nationalities, Guangxi, China

Abbreviations

ACE	Accessibility Consortium of Enterprises
ADB	Asian Development Bank
AFC	Asian Financial Crisis
ANA	All Nippon Airways
ANAP	French acronym for Medico-social Healthcare Institutions
APAEC	ASEAN Plan of Action for Energy
ARDL	Autoregressive distributed lag
ARS	French acronym for Regional Health Agencies
ATIH	French acronym for Technical Agency for Information on Hospitalisation
BSC	Balanced scorecard
BU	Business units
COVID-19	Coronavirus infectious disease
CREF	French acronym for Contracts for the Return to Financial Sustainability
CSR	Corporate social responsibility
D&I	Diversity and inclusion
DGF	French acronym for global operating allowance
DPC	Diagnosis Procedure Combination
EBIT	Earnings before interest and taxes
ECB	European Central Bank
EMA	Environmental management accounting
ERP	Enterprise resource planning
ERPT	Exchange rate pass-through
ESF	European Social Fund
ESG	Environmental, social and governance
FFS	Fee-for-service
FIBS	Finnish Business & Society
FTAs	Free trade agreements
GDP	Gross domestic product

GFC	Global financial crisis
GHM	French acronym for diagnosis-related groups (DRG)
GHS	French acronym for Health Insurance Companies by Homogeneous Hospital Stay Group
GRI	Global Reporting Initiative
GVN	Government of Vietnam
HAD	French acronym for home hospitalisation
HPST	French acronym for Hospital Patient Health Region Act
HQ	Headquarters
HRD	Human resource development
HRM	Human resource management
ICF	International Classification of Functioning
ICF	International Classification of Functioning
IFAC	International Federation of Accountants
IIRC	International Integrated Reporting Committee (Renamed as the International Integrated Reporting Council IIRC)
IMF	International Monetary Fund
IP	Intellectual property
JEMAI	Japan Environmental Management Association for Industry
KPI	Key performance indicators
LOLF	French acronym for Organic Law on Finance Laws
MCO	French acronym for costs of medical, surgical, obstetric
MCOO	French acronym for medicine, surgery, obstetrics and dentistry
METI	Ministry of Economy, Trade and Industry
MFCA	Material flow cost accounting
MFI	Microfinance institutions
MITI	Ministry of International Trade and Industry
MNC	Multinational companies
MOEJ	Ministry of the Environment of Japan
NGOs	Non-governmental organizations
OECD	Organisation for Economic Co-operation and Development
ONDAM	French acronym for National Health Insurance Expenditure Target
PRC	People's Republic of China
R&D	Research and development
RKT	Reverse knowledge transfer
RMB	Renminbi
SARS-Cov-1	Severe acute respiratory syndrome coronavirus 1
SDG	Sustainable Development Goals
SEM	Social Enterprise Mark
SSR	French acronym for follow-up and rehabilitation care
T2A	French acronym for activity-based funding
UN	United Nations
VBP	Vietnam Bank for the Poor
VBSP	Vietnam Bank of Social Policies
VND	Vietnamese Dong

WB	World Bank
WISE	Work integration social enterprises
WITS	World Integrated Trade Solution
WU	Vietnam Women's Union

List of Figures

Chapter 5

Chapter 6

List of Tables

Introduction and Overview

Robert Taylor

Abstract This overview introduces the general context within which the topics of the following chapters may be viewed. Sustainable development is broadly defined, embracing natural capital and Environmental, Social and Governance (ESG) issues, especially in the light of the COVID 19 pandemic. Sino-American rivalry, manifested also in competitive infrastructure projects, is seen as impacting on sustainable development in Asia and the initiatives of the two countries are compared. The role of economic integration in ASEAN, particularly relating to digital transformation, is assessed.

Keywords Sustainable development · Environmental social governance · COVID 19

The following chapters, derived mainly from the revised versions of papers presented at the 25th International Euro-Asia Roundtable and Research Conference held in 2020 and 2021, focus on sustainable development, embracing also Natural Capital and Environmental, Social and Governance issues, as outlined below. Sustainable development was originally conceived of in the face of global warming, itself caused by carbon emissions, especially as the use of fossil fuels resulted in environmental degradation. Latterly, however, the term has been more broadly defined to embrace social justice and inequalities, whether in education, health provision, educational opportunity as well as human resource management directly related to employment and wider areas of corporate responsibility.

Thus it can be argued that climate change and environmental degradation have had a devastating impact on what may be defined as Natural Capital, thereby affecting all forms of human activity. Natural Capital which impacts on all areas of life has been undervalued; tolerable temperatures, air quality, drinkable water, suitable land for food production and a healthy thriving ecosystem are all under threat.

R. Taylor (✉)
University of Sheffield, Sheffield, UK
e-mail: r.i.d.taylor@sheffield.ac.uk

B. Andreosso-O'Callaghan et al. (eds.), *Sustainable Development in Asia*, Contributions to Economics, https://doi.org/10.1007/978-3-030-94679-1_1

The main regional concern of this book is Asia, an area where Sino-American rivalry is apparent. Given, however, the need for global action on sustainable development, there is the challenge of cooperation in, for example, corporate responsibility in pricing the costs of carbon emissions via the allocation of capital by financial markets (Armstrong, 2021).

This brings into focus the definition of Environmental Social Governance (ESG), whereby socially conscious investors may screen potential investments. Firstly, there are environmental criteria by which how a company performs as a steward of nature may be assessed. Secondly, social responsibilities form the basis on which relations with suppliers, customers and the local communities may be judged. Thirdly, governance covers such issues as a company's structural hierarchy, executive pay, auditing and internal controls. More specifically, environmental criteria include energy use, disposal of waste, pollution, natural resource conservation and treatment of animals. Social issues concern business relationships, working conditions and employee health and safety, in addition to stakeholder interests. Governance areas include legality, transparent accounting, avoiding conflicts of interest in choosing board members and preventing the use of political contributions to gain undue favours (Investopedia, 2021).

Sustainable development initiatives are taking place against a background of rivalry for global dominance on the part of the world's greatest sources of environmental pollution, China and the United States. Conflict between the two powers proceeds on a number of economic and political fronts. Globally, the COVID-19 crisis, with its impact on employment, health and increasing national debt, has brought a resurgence of national industrial policy. It is ironic that the United States, in seeking to curb China's power and constantly complaining about unfair Chinese state subsidies, is restoring what is, similar to Franklin Roosevelt's New Deal, essentially an industrial policy, at both home and abroad. While the United States' withdrawal from Afghanistan may seemingly present China with an unparalleled opportunity for influence, the situation is nevertheless fraught with danger. Militarily, the Chinese have in the past received assurances from the Taliban that Afghan territory will not be used as a staging ground for attacks within China by Uighur separatists but there is no guarantee that extremists will not use Afghanistan territory to regroup. There is, however, enormous potential for Chinese economic influence; China has already donated medical aid to Afghanistan as well as a solar power station. China has also become one of Afghanistan's largest trading partners. In addition, Afghanistan also offers China opportunities to fund infrastructure building and access industrial materials like lithium, iron and cobalt. This potential could, however, be negated if the Taliban victory leads to regional instability. Any unrest could disrupt China's Belt and Road programme, designed to finance and build infrastructure across Asia; at the same time local security could be jeopardized (Zhou, 2021).

To counter China's global economic influence, the Biden administration has resorted to an industrial policy at home and abroad. As a democratic alternative to China's loans to developing countries, America's build back better for the world plan will grant nations improved access to financing for low carbon projects, including wind farms and railways. Now hailed as a green Marshall Plan, its objective is to increase climate funding from multilateral development banks as well as the private sector (US-China Business Council News Overview, 2021b).

Similarly, there is emerging United States-EU cooperation to confront Chinese influence in both Europe and the Asia-Pacific. Currently 10 per cent of EU exports go to China and 22 per cent of the Union's imports come from that country. China's Belt and Road infrastructure project impinges on Europe from Asia and the EU is adopting offensive mechanisms to address its challenges. For example, the 2018 Europe-Asia Connectivity Plans offers security, trade and cultural alternatives. This is in tandem with the Indo-Pacific Industrial Initiative, launched in 2018 (Odgaard et al., 2020).

In spite of being perceived as a global threat to US predominance, China nevertheless faces enormous problems under the Natural Capital and ESG rubrics. China's environmental pollution impacts on every area of economic life. Observers have pointed out the importance of conservation by highlighting the linkage between biodiversity and human health. Human activity has degraded ecosystems and ecological barriers which limit disease transfer, resulting in the COVID 19 pandemic.

As an example of Chinese commitment to sustainable development may be cited China's streamlining of the administration of its 12,000 conservation areas under a unified protection system in 2018 (Guo et al., 2021).

Importantly, in attempts to reduce carbon emissions, China's new electric vehicle (NEV) sales have exceeded one million units for three consecutive years, with a ranking of first globally for three consecutive years. The use of these vehicles has been increasingly encouraged (US-China Business Council News Overview, 2021i). Moreover, representing the world's second largest economy and responding to global opinion, China's leaders have pledged to bring down the country's carbon emissions to a peak by 2030 and reach carbon neutrality by 2060. Structured rules for companies and provinces are being laid down to achieve these goals. Yet these policies and measures are to a degree vitiated by current increases in coalmining output (US-China Business Council News Overview, 2021f).

Simultaneously, China is facing demographic change, with a shrinking labour force, resulting in repercussions for social cohesion, health, education and human resource management. Because of the ageing of the population China faces a pension crisis, and raising the retirement age will only buy time. Pension provision is threatened because of a shrinking working age cohort and a rapidly declining birth rate. In response the Chinese government has pledged to lower the costs of childbirth, parenting and education by 2025. Couples may now have three children, an encouragement to increase the birth rate. These measures, however, will need time to take effect. In response, in the Fourteenth Five Year Plan, released in July 2021, the government aimed to expand coverage of the basic state pension insurance system managed by provincial authorities and encourage the growth of the occupational private pension sectors, according to a Nikkei report. (US-China Business Council News Overview, 2021h).

Working parents are nevertheless in any case facing the rising cost of education, especially extra private tutoring, even though the financial activities of the company providers have recently been curbed by the state authorities. In addition, at the same time ageing parents need to be supported. Likewise, general health costs have also increased, although private insurance has become more widespread. As in the provision of healthcare, there is a wide urban-rural quality gap in the field of education. Moreover a considerable personal income differential exists between the cities and the countryside, despite the fact that, according to an official source, the gap has been narrowing, as the per capita disposable income of rural residents reached 9248 yuan (about US $1426) in the first half of 2021, up 14 per cent year on year in real terms after deducting price factors (US-China Business Council News Overview, 2021c).

Such differentials are largely based on occupational statistics and the key to Xi Jinping's aim to end poverty and build a moderately prosperous society is the enhancing of technological skills. A current reflection of income inequality, again an urban-rural phenomenon, is the fact that the richest 20 per cent of the population earn ten times more than the poorest 20 per cent (US-China Business Council News Overview, 2021g). In recent decades urban labour intensive industries have been staffed by technologically unskilled rural migrants, but now enhanced skills for knowledge intensive sectors will be at a premium, given that China also falls behind other advanced economies in productivity, itself based on output and time factors. Knowledge workers require more sophisticated forms of control, as evidenced by the adoption of Western style human resource management, first utilized in Sino-foreign joint ventures but now increasingly present in native Chinese enterprises. In the knowledge intensive sector employees have more initiative and decision-making powers, especially in services, where understanding of information technology in dealing with clients is critical. This necessitates continual training, particularly necessary if rural recruits are to be inducted into the knowledge economy. Thus education and training, as always, may serve as instruments of social mobility, thereby helping to reduce social and regional inequality which threatens the national cohesion crucial if China is to compete successfully with the United States (Wang, 2020; Guo & Xiao, 2017).

The countries of Southeast Asia, in a context of Sino-American rivalry, also face, like China, similar problems relating to the depletion of natural capital and other hindrances to sustainable development. On a number of fronts China and the United States are competing for influence. The COVID 19 crisis has brought into sharp relief the poverty and overcrowding prevalent in many Asian cities. Given that the rapid roll out of the COVID 19 vaccine is seen as essential to contain the pandemic, China and the United States have been at pains to establish their credentials by promoting distribution of vaccines. In June 2020 Xi Jinping promised US $100 million for the distribution of vaccines mainly to developing countries. In order to close the gap with China the United States has already donated millions of vaccines to Southeast Asian countries (US-China Business Council News Overview, 2021a, 2021d, 2021e).

There was brief reference above to the link between biodiversity and human health. Such sustainable development challenges are apparent in Southeast Asia, the fastest growing economic region in the world, where there is need to match energy demand with green supply during transition to a lower carbon economy. However, even attempts at greener energy may involve costs. Hydropower is seen as a cleaner source than fossil fuels and yet dams in the Upper Mekong River Area have brought environmental costs, notably adverse effects on agriculture for energy exporters like Laos, Cambodia and Myanmar, the major beneficiary being China which has built eleven dams in the Upper Mekong area and is financing six more in Laos and Cambodia. China remains a major player regarding infrastructure in Asia via the One Belt One Road and Maritime Silk Road projects which belatedly the United States has sought to counter through its Indo-Pacific initiative launched in 2018 and the infrastructural Blue Dot initiative in cooperation with Australia and Japan. In addition, the EU is also adopting offensive measures to address the challenges posed by China's Belt and Road initiative. The 2018 Europe-Asia Connectivity Plan is one alternative, ranging across security, trade and cultural issues. Nevertheless ASEAN will determine the pace of sustainable development in the region. But currently the key obstacle to coordination among Southeast Asian nations is that sub-regional energy strategies are independently decided by individual countries (Han, 2021; National Bureau of Asian Research, 2021; Odgaard et al., 2020). What is required is action at ASEAN level to achieve a balance between economic development, sustainable energy use, social well-being and environmental sustainability.

A region wide sustainable development policy in Southeast Asia is constrained by the fact that its states are not economically integrated in the sense that EU countries are, and one indication of this is that progress has been slow in solving the problem of industry-induced haze across national borders. While at regional level ASEAN has succeeded in shaping a common environmental framework, to date the emphasis on consensus at regional level has proved inadequate to deal with immediate emergencies. The need is for more effective systems and procedures for environmental governance. A review of progress towards reducing carbon emissions indicates that to date renewables like solar and wind power have contributed a negligible amount to electricity generation. One alternative believed to have potential as a clean energy source is hydrogen which can be produced through fossil fuels, though unfortunately this produces some carbon emissions, or via renewables. There have been some tentative moves to explore the use of hydrogen; Japanese and Singapore scientists have been working together to promote the development of hydrogen as a clean fuel. Hydrogen policy was endorsed in the ASEAN Plan of Action for Energy (APAEC) in 2015. Nevertheless further investment is needed in a commitment to energy policy, whereby the use of hydrogen is promoted in transportation and industry. The electricity governance among ASEAN nations needs to be improved with better coordination at regional level. (Robinson & Koh, 2002; Han, 2021).

If progress towards sustainable development has been inhibited by a lack of consensus at regional level, similarly non-existent monetary union and slowly emerging political integration have been barriers to ASEAN's digital transformation, crucial for both greening the economy and building back from the pandemic (Gillispie, 2021).

At the end of 2020 the Asia-Pacific had 2.3 billion internet users, although millions still remained offline. A barrier to further internet consumer growth has been inadequate network infrastructure. Significantly, 65 per cent of all subscribers in the Asia-Pacific region are on 4G. One pioneer in 5G projects is South Korea, especially via the country's New Southern Policy Plus, and there are also roles to be played by the Korean ASEAN Infrastructure Fund and the Asian Development Bank in helping to promote national strategies in areas connected to digital development like enacting laws governing digital business activities and aiding the public and private sectors in adopting new technical standards (ibid.). Currently, digital transformation in Southeast Asia is potentially a legal minefield. What is required is a unified intellectual property (IP) system to guarantee protection for innovation, patents and commercialization, practices which are at present threatened by variation in national legal systems. No supranational Court of Appeal exists in ASEAN to resolve disputes and there is no final supranational appellate judicial body able to interpret or enforce a domestic IP law. In fact, the success of the ASEAN Economic Community will depend to a great extent on the rapid harmonization of IP norms and practices (Fowler, 2021).

Thus while the Asian region remains the scene of Sino-American rivalry, further integration under ASEAN represents the best hope of addressing the challenges presented by the pandemic and climate change.

In summary, while in popular parlance sustainable development has been conceived of in terms of reaction to carbon emission induced climate change, its remit is now seen as much wider, encompassing natural capital and ESG, that is, issues relating to both the physical environment and the conduct of industrial and service employers regarding their employees, stakeholders and clients. Moreover the link between biodiversity and human health has been highlighted by the COVID 19 pandemic. China and the United States, the greatest global polluters, are economic and political rivals. The Biden administration has sought to curb China's economic influence through a new industrial policy and a green Marshall Plan as well as via the Indo-Pacific Infrastructural Initiative, launched in 2018. China, however, is now suffering, as are other advanced economies, from an ageing population, with consequent implications for healthcare provision, in addition to resources for education and other demands of human resource management. Remedial action has been initiated through the provision of extended healthcare and enhanced educational opportunity, through which the knowledge economy and social mobility may be furthered. In turn, the reduction of social and regional inequality is key to maintaining the national cohesion necessary if China is to compete successfully with the United States. That rivalry is apparent in Southeast Asia where under ASEAN steps have been taken towards economic integration but a lack of political and monetary union has tended to inhibit concerted action on climate change, even though there have been belated moves, for example, in the development of hydrogen as an energy source. As pressing is the issue of digital transformation. There is a need for a regional IP system, guaranteeing protection. There are also national legal barriers, for instance, to interpretation and enforcement at the regional level.

The global and regional challenges presented by climate change and the COVID 19 pandemic form the context of the following chapters.

The following studies cover various areas within the overall remit of sustainable development and Natural Capital. A crucial issue not always adequately examined by scholars is addressed in Jiang's chapter on the Reverse Knowledge Transfer (RKT) of diversity management practices in multinational companies. Her case study of French subsidiaries in Singapore assesses how expatriates practise diversity management and the extent to which such experience is communicated to headquarters.

Futugami and Kettunen consider another aspect under the broad remit of Natural Capital, namely, measures to enhance the inclusion of the disabled in employment; they discuss the human resource development of such employees in Japan and Finland. Their chapter's conclusion indicates future challenges and implications for policy.

Morales and Andreosso-O'Callaghan study business as usual in Hong Kong amidst social unrest. Attempts by the CCP to attenuate the democratic rights and liberal values enshrined in the retrocession of the former colony to China in 1997 have sparked not always peaceful protests by Hong Kong demonstrators against the alleged violation of human rights, with social media playing a key part in the organization of protests. The chapter considers whether instability in Hong Kong will undermine its status as a major Asian financial centre.

Madi, Morales and Andreosso-O'Callaghan in their chapter examine China's connections with politically volatile Middle Eastern countries in the context of the conflict between the CCP's stated commitment to sustainable development and the continuing need for fossil fuels. It is suggested that in seeking to reduce coal dependency, the Chinese leaders are moving towards a new energy model based on oil.

Uprasen's topic is rising public debt in developing countries, occasioned particularly by measures directed against the COVID 19 crisis, an example being Thailand, with implications for the country's future economic growth. Nevertheless the findings indicate that a rise in total public debt contributes to economic growth. The conclusion, however, is cautious, given that the money is used to support consumption rather than contributing to productive sectors.

Morales and Andreosso-O'Callaghan in their chapter relating to the world's top five financial centres demonstrate that stock markets have been unsettled by significant levels of volatility, caused largely by such issues as the ongoing US-China trade war, the UK's divorce from the EU and social unrest in Hong Kong. Such volatility in financial markets is seen as having spillover effects across financial hubs. Significantly, the question is raised as to whether drops in retail, consumer services and transport businesses on Asian and Western stock markets could trigger a new global economic and financial crisis.

Financial perspectives continue as Thanh, Morales and Andreosso-O'Callaghan focus on gender imbalance, specifically the role of microfinance in empowering women in Vietnam. The study is supported by a sample of 351 women microfinance borrowers in the Mekong Delta and interviews conducted in financial institutions.

The role of the women's union is identified as assisting female economic independence.

Amann, Jaussaud, Mizoguchi and Nakamura stress the importance of environmental management and related adequate information systems in both the EU and Japan, particularly the latter, since much Japanese published research has not been accessed elsewhere. Environmental management reporting under the aegis of international bodies is assessed in addition to firms' approaches to the environment. Finally, they present cases of innovative firms in the field of environmental management accounting.

Cargnello-Charles, Franchisteguy-Couloume, Jaussaud, Martine and Nakamura compare hospital funding and management control systems in France and Japan, given the key issue of an ageing population which demands greater financial input. In-depth interviews provide data on how the nature of hospital funding in the two countries impacts on hospital management controls. The consequences of the COVID 19 crisis are also considered.

Finally, Tan and Yang's research indicates that the Chinese Renminbi (RMB) is an invoicing currency for Vietnam when the latter is importing goods from abroad. There are two main conclusions to the study. Firstly, the degree of intra-industry trade between Vietnam and China has been increasing. Secondly, while most of Vietnam's trading goods are of low quality relative to China, the years from 2001 to 2016 have seen improvement.

Thus the following chapters have been placed in context.

References

Armstrong, S. (2021, August 16). Making Asia Pacific financial markets fit for climate change. *East Asia Forum Weekly Digest.*

Fowler, P. N. (2021, July 1). *Intellectual property challenges in the ASEAN region.* Commentary from the Centre for Innovation, Trade and Strategy.

Gillispie, C. (2021, June 11). The Asia Pacific's digital transformation. What role can US – South Korea cooperation play. *National Bureau of Asian Research.*

Guo, L., Santamana, C., Meng, H., Davis, R., & Harwath, H. (2021, June 30). *Biodiversity in China: Conserving nature, securing the future.* Chatham House, Webinar.

Guo, S. H., & Xiao, M. Z. (2017). Is encouraging employees' belonging really a good thing? Waiguo Jingji yu Guanli. *Foreign Economics and Management, 39*(8), 40–55.

Han, P. M. (2021). *The role of hydrogen in ASEAN's clean energy future.* National Bureau of Asian Research, Essay from Asia EDGE.

Investopedia. (2021). Accessed 21 July 2021.

National Bureau of Asian Research. (2021, July 10). *Securing the Mekong Subregion's future through transition to renewable energy.* Essay from Asia EDGE.

Odgaard, L., Tellis, A. J., Szalwinski, A., & Wallis, M. (2020). *Europe's place in Sino-US Cooperation.* Strategic Asia.

Robinson, N., & Koh, K. L. (2002). Strengthening sustainable development in regional intergovernmental governance: Lessons from the ASEAN way. *Singapore Journal of International and Comparative Law, 6*, 640–682.

US-China Business Council News Overview. (2021a, June 4). Biden to share 80 million vaccine shots with world to match China. *Nikkei.*

US-China Business Council News Overview. (2021b, June 14). G7 set to agree green belt and road plan to counter China's influence.

US-China Business Council News Overview. (2021c, July 21). Income of China's rural residents up 14.1%. *Reuters.*

US-China Business Council News Overview. (2021d, July 27). Pentagon chief slams China while vowing deeper role in Asia. *Bloomberg.*

US-China Business Council News Overview. (2021e, August 6). China to provide 2 billion COVID 19 vaccines globally this year. *Xinhua.*

US-China Business Council News Overview. (2021f, August 17). China's state planner vows crackdown on projects with high energy use. *Reuters.*

US-China Business Council News Overview. (2021g, August 18). China eyes wealth distribution in push for common prosperity.

US-China Business Council News Overview. (2021h, August 20). China plans $1.72 billion national pension company. *Nikkei.*

US-China Business Council News Overview. (2021i, August 27). China's NEV market penetration rate at 5.4 per cent in 2020: Industry report. *Xinhua.*

Wang, X. B. (2020). New thinking regarding effective management of human resources in work units. *Zhongwai Jeyejia, 3*, 106–114.

Zhou, B. (2021, August 23). China stands ready to fill Kabul's void. *New York Times* International Edition.

Sustainable Development of Multinational Companies in Asia: Reverse Transfer of Diversity Management Knowledge to Headquarters

Cuiling Jiang and Marion Besse

Abstract For the sustainable development of multinational companies, one of the crucial issues for headquarters (HQ) is to value and integrate the knowledge acquired by expatriates during their international assignments. This chapter aims to investigate the Reverse Knowledge Transfer (RKT) of diversity management practices in multinational companies (MNCs). More specifically, we explore the factors that may hinder expatriates' willingness and engagement in the RKT. With the data collected in French subsidiaries in Singapore, by capturing how French expatriates perceive and practice diversity management while working in the French subsidiaries in Singapore, and what organizational supports have been put in place to ease the RKT, the findings reveal the expatriates' silence and the reasons behind the weak transfer of their diversity management knowledge to HQ. The results highlight the importance for both HQ and expatriates to pay attention to the reverse transfer of diversity management knowledge. Concrete policies and practices that foster RKT are outlined at the end of the chapter.

Keywords Diversity management · Expatriate · French subsidiaries · Reverser knowledge transfer (RKT) · Singapore · Sustainable development

1 Introduction

The concept of sustainability has generated the increasing attention in different domains, which is not only linked to environmental aspect, but also concerns the durability or continuity of business. Among the different key success factors to organizations, firm-specific knowledge is proved to be the resource of competitive

C. Jiang (✉)
Kedge Business School Bordeaux, Talence, France
e-mail: cuiling.jiang@kedgebs.com

M. Besse
Paris, France
e-mail: marion.besse@kedgebs.com

B. Andreosso-O'Callaghan et al. (eds.), *Sustainable Development in Asia*, Contributions to Economics, https://doi.org/10.1007/978-3-030-94679-1_2

advantages (Spender & Grant, 1996) that lead to organizational sustainability. In particular, when firms start to expand the business across borders, knowledge flows within multinational companies (MNCs) become extremely valuable (Crespo et al., 2014; Inkinen, 2016). Past research has pointed out that knowledge transfer within MNCs can enhance innovation (Phene & Almeida, 2008; Tsai, 2002), improve subsidiary performance (Fang et al., 2007), and facilitate the implementation of global strategies (Ambos et al., 2006). While it is common for HQ to transfer knowledge to foreign subsidiaries, more reverse knowledge transfer (RKT: from foreign subsidiary to HQ) exists and expatriates play the major role in the RKT process (Caligiuri & Bonache, 2016). Prior research argues that MNCs are often failing when it comes to acknowledge expatriates as key agents of knowledge transfer within the MNCs (Burmeister & Deller, 2016). We know little whether expatriates' knowledge has been systematically paid attention to by HQ. If the answer to the question is yes, how can expatriates' knowledge be integrated and benefit group-wide operations? If the answer to the question is no, what are the reasons that lead to the failure of knowledge transfer from expatriates to HQ?

This chapter aims to use French MNCs in Singapore as the research focus. We investigate how French expatriates in the Singaporean subsidiaries are willing to share their diversity management knowledge with HQ. We aim to enrich our understanding on expatriates' RKT and make the following contributions. First, our study comprehensively shows the picture of how French expatriates are involved in knowledge transfer from Singaporean subsidiaries to HQ, identifying the factors that may ease or hinder the RKT, and pointing out the relevant consequences. Second, Singapore provides an ideal context for our study, which is a city state that attracts more foreign direct investment in the association of Southeast Asia (ASEAN) and which has the highest level of cultural diversity in Asia. By investigating French expatriates in Singapore, we are able to see the richness of knowledge they gain in managing cultural diversity, and explore how HQ have integrated these valuable knowledges into global diversity management strategies. To the best of our knowledge, this is the first study that targets French companies' diversity management in Singapore.

The logics behind our research design that focuses on French MNCs in Singapore and the diversity management, are twofold. First, more than two thirds of French Investments in ASEAN are in Singapore (Embassy of France in Singapore, 2020). Around 800 French MNCs have set up the business in Singapore, such as ST Microelectronics (1st French employer in Singapore with around 5000 employees). Attracted by ease of doing business index (Singapore ranks No. 3 in anti-corruption in 2018, and ranks No. 1 in best business environment in the Asia Pacific and in the world in 2018), highly educated labor force, free trade zone of ASEAN, Singapore has successfully attracted foreign direct investments from different countries of origin. The increasing number of French firms in Singapore reveals the need to send expatriates to work in the subsidiaries. However, we have little knowledge on expatriate management in French subsidiaries in Singapore (Lakshman & Jiang, 2016) and expatriates' knowledge transfer. Meanwhile, Singapore has shown the ability to manage diversity, with the population composed of Chinese, Malays,

Indians, and all other nationalities. Furthermore, Singapore celebrates its multicultural heritage through embracing four official languages (e.g. Chinese, English, Malay, and Tamil) and different religions (e.g. Buddhism, Christianism, Islam, and Taoism). Working in Singapore allows each individual to practice diversity management to a great extent on a daily basis. To the best of knowledge, no studies have been conducted on the transfer of diversity management practices within MNCs in Singapore. Therefore, this study aims to address the gaps by giving answers to the two research questions: (1) how do MNCs interact with expatriates to create the transfer of diversity management knowledge and achieve the sustainable development? (2) what are the barriers that hinder expatriates' motivation in the transfer of diversity management knowledge and which may further inhibit MNCs from achieving sustainability?

2 Literature Review

2.1 RKT's Success Conditions

RKT starts from foreign subsidiaries to HQ, which is a complex process that requires the mechanisms to ensure knowledge creation, development, and sharing (Fey & Furu, 2008). As indicated by Gupta and Govindarajan (2000), during the RKT, the involvement of foreign subsidiaries in knowledge outflows to HQ varies, which is affected by two main factors. In order to well structure the factors that may affect RKT's success, we are going to discuss the impacting factors from the perspectives of organization (e.g. HQ) and employees (e.g. expatriates, subsidiary employees, employees at HQ).

2.1.1 From the Perspective of HQ

From the organizational perspective, variables such as organizational support (e.g. Burmeister & Deller, 2016), absorptive capability of HQs (e.g. Nair et al., 2016), repatriates' disseminative capability (e.g. Sanchez-Vidal et al., 2016), and the existence of transmission channels (e.g. Lazarova & Tarique, 2005), are found to affect knowledge transfer from foreign subsidiaries to HQ. Regarding organizational support, it can improve relationship between expatriates and HQ. By ensuring expatriate-organization fit and increasing perceived career and repatriation support, expatriates may develop a deeper commitment and be more likely to transfer their knowledge (Ye et al., 2021). In terms of the absorptive capacity of HQ, it refers to the ability of HQ in "recognizing the value of new information, assimilating it, and applying it to commercial ends" (Cohen & Levinthal, 1990, p. 128). Influenced by the "Not-Invented-here" syndrome (Gupta & Govindarajan, 2000), when subsidiary-level knowledge is context-based, which may not be directly relevant for HQ context (Oddou et al., 2009), the colleagues from HQ will show less interests to subsidiary knowledge. Concerning the availability of knowledge sharing channels, they have formal and informal ones (Ipe, 2003). On the one hand, the formal knowledge sharing channel refers to the planned learning activities, where organizations put in place meetings, conferences, forums, incentives, and even key performance indicators to promote knowledge sharing between subsidiaries and HQ. On the other hand, informal sharing channels refer to irregular and unwritten activities that invite expatriates to share knowledge with others occasionally (e.g. meals, communities, sport clubs). These social interactions are seen as privileged moments for knowledge construction (Noorderhaven & Harzing, 2009), which help to increase trust and communication between expatriates and domestic employees (Connelly et al., 2012).

2.1.2 From the Individual Perspective

From the individual perspective, expatriates play the crucial role in transferring subsidiary-level knowledges to HQ and colleagues from HQ are the knowledge receivers. Previous studies have pointed out that expatriates' disseminative capability and motivation to share knowledge (Minbaeva & Michailova, 2004) affect the effectiveness of RKT. As known, when the knowledge is explicit, it is relatively easier to transfer than the tacit knowledge, because explicit knowledge is codifiability. Furthermore, knowledge sharing requires efforts and time (Lazarova & Tarique, 2005). When colleagues from HQ show the low receptivity and enthusiasm to the subsidiary-level knowledge, either expatriates need to invest more time and energy to justify the valuableness of their knowledge to HQ, or they become demotivated to share knowledge. Furthermore, the quality of the relationship and the frequency of interaction between colleagues of HQs and expatriates should be considered. During the international assignment, expatriates and colleagues from HQ communicate mainly on work-related issues (e.g. reporting, performance evaluation). Besides work, fewer social and informal interactions take place due to the time difference, the different working contexts, and the busy schedule of each other. The relationship between expatriates and colleagues from HQ will then become weaker, which further reduces the knowledge conversion (Burmeister et al., 2018). In addition, it is necessary to pay attention to the relationship between expatriates and subsidiary employees, which may also affect expatriates' motivation and attitudes at work. When expatriates have poor relationship with host country managers and employees, this will ultimately affect expatriates' ability to learn, understand, and transfer the subsidiary-level knowledge (Wang et al., 2009).

2.2 Diversity Management and Expatriates

In recent years, diversity management has attracted considerable attention in international business. The MNC is a community of multilingual (Luo & Shenkar, 2006) where workforce diversity is strongly presented (e.g. religion, nationality, ethnicity, etc.). Therefore, MNCs need to develop and implement the specific programs, policies, and practices to manage diverse workforces effectively and to promote organizational equality (Nkomo & Hoobler, 2014). By promoting diversity within teams, MNCs are more able to understand clients' needs and will meet their expectations much more easily (Hewlett et al., 2013). Further, diversity can enhance creativity and innovation among team members. Research has well demonstrated that heterogeneous teams are more likely to be creative than homogenous ones, as team members have different backgrounds, mindset, and knowledge that help each other become more open-minded (Yadav & Lenka, 2020). As the report of McKinsey Company reveals, "for every 10% increase in racial and ethnic diversity on senior executive teams, earnings before interest and taxes (EBIT) rises 0.8%" (Hunt et al., 2015). Therefore, diversity management is not only beneficial for a company, but it is a "must-to-do" issue. Previous studies have shed light on diversity management, in terms of legislations, human resource management practices, but there is no particular attention paid to expatriates and their roles in diversity management. However, expatriates themselves represent the diversity, who gain valuable knowledge abroad, especially when it comes to managing diversity as they work closely with other cultures and mindsets, even more in a country such as Singapore where multiculturalism is part of the everyday life and where the workforce is very diversified. Therefore, to address this issue, this chapter focuses on diversity management knowledge and investigates how expatriates transfer their know-how in this particular area to HQ. Figure 1 shows the concept model of our study.

3 Method and Data

3.1 Research Design and Settings

This study, by its nature, relies mainly on primary data. First, the research on how HQ and expatriates manage the reverse transfer of diversity management knowledge is underdeveloped. When the questions are related to "how," it is more appropriate to conduct a qualitative research to explore the new phenomenon (Snape & Spencer, 2003). Given that our research aims to gather and understand in depth the personal perception and interpretation of expatriates toward diversity management, it is logical to employ the semi-structural interview approach which allows new ideas to emerge (Alvesson & Ashcraft, 2012).

The interview guideline (see Table 1) is drafted by one of the authors, cross-checked by another author, and reviewed by two academic scholars and practitioners in the field. The interview guideline is composed of main questions and sub questions. The interview process starts with the collection of participants' general information. Then, questions related to expatriates' perception of diversity management in Singapore, benefits and challenges of practicing diversity management, are

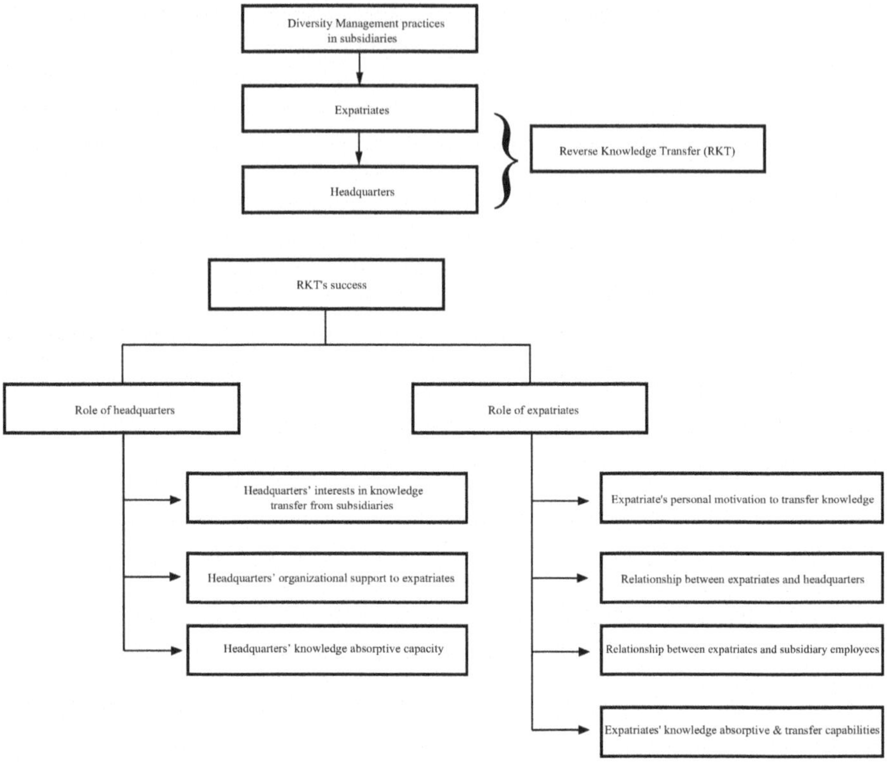

Fig. 1 Concept model

asked. Afterwards, interviewees are invited to explain how HQ promote diversity and inclusion, whether there exists RKT, to which extent that expatriates are involved in RKT of diversity management to HQ. Interviews end with questions about potential barriers that could hinder expatriates' RKT. Some sample questions are: What does Diversity Management mean to you? As an expatriate, what are the organizational supports that can facilitate your RKT in relation to culture diversity management? As an expatriate, how would you share your diversity management knowledge with colleagues at HQ? How would you describe your relationships with HQ and with subsidiary employees?

3.2 Respondent Sample

In total, we have carried out 13 interviews in 2021 (see Table 2); 12 out of 13 (except F9) were French expatriates working or having worked for a French MNC in Singapore. Except F9, all interviewees had previously worked in HQ in France and then assigned to work in Singaporean subsidiary. F9 is a HR Director from

Table 1 Interview guideline

Key questions	Sub questions
Q1. Company and expatriate introduction	• Please introduce yourself. • Please introduce your company and the subsidiary in Singapore.
Q2. What does diversity management (DM) mean to you?	• What is your definition to DM? • What are the examples that show the diversity in your parent company (=headquarters) and in the Singaporean subsidiary?
Q3. To which extent DM is important to you and your parent company?	• Concerning the DM practices, are they transferred from headquarters to Singaporean subsidiary? If your answer is yes, what are they? How do subsidiary employees perceive these headquarters-based DM practices? • If your answer is no, have you developed DM practices in the Singaporean subsidiary? What factors need to be considered when designing the DM practices in Singapore? What are the "made in Singapore" DM practices, any examples?
Q4. What are the benefits and challenges in relation to DM that you would like to highlight?	• From the perspective of headquarters, what are the benefits and other considerations to implement DM practices? • From the perspective of subsidiary in Singapore, what are the benefits and other considerations to have DM?
Q5. What are the organizational supports that are put in place to facilitate the transfer of DM knowledge from Singaporean subsidiary to headquarters?	• Do you think the DM practices that used in Singaporean subsidiaries can be used at headquarters? If your answer is yes, which DM practices can be used at headquarters? How could you share the DM knowledge with headquarters? Through which channels (e.g. forums, meetings, conferences), the DM knowledge can be transferred to headquarters? Any specific examples? If your answer is no, what will be the reasons? • How and how often (if exists) does your company organize social interactions, such as webinars, cafeterias, communities, meals, etc., to keep networking, between headquarters and you, between you and subsidiary employees?
Q6. How would you describe the relationships between you and headquarters, between you and subsidiary employees?	• How would you describe your relationship with headquarters? How often are you in contact with headquarters? For what issues? • Will colleagues from headquarters show interests to your working experience in Singapore in general, and in DM knowledge in particular? • What about your integration in the local teams in Singapore? How did you manage to

(continued)

Table 1 (continued)

Key questions	Sub questions
	integrate yourself with employees in the subsidiary? What have been the main barriers? • At an individual level, what DM knowledge have you achieved when working in Singapore? How do you learn from the subsidiary employees? What are the challenges that you have experienced when working in Singapore?

Malaysia, who is working for a French MNC for Asia Pacific region. Interviews were conducted in French, and then translated into English thanks to notes taken during the interviews. To reach all the interviewees, we firstly sent an e-mail to the target group of participants to introduce to them the research project and the purpose of the interview. We should address the challenge to get the permission to interview the top managers in French subsidiaries in Singapore, which is related to their busy schedules, and parts of them have left Singapore due to the global pandemic (Covid-19). We have contacted 40 companies and we achieved the access to interview 13 companies in the end. Once we get the permission to interview the expatriates, and because of restraint trips in relation to Covid-19, all the interviews are collected through online tools (e.g. Microsoft Teams, Skype, Zoom, and WhatsApp). Each interview lasted between 45 minutes and 120 minutes.

3.3 Data Analysis

For data analysis, we adopt the coding approach (Corbin & Strauss, 2008). The interviews were conducted by one of the authors. Among the 13 interviews, 12 interviews were conducted in French, which is the native language of interviewees and author. The interview with F9 was conducted in English, where the interviewee and author are proficiency in English. During the interviews, detailed notes were taken. Once after each interview, transcription (4 pages in average) is written. The author that conducted the interviews is responsible for preparing transcription and translation, identifying the key themes. The second author is bilingual in English and French, who is in charge of translation verification and identification of key themes as well. The data analysis started by exploring the themes (Braun & Clarke, 2006). Both authors read the transcriptions and identified the themes independently. Then, both authors cross checked the themes that they identified, discussing and deciding the common coding and the emergent themes. For instance, with regard to the components of diversity management in Singaporean subsidiaries, the following codes and subcategories were identified under the theme "nationality, gender, tradition, festivals, culture." The respective interview quotes were "*My company is representative of the diversity, for instance, the Asia Pacific regional director and*

Table 2 Respondents' profiles

Interviewee	Gender	Functional area	Sector	International experience (countries)	Workforce diversity in Singaporean subsidiary (nationality)
F1	Female	Finance	Bank	Singapore, France	Indian, Malaysian, Singaporean, French
F2	Female	Finance	Web services	Hong-Kong, Singapore, France	French, Singaporean, Chinese, Indian, Chinese
F3	Female	Supply Chain	Aerospace	Singapore, France	French, Singaporean, Chinese
F4	Female	Banking	Bank	France, UK, Switzerland, Singapore	Belgian, Indian, Malaysian, Chinese, French
F5	Male	Banking	Bank	China, Netherlands, Singapore, France	French, Indonesian Singaporean, Chinese, Indian
F6	Male	Business Administration	Electronics	China, India, Singapore, France	Singaporean, Chinese, Malaysian, French
F7	Male	Commercial	Sea transport	Belgium, France, Singapore	French, Chinese, Singaporean, Chinese
F8	Male	Finance	Services	US, India, France, Bulgaria, Singapore, China	French, Philippines, Singaporean Malay, Indian, Singaporean
F9	Female	HR	Services	Malaysia	Diverse nationality
F10	Male	Audit	Bank	Japan, France, Singapore	French, Singaporean
F11	Female	Engineering	Analytics services	France, Australia, Singapore	French, British, Canadian, Vietnamese, Indonesian, Singaporean
F12	Female	Project management	Video games	France, Singapore	Canadian, Malaysian, Russian, Ivorian, Singaporean, French
F13	Male	R&D	Video games	Canada, France, Singapore	Indian, Singaporean, French, Burmese

financial direction are French, Human Resource director is Chinese, the chief financial officer for Southeast Asia is Indian, we have a lot of Chinese working in the Singaporean subsidiary" (F2); "*We celebrate employees' traditions, for example, for the Chinese New Year, we offer mandarins to Chinese colleagues to wish them good fortune and wealth. We also celebrate Indians' Diwali, 'la galette des rois' for French. These celebrations show that we respect every single culture in the company*" (F4); "*We are doing our best to implement affirmative actions to increase women employees' number in the subsidiary*" (F8); "*We have diversity scorecard to mark the milestones. In the subsidiary, female employees account for 40–60%*" (F9).

4 Findings

4.1 Current State of RKT of Diversity Management

A key theme across all the interviews was the high diversity level that expatriates experienced in the Singaporean subsidiaries. The dimensions in relation to diversity include but not limit to cultures, traditions, genders, and nationalities. The sample notes are:

> *My company is representative of the diversity, for instance, the Asia Pacific regional director and financial direction are French, Human Resource director is Chinese, the chief financial officer for Southeast Asia is Indian, we have a lot of Chinese working in the Singaporean subsidiary.* (F2)

> *We celebrate employees' traditions, for example, for the Chinese New Year, we offer mandarins to Chinese colleagues to wish them good fortune and wealth. We also celebrate Indians' Diwali, "la galette des rois" for French. These celebrations show that we respect every single culture in the company.* (F4)

> *We are doing our best to implement affirmative actions to increase women employees' number in the subsidiary.* (F8)

With regard to positive aspects of diversity, expatriates reported that they become more sensitive to cultural differences, they develop adaptive methods when working with different cultures while learning from others. The manager F3 described that "*in Singapore, during a meeting or conversation, it is common for people to use silence before giving the answers. In France, people tend to reply to others very quickly.*" By learning and practicing silence when negotiating with clients, F3 is able to pay more attention to listening to clients, to have a second thought and make more deals. At the same time, the interviewed expatriates are highly aware of the challenges to recognize and adapt to each type of diversity. Given that the workforces are more diverse in Singaporean subsidiaries than that at HQ, when there is no cultural training before departure to Singapore, or when expatriates have no experience in working in Asia, or no onboarding activities in Singapore are proposed, it is extremely difficult for expatriates to get integrated with local team members.

A second key theme of current RKT status is that diversity management practices implemented in Singapore are not transferable to France. Ten participants (except F3, F4, and F8) shared this common sense. The reason behind this phenomenon is that colleagues at HQ are not as diverse as those in Singapore, meaning that tools and solutions implemented in the Singaporean subsidiary may not fit the French context. Furthermore, diversity management practices in the Singapore subsidiaries are from HQ in France. In this case, HQ consider that it is not necessary to have RKT and it is a tendency for colleagues from HQ to pay less attention to the valuable diversity management knowledge achieved by expatriates. However, when the teams at HQ are composed of diverse workforce, reverse transfer of diversity management knowledge happens more often. Some sample quotes are shown below:

It doesn't fit the local (hereby French) reality. (F10)

The teams in France are less diverse. (F11)

Nothing special is done in Singapore. The diversity management practices are created and implemented in Paris. (F12)

As HQ and Singaporean subsidiary have very diverse workforce, the good practices created in Singapore can be shared and implemented at HQ. (F8)

Regarding the RKT channel, some companies have implemented the dyadic process/channels to facilitate knowledge transfer between HQ and expatriates. Across interviews, we identify three efficient practices: implementing mentoring programs, developing frequent webinars and roundtables, and increasing number of team meetings and feedback-giving. First, providing each expatriate with a mentor at HQ can create privileged knowledge sharing moments. When it comes to organizing webinars and roundtables, it is a strong formal communication channel. Through webinars and conferences that are related to experience learning or diversity management, expatriates could easily disseminate their knowledge about their experience abroad. This formal moment gives credibility and value to expatriates' knowledge and makes their voices heard within the company. As a result, expatriates are motivated to attend those conferences. Another way to reinforce knowledge sharing is via more frequent feedback-giving and meetings. Covid-19 has definitely changed the ways of working, especially the way how colleagues communicate to each other. From the interviews, we can see that some MNCs are devoted to increase the transparency by giving regular feedbacks to employees about results, performance, and invest in communication tools to facilitate the knowledge exchange. Such an organizational support is well perceived by expatriates. Last but not the least, companies like F12 have set up the formal RKT channel by inviting expatriates to report the subsidiary-level knowledge, which includes diversity management.

In our Asian operation, we have a special mentoring program. For instance, I have a mentee and I am also a mentor. I am the mentor of someone in China, who is not working for me, not reporting to me but I am helping him, giving and brining my insights on how to work. (F8)

We organize roundtables and webinars, we invite employees and clients to share experience, they talk about cultural diversity, challenges, ... all the topics are welcomed ... it is very interesting to join the event. (F9)

We are giving more frequent feedbacks on results, performance. Every week, HQ keep us posted, which allows to reinforce communication and knowledge sharing. (F7)

When a collaboration between 2 studios is over, we have to do "postmortem" analysis. In this report, we have a special part about diversity, not only cultural but diversity as a whole. (F12)

I was invited to share my knowledge with my peers at HQ. It was pretty formal as a presentation, I prepared a PowerPoint to support my speech. I highlighted how life was like in Singapore, positive and negative points, what I have learned in terms of new skills, and how the company could benefit from these skills. (F3)

4.2 The Relationship Between HQ and Expatriates

Relationships between HQ and expatriates are crucial when it comes to RKT. Through analyzing the interviews, we noticed that eight interviewees (except F9, F10, F11, F12, F13) are in close touch with French HQ. Among those who are frequently in contact with HQ, it is purely for business issues. Whereas, for those who are not in touch with HQs, it is mainly because that HQ is not their direct reporting hierarchy. Further, our findings show that when expatriates had the opportunity to work at HQ previously, it is easier for them to build relationship with colleagues at HQ and they are more engaged in RKT.

Purely economic and business linked relationships. (F1)

Not at all at my level. We are working closely with other subsidiaries but not really with HQ. (F12)

We are mainly dealing with regional HQ which are located in Hong Kong. (F10)

It was easier because I had worked in France previously, so I already had some contacts there. I had really good relationships with colleagues at HQ in Paris. (F5)

In my current company, it's very hard to create strong relationship with the HQ as I haven't met them yet. In France people are very attached to face to face and physical contact to create relationship, being abroad doesn't ease the process. It takes time. (F2)

Further, not all the HQ are interested in expatriates' diversity management knowledge. There are different levels of HQ involvement in promoting the RKT of diversity management. For instance, at F3 company, "*French peers and colleagues were really interested about learning from me. Even if the decision was coming from HR team, they were really curious and eager to learn more about my life in Singapore. They were asking questions and everything.*" At F9, "*HQ organize roundtables and webinars to invite employees and clients to share experience... the topics can be but not limited to cultural diversity, challenges ... very interesting*". However, only a few interviewees (e.g. F3, F8, F9 and F11) are convinced that HQ are potentially interested by their knowledge acquired abroad. In fact, due to the context differences, time differences, and busy work schedule of each other, HQ do not seem eager to learn from their peers who had the international experience. As a consequence, the organizational support from HQ is limited.

4.3 The Relationship Between Subsidiary Employees and Expatriates

RKT is a complex and effort-demanding process. To realize RKT, it is necessary for expatriates to learn local diversity management knowledge. Among the challenges claimed by interviewees, language barrier seems to be foremost one that hinders expatriates to learn the best from subsidiary employees. Indeed, not sharing the same language can create misunderstandings, conflicts, in-group/.out-group fall lines... Expatriates and subsidiary employees, even they share the same language (hereby English), they won't have the same way to express their ideas. In addition to the language barrier, cultural differences matter. In Singapore, the mainstream culture values more collectivism and relationship (Lakshman & Jiang, 2016). The French culture is very different from the Singaporean one. The cultural distance makes it complicated for French expatriates to get self-integrated among subsidiary employees, which limits expatriates' cultural learning from locals.

> *As a French, language barrier is hindering conversation, we don't share the same culture, the same way of doing things.* (F11)

> *As a French, sometimes, it's hard to merge within other cultures, it really depends on our own resilience and capability to integrate ourselves.* (F1)

> *It's challenging and time-consuming to create the ties with Chinese/Singapore people, one should prove that we deserve to enter into their close circle.* (F3)

From the interviews, we also identify that being French expatriates in Singapore, not all the subsidiary employees recognize the added value of expatriates properly. The subsidiary employees may perceive expatriates as treats to their job security and career development or expatriates are someone who had poor performance at headquarters and that is why they have to work in the foreign subsidiaries without choice. Hence, the lack of receptivity from local people can prevent expatriates' integration and limit their knowledge sharing to expatriates, due to the considerations such as knowledge protection and defensive intention. Therefore, expatriates may not be able to learn all aspects of diversity management in the Singaporean subsidiaries, which will further affect their RKT of diversity management to HQ.

> *Some colleagues did not understand why French expatriates are working in Singapore. Some of them even misunderstood that expatriates were the poor performer at HQ and that is why they come to Singapore to get a fresh restart.* (F5)

> *The subsidiary employees consider me as a 'spy'. Even I manage to create relationships with them, it's hard to get closer to them, because we are French.* (F3)

To conclude, even though coping with diversity is challenging, all of our participants (except F1) indicated that working with diverse teams was a huge asset to both their professional and personal lives. Among all the benefits that expatriates achieved through working with employees in Singapore, open-mindedness, being more flexible in working methods, and being able to adapt to different situations are the top three advantages of working in Singapore.

4.4 Barriers in RKT of Diversity Management

First, it is linked to the expatriates themselves. For example, F11 is not at ease while sharing knowledge with peers. In fact, he considered that his knowledge sharing would make colleagues at HQ feel he was showing-off. Further, four participants (F6, F7, F8, and F13) revealed that there is an important context difference between what they experience in Singapore and what their colleagues at HQ are experiencing on a daily basis. In other words, colleagues at HQ would not be able to fully understand what expatriation really means if they have not experienced it by themselves. Context matters. It is worthy pointing out that some interviewees hold a kind of self-censorship, who believe that their insights and experiences have no added value, thus, they would not even think of sharing it.

> *Yes, I would love to. But I don't really know how. If it is too formal, people will consider that as ego and knowledge display, not really as a sharing, it would be seen as something top down and I'm not at ease with that. I think doing it in private and informal areas is a better approach.* (F10)

> *It would be relevant if teams in France were diverse, but it is not the case at all. They would not find it relevant; they would not understand, people do not have international experience, they would not understand fully what it involves and implies.* (F13)

> *I am not sure that my feedback and experience would make sense. To be honest in my company we already produce a lot of documents, we have very diverse jobs and positions, I am not convinced that I would be listened to.* (F12)

> *French colleagues with no experience abroad are too far from my reality to understand what I have experienced here.* (F7)

Some expatriates even express their reluctance in RKT of diversity management. Highlighted by F4, we can notice that current sanitary context and economic recession lead colleagues at HQ to perceive expatriates as threats to their job security. If overseas subsidiaries have to be closed for any reason, when expatriates with rich international experience come back to work at HQ, it is possible to have organizational restructure. By feeling inferior to expatriates in terms of knowledge and experience, colleagues at HQ would perceive expatriates' knowledge sharing negatively.

> *HQ are implementing the cost reduction logic, everyone tries to keep the job security, and they (=colleagues at HQ) are pretty scared and frightened about the current context. They are more in a 'survival mode', and us, expatriates coming back from Asia, we represent a 'threat' to them, we are in direct competition with their positions, and we are more skillful and develop cultural intelligence thanks to our international experience, so they are scared and reluctant to activities such as RKT.* (F4)

Another barrier in RKT is related to the fact that colleagues at HQ do not have time to knowledge sharing in diversity management, which does not have direct and immediate impact on firm performance. Considering the high amount of information already shared on a daily basis, to avoid the over-charged workload and information for both HQ and expatriates, it is important to promote some knowledge sharing but not for all areas of expertise. This leads F12 to affirm that knowledge sharing in relation to diversity management would not be seen as a priority. The sample quote is:

> *They would not have time I would say. If managers do not encourage them (=HR stuff at HQ) to do so they would not do it. Every day, we receive tons of mails, and there are some that I consider as very important ones and my colleagues did not even read them. We receive a lot of information, newsletter... people do not have time and would not take time to strategically consider the long-term benefits of knowledge sharing in diversity management.* (F12)

5 Discussion

5.1 Managerial Implications to Promote the RKT of Diversity Management to HQ

Indeed, diversity is seen as both an asset for individuals' professional development and it is deeply beneficial to the companies' sustainable development. As a result, MNCs need to develop solutions at their disposal to promote and encourage diversity on a daily basis. Our case studies suggest several initiatives that HQ may take to foster the reverse transfer of diversity management knowledge.

First of all, it is necessary for HQ to re-consider and carefully assess the value of expatriates' diversity management knowledge. The picture that emerges from our findings shows that majority of MNCs (except F3 and F12) do not insist on the RKT of diversity management enough. In the meantime, all the expatriates that participated in our research expressed the interests in sharing their diversity knowledge with colleagues at HQ and they would appreciate having more sharing opportunities. As a result, MNCs have to seize this opportunity and identify how they can better benefit from the knowledge expatriates acquire abroad in terms of diversity management. To do so, HQ can propose onboarding to expatriates, building relationship with expatriates, allowing new arrivals to get familiar with available knowledge sharing channels. Further, mentoring programs are proved to be efficient in enforcing RKT. From our findings, it is more effective when mentor and mentee do not have supervisor-employee relation. When mentor and mentee are not working in the same team, both parties are more engaged in knowledge sharing in all aspects.

Second, to make knowledge sharing a corporate culture, it is necessary to set up formal and informal channels to ease the knowledge transfer. Some effective and formal knowledge sharing channels are regular webinars and roundtable discussions. Furthermore, companies can consider organizing the best practices sharing per specific topic. For instance, once per year, HQ invite subsidiaries to share their diversity management practices and all the employees are invited to join this group-wide event. Concerning the informal channels, companies can organize the short meetings, which invite employees to share knowledge on all topics that can benefit organizational development.

Third, in order to better value expatriates' knowledge that is achieved in their international assignments, our research confirms the importance to employ human resource management staff that have international working experience and who are curious to different practices. Only in this way, it is easier for HQ to understand the value of expatriates' knowledge and apply it to different areas at HQ and in other subsidiaries. If it is possible, HQ can also employ a diversity manager, who is in charge of group-wide diversity issues (e.g. design and implement key performance indicators linked to diversity management among all the subsidiaries).

Fourth, to promote RKT, expatriates themselves are also the key protagonists when it comes to knowledge sharing. This study confirms that when expatriates have working experience at HQ beforehand, they are more likely to have RKT because they know better where to share knowledge and with whom they could share the knowledge. Here, the relationship between expatriates and colleagues at HQ plays an important role. From our findings, we can see that all the interviewees are interested in knowledge sharing of what they learned in Singapore with others. However, some expatriates do not feel confident about their knowledge. By believing in that they do not bring any added value to HQ, they censor themselves. Further, as a lot of information already circulates within the company, they are afraid that their insights and sharing will take too much time of their colleagues at HQ. In this case, HR teams should value expatriates' knowledge, pointing out how their knowledge can be useful to other functions in the companies. All in all, when expatriates are able to "market" their know-how achieved in the international assignments, when knowledge sharing and diversity are parts of corporate cultures, when HQ are sensitive to listen to expatriates and integrate their knowledge into global practices, RKT will become a more straightforward and self-initiated process.

RKT is affected by the expatriates' local integration and learning from local capability. If expatriates have challenges in getting integrated to the local teams, it will be also challenging for them to learn from the subsidiary colleagues. As a result, expatriates are not likely to share the local knowledge with HQ. To ease expatriates' integration in the subsidiaries, HQ should provide multicultural training before expatriates' departure to foreign countries. The common mistake that MNCs often make is that they believe expatriates can work well in all country contexts without preparation. This assumption, in fact, has underestimated the complexity of each country context and overestimated expatriates' cultural intelligence and adaptation skills. Furthermore, during the expatriation, organizational supports, such as constant communication with expatriates, paying attention to expatriates' and their family members' wellbeing, employing at least two people of similar background in foreign subsidiaries, selecting expatriates that have experience in relation to diversity to work in foreign subsidiaries, are found to be effective in facilitating RKT.

Finally, HQ should pay attention to the subsidiary team composition, promoting diversity while staffing at least one team member that shares similar background as that of expatriates to facilitate expatriate integration. Otherwise, diversity can be more harmful than beneficial to expatriates themselves, especially at the beginning of their expatriation to a host country. As revealed in our findings, some subsidiary employees perceive expatriates negatively. On the one hand, subsidiary-level HR department should clarify expatriates' values to employees. On the other hand, expatriate selection is a key issue. Firms should privilege sending the expatriates that have cultural intelligence, sensitivity to diversity, relevant working experience to work in the foreign subsidiaries, which can pave the way for expatriates' integration into local teams.

6 Conclusion

This study has some limitations. First, even though our data have achieved saturation effect, with a sample of 13 companies and 6 companies are specialized in finance/ banking sector, it is difficult for this study to have generalizability of findings. Second, most of our participants (except F4, F8, F9, and F12) refer diversity only to its cultural dimension. Hence, our findings are mainly linked to expatriates' knowledge in managing cultural diversity. But diversity concerns also gender, sexual orientation, age, disabilities, education... in this vein, our results can be biased. Third, our research only investigated French expatriates working in Singapore. It is worthy paying attention to the period of time in which our research occurred. During tough times such as Covid-19, a country like Singapore decided to curb the number of expatriates entering the country to favor local employment. As a result, the moment in which we carried out our interviews was not the most favorable for MNCs to implement Diversity Management practices, as diversity was slowly going down.

Future research may address all the limitations above. First, it is important to have a larger number of samples, in order to have generalized and closer-to-reality results. Second, it would be very interesting to interview employees at HQ, whose perspectives can enrich the findings by pointing out how they perceive RKT of diversity management and reducing the information asymmetry given by one interviewee per company. Third, we recommend future research to have a more diversified sample of interviewees, especially when it comes to the sectors. We are aware of how the sector the company is operating in can affect its vision in terms of diversity. It would be fruitful for verifying the current findings and generating emergent results through having companies from as more diverse sectors as possible to join the research.

References

Alvesson, M., & Ashcraft, K. (2012). Interviews. In G. Symon & C. Cassell (Eds.), *Qualitative organizational research* (pp. 239–257). Sage Publications. https://doi.org/10.4135/9781526435620.n14

Ambos, T. C., Ambos, B., & Schlegelmilch, B. B. (2006). Learning from foreign subsidiaries: An empirical investigation of headquarters' benefits from reverse knowledge transfers. *International Business Review, 15*(3), 294–312. https://doi.org/10.1016/j.ibusrev.2006.01.002

Braun, V., & Clarke, V. (2006). Using thematic analysis in psychology. *Qualitative Research in Psychology, 3*(2), 77–101. https://doi.org/10.1191/1478088706qp063oa

Burmeister, A., & Deller, J. (2016). A practical perspective on repatriate knowledge transfer: The influence of organizational support practices. *Journal of Global Mobility, 4*(1), 68–87. https://doi.org/10.1108/JGM-09-2015-0041

Burmeister, A., Lazarova, M. B., & Deller, J. (2018). Repatriate knowledge transfer: Antecedents and boundary conditions of a dyadic process. *Journal of World Business, 53*(6), 806–816. https://doi.org/10.1016/j.jwb.2018.06.004

Caligiuri, P., & Bonache, J. (2016). Evolving and enduring challenges in global mobility. *Journal of World Business, 51*(1), 127–141. https://doi.org/10.1016/j.jwb.2015.10.001

Cohen, W. M., & Levinthal, D. A. (1990). Absorptive capacity: A new perspective on learning and innovation. *Science Quarterly, 35*(1), 128–152. https://doi.org/10.2307/2393553

Connelly, C. E., Zweig, D., Webster, J., & Trougakos, J. P. (2012). Knowledge hiding in organisations. *Journal of Organisational Behavior, 33*(1), 64–88. https://doi.org/10.1002/job.737

Corbin, J., & Strauss, A. (2008). *Basics of qualitative research: Techniques and procedures for developing grounded theory* (3rd ed.). Sage Publications.

Crespo, C. F., Griffith, D. A., & Lages, L. F. (2014). The performance effects of vertical and horizontal subsidiary knowledge outflows in multinational corporations. *International Business Review, 23*(5), 993–1007. https://doi.org/10.1016/j.ibusrev.2014.03.002

Embassy of France in Singapore. (2020). Economic relations. Retrieved October 15, 2021, from https://sg.ambafrance.org/Economic-Relations

Fang, Y., Wade, M., Delios, A., & Beamish, P. W. (2007). International diversification, subsidiary performance, and the mobility of knowledge resources. *Strategic Management Journal, 28*(10), 1053–1064. https://doi.org/10.1002/smj.619

Fey, C. F., & Furu, P. (2008). Top management incentive compensation and knowledge sharing in multinational corporations. *Strategic Management Journal, 29*(12), 1301–1323. https://doi.org/10.1002/smj.712

Gupta, A. K., & Govindarajan, V. (2000). Knowledge flows within multinational corporations. *Strategic Management Journal, 21*(4), 473–496. https://www.jstor.org/stable/3094239

Hewlett, S. A., Marshall, M., & Sherbin, L. (2013). Diversity can drive innovation? *Harvard Business Review*. Retrieved October 15, 2021, from https://hbr.org/2013/12/how-diversity-can-drive-innovation

Hunt, V., Layton, D., & Prince, S. (2015). Why diversity matters. McKinsey. Retrieved October 15, 2021, from https://www.mckinsey.com/business-functions/people-and-organizational-performance/our-insights/why-diversity-matters

Inkinen, H. (2016). Review of empirical research on knowledge management practices and firm performance. *Journal of Knowledge Management, 20*(2), 230–257. https://doi.org/10.1108/JKM-09-2015-0336

Ipe, M. (2003). Knowledge sharing in organisations: A conceptual framework. *Human Resource Development Review, 2*(4), 357–359. https://doi.org/10.1177/1534484303257985

Lakshman, S., & Jiang, C. (2016). Executive nationality choices in subsidiaries: Evidence from French multinationals in Asia. *Asia Pacific Journal of Human Resources, 54*(4), 498–517. https://doi.org/10.1111/1744-7941.12105

Lazarova, M., & Tarique, I. (2005). Knowledge transfer upon repatriation. *Journal of World Business, 40*(4), 361–373. https://doi.org/10.1016/j.jwb.2005.08.004

Luo, Y., & Shenkar, O. (2006). The multinational corporation as a multilingual community: Language and organization in a global context. *Journal of International Business Studies, 37*, 321–339. https://doi.org/10.1057/palgrave.jibs.8400197

Minbaeva, D. B., & Michailova, S. (2004). Knowledge transfer and expatriation in multinational corporations: The role of disseminative capacity. *Employee Relations, 26*(6), 663–679. https://doi.org/10.1108/01425450410562236

Nair, S. R., Demirbag, M., & Mellahi, K. (2016). Reverse knowledge transfer in emerging market multinationals: The Indian context. *International Business Review, 25*(1), 152–164. https://doi.org/10.1016/j.ibusrev.2015.02.011

Nkomo, S., & Hoobler, J. M. (2014). A historical perspective on diversity ideologies in the United States: Reflections on human resource management research and practice. *Human Resource Management Review, 24*(3), 245–257. https://doi.org/10.1016/j.hrmr.2014.03.006

Noorderhaven, N., & Harzing, A.-W. (2009). Knowledge sharing and social interactions within MNEs. *Journal of International Business Studies, 40*(5), 719–741. https://doi.org/10.1057/jibs.2008.106

Oddou, G., Osland, J. S., & Blakeney, R. N. (2009). Repatriating knowledge: Variables influencing the "transfer" process. *Journal of International Business Studies, 40*(2), 181–199. https://www.jstor.org/stable/25483370

Phene, A., & Almeida, P. (2008). Innovation in multinational subsidiaries: The role of knowledge assimilation and subsidiary capabilities. *Journal of International Business Studies, 39*(5), 901–919. https://doi.org/10.1057/palgrave.jibs.8400383

Sanchez-Vidal, M. E., Sanz-Valle, R., & Barba-Aragon, M. I. (2016). Repatriates and reverse knowledge transfer in MNCs. *The International Journal of Human Resource Management, 29*(10), 1767–1785. https://doi.org/10.1080/09585192.2016.1216876

Snape, D., & Spencer, L. (2003). The foundations of qualitative research. In J. Ritchie & J. Lewis (Eds.), *Qualitative research practice: A guide for social science students and researchers* (1st ed.). SAGE Publications.

Spender, J. C., & Grant, R. M. (1996). Knowledge and the firm: Overview. *Strategic Management Journal, 17*(S2), 5–9. https://doi.org/10.1002/smj.4250171103

Tsai, W. (2002). Social structure of "coopetition" within a multiunit organization: Coordination, competition, and intraorganizational knowledge sharing. *Organization Science, 13*(2), 179–190. http://www.jstor.org/stable/3085992

Wang, S., Tong, T. W., Chen, G., & Kim, H. (2009). Expatriate utilization and foreign direct investment performance: The mediating role of knowledge transfer. *Journal of Management, 35*(5), 1181–1206. https://doi.org/10.1177/0149206308328511

Yadav, S., & Lenka, U. (2020). Diversity management: A systematic review. *Equality, Diversity and Inclusion, 39*(8), 901–929. https://doi.org/10.1108/EDI-07-2019-0197

Ye, X., Wang, Z., Zhang, Y., & Li, H. (2021). How do knowledge governance mechanisms impact on repatriate knowledge transfer intention? The moderating role of perceived career and repatriation support and person-organization fit. *Management Decision, 59*(2), 324–340. https://doi.org/10.1108/MD-03-2019-0305

Employment and Human Resource Development of Disabled People in Japan and Finland: A Comparative Study from the Perspective of Diversity, Inclusion, and Decent Work

Shiho Futagami and Erja Kettunen

Abstract By analyzing the best practices in Japan and Finland, this study addresses the measures taken in those countries for enhancing the inclusion of disabled people in working life. The study reviews the existing research on diversity, inclusion, and decent work as well as the support programs for people with disabilities, and compares Japan and Finland in supporting the employment and human resource development (HRD) of disabled people from the perspective of diversity, inclusion, and decent work. The study considers the cases of the Accessibility Consortium of Enterprises (ACE) from Japan and the "Leap to Labour!" and "ILONA" projects of social firms from Finland in supporting the employment and HRD of disabled people. The conclusion section of the study highlights both the future challenges and opportunities in this area and provides a list of the policy implications.

Keywords Employment · Human resource development (HRD) · Diversity · Inclusion · Decent work · Disabled people

1 Introduction

There are an estimated one billion people with disabilities globally, with about 80% of them living in developing countries (WHO, 2011). Around 800 million disabled people are of working age, and many of them face challenges in finding equal opportunities for employment due to attitudinal, physical, and informational barriers (ILO, 2015a). However, access of people with disabilities to decent work is

S. Futagami (✉)
Graduate School of International Social Sciences, Yokohama National University, Yokohama, Japan
e-mail: futagami-shiho-hv@ynu.ac.jp

E. Kettunen
Turku School of Economics, University of Turku, Turku, Finland
e-mail: erja.kettunen-matilainen@utu.fi

B. Andreosso-O'Callaghan et al. (eds.), *Sustainable Development in Asia*, Contributions to Economics, https://doi.org/10.1007/978-3-030-94679-1_3

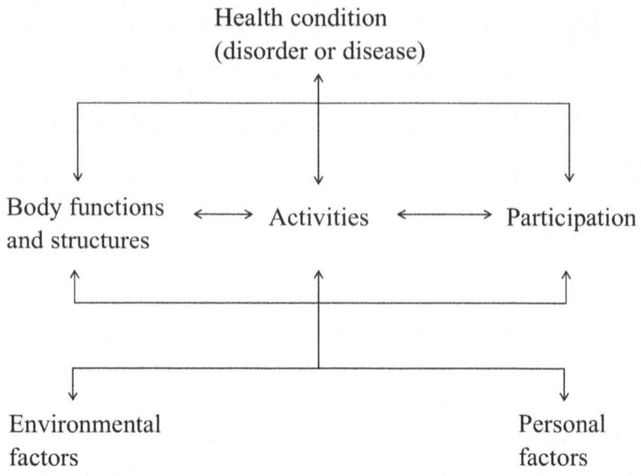

Fig. 1 Representation of the International Classification of Functioning, Disability and Health. (Source: WHO, 2011)

important both as an essential right and in terms of the economic advantages it brings (ILO, 2015b).

Disability is complex, dynamic, multidimensional, and contested (WHO, 2011). While there is no internationally uniform way to precisely define disability or to compare data across countries (WHO, 2011), what is common is that disabilities often lead to unemployment, exclusion, and poverty. The International Classification of Functioning, Disability and Health (ICF), adopted as the conceptual framework for the 2011 WHO *World Report on Disability*, understands functioning and disability as arising from a dynamic interaction between health conditions and contextual factors, both environmental and personal (WHO, 2011, pp. 4–5). It is called a "bio-psycho-social model" (see Fig. 1).

As shown in Fig. 1, health conditions, together with environmental and personal factors, affect a person's possibilities in respect of activities and participation in society such as participation in employment. Environmental factors are diverse and include technology, support, and relationships, services, and policies. The environment can be improved by legislation, policy changes, capacity building, and technology in order to increase the accessibility of disabled people to support services and employment (WHO, 2011, p. 4).

Many countries such as Japan and Finland have introduced specific programs to support and enhance the employment prospects of disabled people and help them develop their employment capacities. Both Japan and Finland are advanced high-income countries with high levels of education and human development, and relatively homogeneous populations.[1] However, they also have marked differences, such as population size, societal histories, and social and value systems related to diversity and inclusion. These similarities and differences make it apposite to

[1] These are indicated by their GDP per capita (PPP) that is currently USD 51,000 for Finland and USD 42,000 for Japan (World Bank, 2021), as well as their human development index ranking where Finland ranks 11th and Japan 19th among 189 countries (UNDP, 2021).

compare the two countries in respect of their support for the employment and human resource development (HRD) of disabled people. Thus, this study focuses on the employment and HRD of the disabled in Japan and Finland from the perspective of diversity, inclusion, and decent work. Here, HRD is defined as "a process of developing and unleashing expertise for the purpose of improving individual, team, work process, and organizational system performance" (Swanson & Holton, 2009, p. 4).

The aim of the study is to compare the current employment situation of disabled people and the respective HRD support measures in the two countries. Specific interest is focused on the HRD support organized by the private and non-governmental sectors to complement the state support for people with disabilities. Our research question is this: *What kinds of measures are taken by non-state actors in Japan and Finland for enhancing the inclusion of disabled people in working life?* The measures are analyzed from the viewpoint of best practices in the employment and HRD of people with disabilities in the two countries. Best practices are understood in this study as practices that display their effectiveness in the employment and HRD of people with disabilities from the perspective of diversity, inclusion, and decent work. At the same time, these best practices balance business goals with disabled inclusion. Industry-university-government collaboration plays a role as an employment and HRD support cluster for people with disabilities in both countries.

The rest of the chapter is structured as follows: first, the existing literature on diversity, inclusion, and decent work is reviewed especially concerning people with disabilities in the workplace, as well as the extant research on support for the employment of disabled people. Second, the data and method of the study are described, and third, the findings from the case studies on the support programs from Japan and Finland are presented. Finally, the chapter discusses the main findings of the research vis-à-vis prior research and presents the study's conclusions and policy implications.

2 Diversity, Inclusion, Decent Work, and the Employment of Disabled People

2.1 Diversity and Inclusion

Diversity represents all the ways people are unlike and alike, differences and similarities in age, gender, race, religion, ethnicity, sexual orientation, disability, and socioeconomic background. Loden and Rosener (1991) suggest distinguishing between primary and secondary dimensions of diversity where the former includes immutable differences such as age, ethnicity, gender, and physical abilities, and the latter includes mutable differences such as education, geographic location, income, religious beliefs, and work background. Gardenswartz and Rowe (2003) develop the

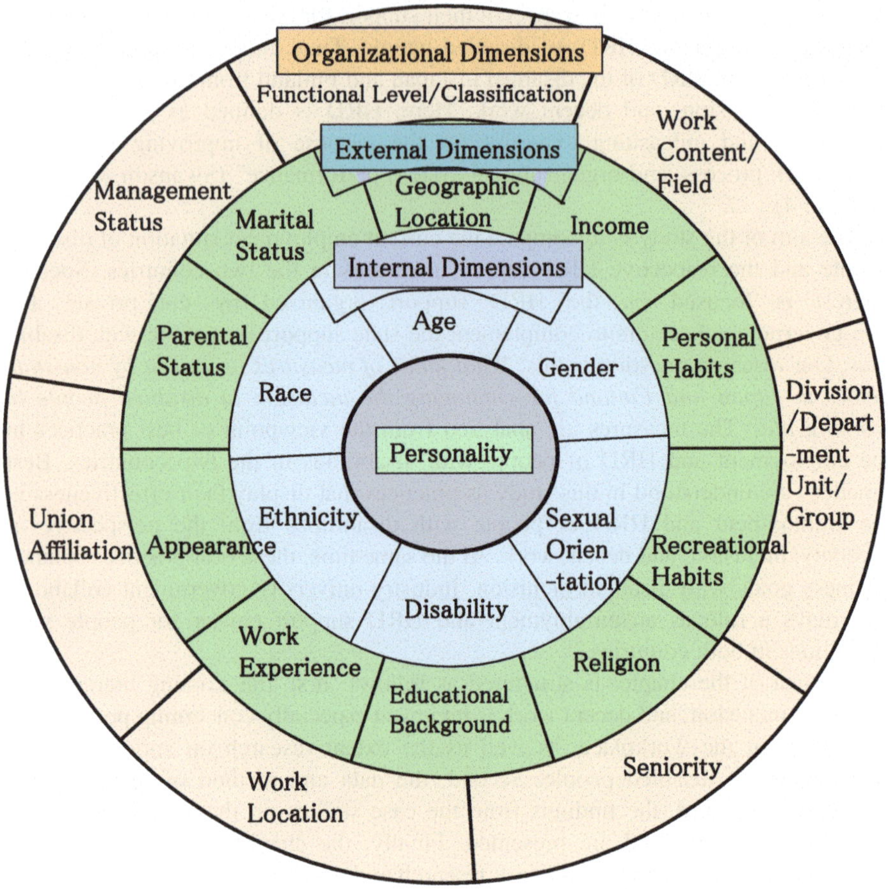

Fig. 2 The Dimensions of Diversity Wheel. (Sources: Loden & Rosener, 1991; Gardenswartz & Rowe, 2003)

concept of diversity and include dimensions that exist as internal, external, and organizational layers around personality. They have identified a "diversity wheel" (see Fig. 2) consisting of four layers of diversity: personality in the center of the wheel; internal dimensions such as age, gender, and disability in the second layer; external dimensions such as geographical location, religion, and educational background in the third layer; and organizational dimensions are in the outermost layer and include work content or field, seniority, etc. Disability should be respected as part of diversity (ILO, 2015a).

Diversity and inclusion are often used interchangeably where the two are not clearly distinguished, but the two are different concepts. Inclusion is a sense of belonging; feeling respected, valued for who you are; feeling a level of support and commitment from others so that you can do your best (Miller & Katz, 2002). Shore et al. (2011) define inclusion as the degree to which an employee perceives that he or

	Low Belongingness	High Belongingness
Low Value in Uniqueness	**Exclusion**	**Assimilation**
High Value in Uniqueness	**Differentiation**	**Inclusion**

Fig. 3 Inclusion framework. (Source: Shore et al., 2011)

she is an esteemed member of the work group through experiencing treatment that satisfies his or her needs for belongingness and uniqueness. A person's perception of high belongingness and high uniqueness results in a feeling of inclusion, whereas perceiving low belongingness and low uniqueness turns into a feeling of exclusion. Shore et al. (2011) present this as a 2×2 framework of inclusion in which they propose that uniqueness and belongingness work together to create feelings of inclusion (Fig. 3). An individual is treated as an insider and also allowed/encouraged to retain uniqueness within the work group. Therefore, from this definition of inclusion, it also emerges that inclusion is more advanced than diversity because inclusion moves beyond counting demographic differences to showing how these demographic differences can make a difference if people are working together to achieve organizational objectives (Roberson, 2006; Shore et al., 2011). It can be assumed that the employment and HRD support programs have the potential to increase the feelings of inclusion for people with disabilities.

Inclusion is also an important concept for the Sustainable Development Goals (SDGs), the 17 globally agreed goals that the United Nations General Assembly has adopted at its summit in 2015. They pledge that no one will be left behind and envisage a world in which every country enjoys inclusive and sustainable economic growth and decent work for all (United Nations, 2015). By 2030, Goal number 10 aims to empower and promote the social, economic, and political inclusion of all, irrespective of age, sex, disability, race, ethnicity, origin, religion, or economic or other status.

Diversity and Inclusion (D & I) has become a key concept for Human Resource Management (HRM) and refers to the strategy of fair treatment, equal opportunities, and non-discrimination of actual and potential workforce in organizations. Diversity management is an increasingly researched topic (Jonsen et al., 2021; Farndale et al., 2015) addressing the advantages and disadvantages of diversity as performance effects on the company. The advantages include positive effects on performance; gender diversity, age diversity, and nationality diversity especially lead to a positive performance by the company (Catalyst, 2015; Farndale et al., 2015; McKinsey &

Company, 2012). The performance effects are primarily analyzed on the premise of the resource-based view of the firm (Barney, 1991) stipulating that the heterogeneity of human resources rather than homogeneity of human resources leads to competitive advantages and thus motivates diversity and its management.

Therefore, D & I is nowadays part of company branding, as indicated by Jonsen et al. (2021), who examined the websites of 75 major companies in five countries: France, Germany, Spain, the United Kingdom, and the United States. They show that D & I branding has become mainstream with two main implications: a focus on diversity is particularly useful to attract talent, while a focus on inclusion seems particularly beneficial when a company aims to appear to be an employer of choice. According to Jonsen et al. (2021), disability is one of the most frequently listed dimensions among diversity dimensions, as 65% of the companies mention it and often list concrete measures taken to promote awareness as well as the inclusion of people with disabilities. In their survey, most French companies report having action plans for disabled employment given that the financial consequences of not complying with the rules governing disability are high when companies do not reach the mandatory quota of 6% of employees (Jonsen et al., 2021). A similar process is in place in Germany. In these cases in both countries, companies employ people with disabilities because of mandatory compliance requirements. However, not all countries impose such compliance rules on companies; the employment of the disabled is voluntary and supported financially by government, such as in Finland.

2.2 Decent Work

Decent work is defined by the ILO (2015b, p. 157) as "productive work in which rights are protected, which generates an adequate income, with adequate social protection." In other words, decent work guarantees a fair income with protection of human rights and safety at work. The problem of disabled people, however, is the lack of employment altogether. People with disabilities have higher unemployment rates and are more likely to be economically inactive than non-disabled people (ILO, 2015b). Access of people with disabilities to decent work is important both as an essential right and in terms of the economic advantages it brings (ILO, 2015c). Work is central to people's well-being. In addition to providing income, work can pave the way for broader social and economic advancement, strengthening individuals, their families, and communities. Such progress, however, hinges on work that is decent. Decent work sums up the aspirations of people in their working lives (ILO, 2015b).

The primary goal of the ILO is to promote opportunities for women and men to obtain decent and productive work, in conditions of freedom, equality, security, and human rights (Futagami & Muramoto, 2017). Decent work is considered as being comprised of four components (Fig. 4), that is, rights at work, employment, social security, and social dialogue (Futagami & Muramoto, 2017; Ghai, 2002, 2003, 2006). Employment especially is a vital component of decent work (Ghai, 2005). Employment in the decent work paradigm refers not just to wage jobs, but to work of

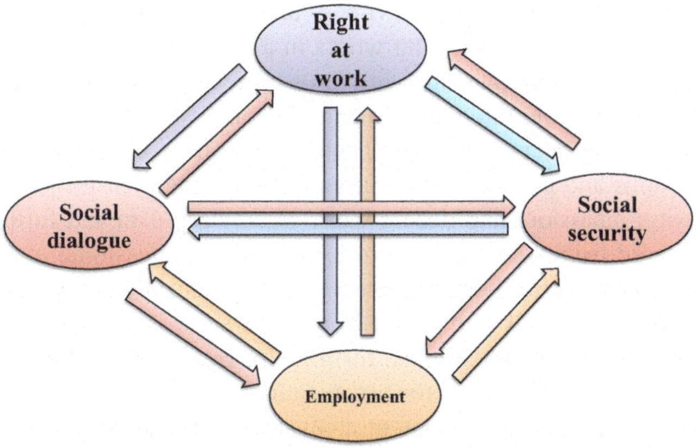

Fig. 4 Decent work components. (Source: Modified from Ghai [2006])

all kinds: self-employment, wage employment, and work from home. It also refers to full-time, part-time, and temporary work, and to work done by women, men, and children (Ghai, 2006). For decent work to be actualized, certain conditions must be satisfied. There should be adequate employment opportunities for all those who seek work (Ghai, 2006). Work should yield a remuneration that meets the essential needs of the worker and family members (Futagami & Muramoto, 2017; Ghai, 2006, p. 10).

To achieve this goal, the ILO has implemented a Disability Inclusion Strategy and Action Plan. The ILO works to increase the employability of people with disabilities, to support employers becoming more inclusive, and to promote enabling legislative and policy environments incorporating these goals (ILO, 2015c). Disability inclusion refers to promoting and ensuring the participation of people with disabilities in education, training, and employment and all aspects of society and providing the necessary support and reasonable accommodation so that they can fully participate (ILO, 2015a). However, the implementation of this strategy is up to individual countries and their governments and other institutions on whether and how such support is carried out. Some countries have support programs for people with disabilities organized by non-governmental actors, such as networks of corporations, disability associations, or other non-governmental organizations (NGOs).

To sum up, the employment and the human resource development of people with disabilities are important from the perspective of diversity, inclusion, and decent work in the workplace.

3 Data and Method

This is a qualitative comparative study that draws from a variety of source materials, such as expert interviews, national reports, and international comparative reports (e.g., WHO, ILO, Eurostat). Triangulation from multiple sources helps establish evidence on the studied phenomena. Primary data were collected in personal interviews with a personnel manager, who works in a consortium of business organizations for the case study on Japan, and with three professionals who work in disability organizations that promote the employment of people with disabilities for the case study on Finland. The interviews lasted from about half to one-and-a-half hours and dealt with the aims and practices of the organizations and their projects in working toward diversity, inclusion, and decent work. Secondary data and further information were gathered from webpages, reports, articles in professional magazines, and internet sources concerning both the interviewed organizations and their peer disability organizations as well as relevant Ministries, such as the Ministry of Health, Labour and Welfare, Japan, the Finnish Institute for Health and Welfare, the Cabinet Office, Japan, and other public sector organizations.

A combination of qualitative content analysis and qualitative narrative research was carried out to analyze the data. For content analysis, relevant key words and phrases were picked from the material according to code words such as "employment," "support," "social firm," "education," "training," and "human resource development." In addition, narrative research was conducted since all the interviewees represented organizations that implement the support programs and have been developing and carrying out the projects. Narrative research is a suitable method to explore the personal experiences and insights of the professionals about the processes and their outcomes (Overcash, 2003). Based on in-depth theme interviews, it reaches beyond what can be achieved by questionnaire research.

4 Employment and Human Resource Development of Disabled People: Findings from Japan and Finland

4.1 The Employment Situation and Support for Disabled People in Japan

4.1.1 Current Situation of People with Disabilities

The number of people with disabilities in Japan is 9,635,000, which is 7.6% of the population. The number of people with physical disabilities is 4,360,000, the number with intellectual disabilities is 1,082,000, and the number with mental disabilities is 4,193,000. The number of people with physical and intellectual disabilities is based on a survey on the difficulties in life that is sent to people at home who have a disability certificate, and the number with mental disabilities is based on the number of patients who have seen doctors in hospitals.

In Japan, the Act on Employment Promotion of People with Disabilities was originally enacted in 1960. It regulates the quota system for the employment of people with disabilities since 1976. The statutory employment rate was originally set at 1.5% and was raised to 1.6% in 1988, 1.8% in 1998, 2.0% in 2013, and 2.2% in 2018. Since March 2021, the statutory employment rate has been increased to 2.3%.

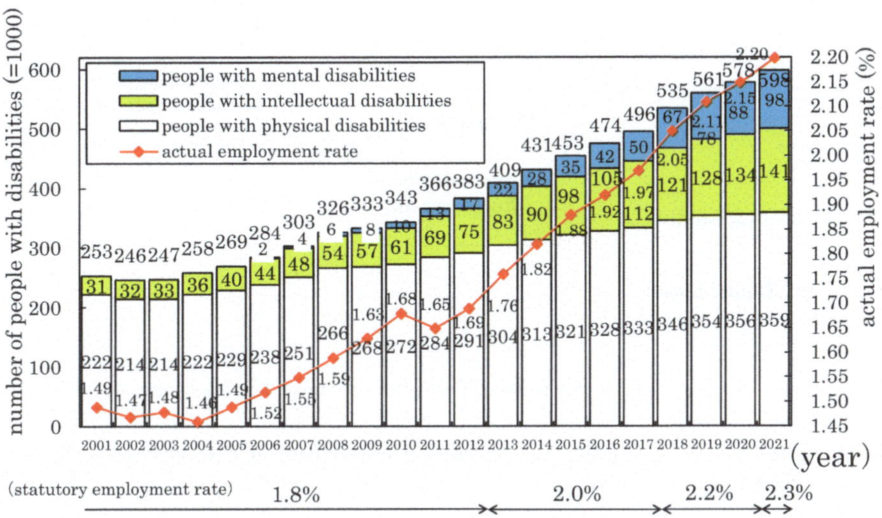

Fig. 5 The number of people with disabilities in regular employment. (Source: Cabinet Office, Government of Japan [2021] Annual Report on Government Measures for People with Disabilities 2021)

Under the levy and grant system for the employment of people with disabilities, employers in companies that do not satisfy the statutory employment rate are required to pay levies, while employers whose percentage of employees with disabilities exceeds the specified levels receive grants (Futagami et al., 2017).

The base for the calculation of the statutory employment rate originally included only people with physical disabilities; since 1998 it has also included people with intellectual disabilities, and since 2018 people with mental disabilities.

However, the number of people with disabilities in regular employment who are working in regular firms in Japan was only 597,786[2] in 2021, which means that their actual employment rate is 2.20%, as seen in Fig. 5. The number with physical disabilities in regular employment is 359,067.5, the number of with intellectual disabilities is 140,665, and the number with mental disabilities is 98,053.5. As such, only 47.0% of regular firms in Japan attained the 2.3% disabled employment quota required by law in 2021. Therefore, the employment challenges of the disabled are very severe, even though a quota system for the employment of people with disabilities exists in Japan.

[2]One part-time disabled worker is counted as 0.5 and one full-time severely disabled worker as two in the Japanese statistics.

Fig. 6 Vision of Accessibility Consortium of Enterprises. (Source: The interview with ACE)

4.1.2 Case Study in Japan: Accessibility Consortium of Enterprises (ACE)

This section discusses the case study on the Accessibility Consortium of Enterprises (ACE) as one of the most successful endeavors by Japanese companies to promote diversity, inclusion, and decent work in the workplace. Originally, ACE was initiated by IBM Japan and was joined by other Japanese big companies such as Japan Airlines, All Nippon Airways, Nissan motor company, and Asahi Beer. There were 24 companies involved at its establishment in September 2013. In 2021 the number of member companies was increased to 34. The main aim of ACE is the realization of an inclusive society and the employment of people with disabilities in Japan (interview, with ACE (2016)). This target is to be reached through a three-step process, as shown in Fig. 6.

As can be seen in Fig. 6, the first step in the process is called Compliance. In this step, the ACE member companies aim to attain the statutory employment rate, that is, to employ disabled people to make up 2.3% of the companies' workforce. Many of the companies have already attained this objective. The second step is formulated as Corporate Social Responsibility. In this step, ACE member companies aim to employ more people with disabilities in response to their Corporate Social Responsibility obligations, for example, to promote the employment of the disabled. Some of the companies have already reached this step. The third step is named Realization of Inclusive Society. In this step, the ACE companies aim to employ and develop people with disabilities from the perspective of diversity and to realize an inclusive society. They employ people with disabilities in their core businesses and utilize them as strategic human resources in tasks that require high-skilled employees such as in research and development (R & D) in order to secure competitive advantages, instead of recruiting them for low-skilled routine work. In the future, ACE aims to promote this kind of employment throughout Japan. Currently the objective of ACE is in the fulfillment this step. It is a target for the future, not yet fully realized.

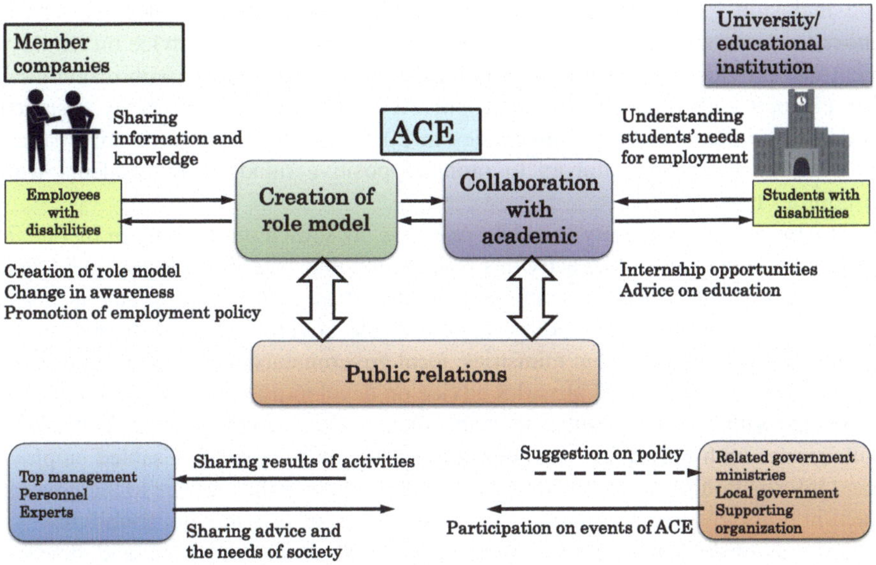

Fig. 7 Activities of Accessibility Consortium of Enterprises. (Source: The interview with ACE)

In addition to employing people with disabilities, ACE carries out other activities to promote diversity, inclusion, and decent work for them. The main activities of ACE can be divided into three parts, as can be seen in Fig. 7.

The first type of activity is the *creation of a role model* for employees with disabilities, as shown in the upper left side of Fig. 7. This is done by networking and sharing information and knowledge among the member companies, which also includes increasing the general awareness and the promotion of an inclusive employment policy. Events such as ACE FORUM are arranged where experts give lectures on disability, and good practice companies and employees are awarded as role models. The ACE FORUM takes place regularly once a year. An ACE award is given to a role model employee and also to a role model company every year. As an example of awarding an employee, ACE in 2019 awarded its highest honor to an employee with a hearing disability for their contribution on co-developing an innovative hearing device to be used with smartphones (Nikkei Asia, 2020).

Seminars and workshops take place to promote awareness on diversity and the employment of people with disabilities. For example, ACE Challenge seminars provide disabled workers of member companies with guidance for career development. The seminars also provide an opportunity to develop the strengths of disabled workers using a tool called strength finder. Seminars take place regularly mainly in big member companies' premises in Tokyo; the latest seminar was held at IBM Japan.

The second type of ACE's activity is *collaboration with academics*, as shown in the upper right side of Fig. 7. University lecturers specialized in HRM, disability, and inclusion give lectures at ACE FORUMs on disability management. ACE understands disabled students' needs for employment and gives advice on employment and provides internship opportunities to university students with disabilities. For example, 15 member companies of ACE accepted 95 university disabled students as interns from 31 universities in 2019. Collaborating with universities, ACE conducts career seminars to promote positive mindsets by students with disabilities toward work.

The third type of activity is *public relations*, as shown on the bottom of Fig. 7. ACE shares the results of its activities with the top management, HR personnel, and experts in Japanese companies, and they, in turn, share their advice and the needs of society. ACE also provides policy advice to the government at different levels, including related government ministries, local governments, and supporting organizations. For example, ACE provides advice on developing screen reading software for people with visual disabilities to enable them to become independent. Thus, ACE collaborates with universities and educational institutes, supplies disabled employment information packages to companies, and provides policy advice to the government in order to solve problems on the employment of people with disabilities.

As previously stated, ACE utilizes a "strength finder" to train and develop disabled workers. The strength finder was originally a self-assessment tool for human resource development introduced by Gallup in the United States (Buckingham & Clifton, 2001). ACE has modified and developed the strength finder for disabled workers. Disabled workers in ACE programs focus on developing their strengths and talents rather than fixing their shortcomings. It is therefore a "resource-oriented approach" instead of a "deficit-oriented approach" and is popular among the disabled in the workplace.

For example, the All Nippon Airways (ANA) group, a member company of ACE, employs about 1200 disabled employees out of a total 45,849 employees, which is 2.68% of the total employment in 2020. The disabled employees include those with physical disabilities (50%), employees with intellectual disabilities (25%), and employees with mental disabilities (25%) (Futagami & Muraki, 2017).

In 2012, the ANA Group established the Employment Promotion Office for people with disabilities aimed at increasing the employment of people with disabilities at the ANA Group (Futagami & Muraki, 2017). In 2015, the CEO of the ANA Group launched the ANA Group Diversity & Inclusion Promise (Futagami & Muraki, 2017). In order to promote greater understanding and the employment of people with disabilities throughout the Group, in 2015 more than 50 human resources staffs from the Group companies gathered to discuss "the 36 K-Employee Kickoff", the ANA Group's Code of Conduct for the Employment of People with Disabilities. Based on "the 36 K-Employee Kickoff" the ANA Group aims at increasing employee understanding of the Group policies regarding the employment of people with disabilities and how all employees can play an active role in improving the work environment (Futagami & Muraki, 2017).

In sum, ACE can be considered as a best practice organization because of three success factors. The first success factor for ACE is the setting up of a consortium or network of companies which aims to realize an inclusive society, and to employ and develop people with disabilities. The second success factor for ACE is the industry-university-government nature of its collaboration activities. Thus, not only companies, but also universities and the government collaborate in order to solve problems on the employment and HRD of people with disabilities. It is an employment and HRD support cluster for the disabled. The third success factor for ACE is its resource-oriented approach to HRD for employees with disabilities, which is very important from the perspective of diversity, inclusion, and decent work.

4.2 Employment and Support for Disabled People in Finland

4.2.1 Current Status of People with Disabilities

In Finland, the number of working-age people who have a disability or a chronic illness is 1.9 million; however, this figure also includes people with food allergies, which do not hinder employment. The number of people who get benefits for disabilities is about 240,000, which is 7% of the working-age population and comparable to other Nordic countries (6–8%). According to surveys, around 600,000 people in Finland find that their illness or disability affects their work or work opportunities. Therefore, the Finnish social and health sector commonly refers to "partial work ability" instead of "disability." Over 300,000 people with partial work ability are constantly in employment part-time, temporarily, or permanently (Mattila-Wiro & Tiainen, 2019). Compared to other European Union countries, Finland ranks high in the employment of disabled people which in 2011 was 61% for people aged 15–64 (Eurostat, 2014, p. 2), exceeded only by Sweden (66%) and Luxembourg (63%).[3] These figures are much higher than the 23% for Japan in 2003 (WHO, 2011, p. 238) although there is a time gap and definitions may vary between the two data sources. In many European countries, the employment rate of disabled people has increased between 2003 and 2011 as shown by the WHO and Eurostat figures.

People with disabilities are represented, and their employment is promoted by several disability organizations with different objectives in Finland, all of which are monitored by the Finnish Disability Forum (*Vammaisfoorumi*). One central organization is the Finnish Neuromuscular Disorders Association (*Lihastautiliitto*), which represents people with difficult physical disabilities such as the motor neuron disease ALS.[4] People with neuromuscular disabilities often need a wheelchair and/or a

[3]In Eurostat, the employment rate is calculated by dividing the number of people with disabilities aged 15–64 in employment by the total population in the same age group. Disability is defined as a self-reported limitation in the activities of everyday life (Eurostat 2014, p. 5). For further information on national differences in data collection, see, for example, Eurostat (2015), and on different definitions for disabilities, see Eurostat (ibid., pp. 94–95).

[4]*Amyotrophic lateral sclerosis.*

Table 1 Objectives of the OTE project

Employer	• Increased availability of work • Proven methods for enabling persons with partial work ability to stay in their work • Lower threshold for employing persons with partial work ability • Less prejudice towards persons with partial work ability
Person with partial work ability	• Easier access to employment • Support for access to employment, returning to work and continuing in one's work • Increased income • Increase in equality, participation and wellbeing
System/society	• Efficient and customer-oriented service system • Collaboration between different parties brings results • Reduced costs from non-participation in society and employment • Reduced inequality

Source: Adapted from Mattila-Wiro and Tiainen (2019)

personal assistant and therefore have difficulties in finding employment, even if they are highly educated.

In Finland, special-needs education is organized for disabled children and young people from the pre-school level to high school and vocational school level. Depending on the level of a person's disability, they are placed either within regular schools or in special schools. There are several special vocational schools for disabled people. Special services for people with intellectual disabilities include, for example, work activities and non-work daytime activities (Ministry of Social Affairs and Health, 2021). Around 9000 people with intellectual disabilities participate in work activities and ca. 5000–6000 people in other daytime activities in sheltered workshops or day centers (FAIDD, n.d.).

One longstanding problem in Finland for people with disabilities was the existence of the national income policy[5] that hindered efforts to improve their employment situation. Young disabled people were already granted a pension at the age of 16. The pensions were very small, and many recipients lived in poverty. Furthermore, because of these pensions they could not apply to the employment office for job opportunities, and thus the system did not support part-time work even if they wanted to work, according to the interview with Verainen (2019). However, the government subsequently initiated a key project for the employment of people with partial work ability. The project "Career opportunities for people with partial work ability" (Osatyökykyisille tie työelämään), known as the OTE key project, was carried out in 2015–2018 as a collaborative effort between the Ministry of Social Affairs and Health and the Ministry of Economic Affairs and Employment. Table 1 shows the impact of the OTE on employers, people with partial work ability, and society as a whole.

[5]Up to 2008, the national income policy in Finland was based on tripartite agreements between trade unions, employers' organizations, and the Finnish government.

Currently people with partial work ability are allowed to search for work, and there have been good results. The methods of the OTE project were to train 700 work ability coordinators (i.e., professionals who help disabled people to identify their personal strengths and find a place in working life),[6] develop online services, and organize seminars and promotional events on working life. Furthermore, OTE strategies included increasing their media visibility and promoting changes to legislation to improve the position of people with partial work ability in the labour market. The main changes achieved by OTE include the increased employment rate of people with partial work ability, promoting positive attitudes by employers toward people with partial work ability, promoting the passing of new legislation to improve the position of people with partial work ability in the labour market, and making the support service system more efficient and customer oriented (Mattila-Wiro & Tiainen, 2019).

In addition, Finnish disability organizations have initiated two projects that are considered in this study as best practices in Finland: the *Leap to Labour!* project for employing people with disabilities and the ILONA project supporting social firms, as discussed next.

4.2.2 Case Study in Finland: The Leap to Labour! And ILONA Projects

Leap to Labour!

In 2006–2008, the Finnish Neuromuscular Disorders Association[7] launched the project *Leap to Labour! (Sisäänheitto työelämään)* aimed at creating a model to enhance the employment of people with disabilities through cooperation with companies and disability organizations. The project was financially supported by RAY (Finland's Slot Machine Association).[8] Eleven disability organizations were involved and brought together their job-seeking members with companies that needed workers. The project also aimed at encouraging public debate about corporate social responsibility. Publicity campaigns were carried out in order to promote awareness on disabilities in companies, influence attitudes, and gradually change organizational cultures. Breaking down prejudices create the conditions for negotiating work contracts (Idström & Stenroos, 2013, p. 10). Altogether 231 disabled

---

[6] Work ability coordinators may work in social care services, health care, occupational health care, educational institutions, and companies.

[7] This is an association that represents the around 15,000 people in Finland with some kind of neuromuscular disease or disorder.

[8] RAY (Raha-automaattiyhdistys) was a government-owned non-profit gaming association that by law distributed its profits to domestic charities. In 2017, RAY was merged with Veikkaus Oy, the Finnish government-owned betting agency, which, as well, distributes its profits as determined by law to Finnish Ministry-specific beneficiaries to support health and social welfare, sports, science, arts, and youth work. In 2019, Veikkaus distributed over one billion euros to these functions through different Ministries (Veikkaus, 2020).

people took part by providing their CVs which was a prerequisite for participating. Of the participants, 40% were either wholly or partially on pension support, or on supported rehabilitation.

Crucially, the interaction between the disabled and the companies was based on face-to-face meetings. The person who roll-called the disabled job seekers to visit the companies was a disabled person herself. Working as the project manager, she could exemplify to employers the capabilities of disabled people, according to the interview with Verainen (2019). This had a strong positive impact on the attitudes of the company managers and helped get rid of the stereotype that disabled people cannot operate without help from others (ibid.). By providing this example, the project manager enhanced the perception among employers that people with disabilities can be very capable employees. They also have diverse capabilities. Furthermore, the participating disability organizations provided information on the various special needs of the disabled applicants which proved to be very useful for the companies concerned.

Contacts with the business sector were established through two main employer partners of the project, the Finnish Business & Society (FIBS) and Manpower Inclusive. The FIBS is a network of over 300 Finnish companies and organizations promoting sustainable and responsible businesses that aims to raise awareness about diversity management, human rights, and the SDGs (FIBS, 2020). Manpower Inclusive is a temporary employment agency that hires out workers that has social firm status and promotes workplace diversity and equality (Lämsä, 2012, p. 13). Cooperation between disability organizations and FIBS started in 2003 when the CVs of disabled job seekers were circulated to FIBS member companies. In 2006, the project *Leap to Labour!* enabled its project manager to start visiting the companies and present both the skills and special needs of the potential employees and, if needed, also to arrange face-to-face meetings in the companies' premises. A website was created listing open positions and sharing related information. Local and regional meetings were arranged in five cities in Finland to bring together job seekers, companies, and employment officials and to share information about support methods that help disabled people's employment prospects. This turned out to be important in increasing the number of people who were eventually hired (Verainen, 2013, pp. 139–141).

Of the 231 disabled people who took part in the project, 76 got employment: 18 got permanent employment, 31 fixed-term employment, 10 an internship, and 12 a work trial, and 5 salaried freelance work. These relatively high employment numbers derived from the personal meetings and the local and regional meetings. The jobs were diverse, such as IT support, financial administration, IT manager, administrative assistant, and purchase ledger (interview, Verainen, 2019). Typically it was office work: help desk, customer guidance, and customer service. The employers were social and health sector associations, the third sector, and private companies.

The project has been successful, and information about the project has been widely circulated. Since 2011, the project has a Facebook page *Sisäänheitto työelämään* (Leap to Labour!) for announcing job vacancies. The page is followed by about 500 disabled people searching for work. The open positions are mostly in the third sector, in the social and health sector associations. In order to help the associations hire new employees, a support funding program *Vacant Job* has been established. This program gives funding to social and health sector associations, such as disability organizations and NGOs in the health and social sectors, for employing (1) people with partial work ability or (2) people under 30 years of age who are outside of working life. The grants are issued by the Ministry of Social Affairs and Health, and associations can apply for one-year funding for 100% of salary costs to employ people for 12 months; the maximum sum is 50,000 euros per person per year (Paikka auki, 2020). This funding is important because by law, associations cannot make a profit and thus they do not have extra money to hire new people. A related project is *Yritystä!* (*Entrepreneurship*),[9] which aims to develop and enhance the employment prospects of disabled people via entrepreneurship as well as promoting their networking and creation of new businesses (interview, Verainen, 2019). This project was funded by the Funding Centre for Social Welfare and Health Organizations during 2016–2019 and administered by the Finnish Association of People with Physical Disabilities (Yritystä, 2020).

The *Leap to Labour!* project is an example of good practice because of its contribution to the disability field at large. The project is innovative in creating cooperation networks between the disability organizations and companies—a practice which was unknown in Finland until 2006. It offers consulting services and information to companies and has a register of job seekers. It is essentially an experiment in marketing the skills of disabled people and giving accurate information about disabilities to the companies. The project manager, a disabled person herself with an academic education, is a positive example in influencing the perceptions of both potential employees and employers. As a result, some companies have modified their recruitment procedures to promote equality, for example, by emphasizing positive attitudes toward diversity in job advertisements, restructuring electronic application forms to help the disabled to apply for vacancies, and arranging job interviews to provide fair treatment to all interviewees (Verainen, 2013, pp. 144–145). The project has enhanced awareness on diversity, inclusion, and social responsibility among Finnish businesses.

ILONA Project

The second example of best practice is the ILONA project that focuses on social firms and social entrepreneurship as a path to meaningful employment for partially disabled people. A social firm is a business that creates added value for society and aims to support the employment of people who have difficulties getting work. There are different operational definitions in the different EU countries for social

[9] Translation by authors. The Finnish word *yritystä* has many meanings, such as “making an effort,” “a company,” or “a trial.”

enterprises. In Finland, their institutionalized forms include the legally approved and registered "Work integration social enterprises" (WISE) and those that have received the social enterprise hallmark, Social Enterprise Mark (SEM).[10] Currently, there are 37 WISE and 214 SEM social enterprises in Finland, in addition to non-profit welfare organizations and cooperatives that operate similarly to social enterprises (European Commission, 2019). According to Finland's law on social enterprises, social firms can get support for salaries from the public employment and business services provider (*TE-palvelut*)[11] when at least 30% of their staff are people with disabilities, long-term illness, or are long-term unemployed (TEM, 2020). The total number of employees in WISE and SEM types of social enterprises is 272 and 18,750, respectively (European Commission, 2019, p. 33).

The ILONA project is being carried out between 2018 and 2021 and is funded by the European Social Fund (ESF). The main executor of the project, Silta-Valmennusyhdistys is a non-profit association that offers services to the public sector in coaching hard-to-employ people to improve their vocational and studying abilities.[12] Its collaborators are Vates Foundation, Helsinki Metropolitan Area Reuse Centre Ltd., Diaconia University of Applied Sciences (Diak), and the National Institute for Health and Welfare. In the preparatory phase of the ILONA project, a study was conducted on domestic and international experiments in social entrepreneurship for partially disabled people (Siltavalmennus, 2020). A cooperation network between Finland and Europe was created.

The purpose of ILONA is to find innovative solutions for people who are the most challenged in finding employment. The project is carried out in cooperation with international partners with whom best practices and models are shared. With comparative information from abroad, the project assesses different international models to advance the employment of people with partial work ability and to decide which model would be best suited for Finland. A special interest is maintained in the policies and good practices related to social firms and social entrepreneurship, and the aim is to create better prerequisites for them, according to the interview with Lindberg (2019). This is done by evaluating them against the Finnish societal and legislative framework. The project tests new methods for employment in social firms and in social entrepreneurship in sectors where labour demand is high such as social and health care, and elderly care (Ilonahanke, 2020a). The circular economy and sustainable development are also emphasized.

---

[10] Whereas a WISE entity (*sosiaalinen yritys*) offers employment opportunities to the disabled and long-term unemployed, SEMs (*yhteiskunnallinen yritys*) are intended for businesses that address social or ecological issues and invest the majority of their profits in promoting their social aims (European Commission, 2019, p. 18).

[11] TE is an abbreviation for *työ ja elinkeino* (work and business).

[12] Silta-Valmennusyhdistys provides supported learning environments, work coaching, and workshops for working-age people with disabilities and people suffering from long-term unemployment, young people, and substance abuse rehabilitees with the aim of increasing societal equality, participation, and welfare.

In practice, the ILONA project creates new forms and models of training that are effective in orienting disabled people to the open labour market. It includes two innovative group experiments and targeted training for the promotion of operational capacity and the employment of people with partial work ability. The two experiments are organized by the Helsinki Metropolitan Area Reuse Centre (in Helsinki) and Silta-Valmennusyhdistys (in Tampere). The Diaconia University of Applied Sciences has an advisory role in both experiments.

The first employment promotion experiment was held in spring 2019 at the Helsinki Metropolitan Area Reuse Centre Ltd.[13] This was a recruiting event for drivers in the logistics section of the Reuse Centre in cooperation with two medium-sized companies. Furthermore, the Reuse Centre has started group training programs that last 2–6 months aimed at improving the working capacity and performance of their workers. The ILONA project also develops methods for Finnish language training for drivers from migrant backgrounds. Recruitment events will be further developed into a permanent feature of the Reuse Centre in cooperation with large- and medium-sized companies in order to create opportunities for employment going from the intermediate labour market toward long-term employment in the open job market (Ilonahanke, 2020b; interview, Munther, 2020).

In addition, the second employment promotion experiment of the ILONA project will be organized in the city of Tampere. This will be training programs for disabled people to work in elderly care, organized by Silta-Valmennus in the Tampere region (ibid.).

The results of these two employment promotion experiments are evaluated by the project partner, the Finnish Institute for Health and Welfare with the help of the *Abilitator* (*Kykyviisari*, "ability pointer") for the measurement of the participants' work ability. The Abilitator is a method originally developed by the Finnish Institute of Occupational Health for the assessment of people's work ability, a project funded during 2014–2020 by the European Social Fund (Kykyviisari, 2020). Good work ability not only is worth pursuing for the sake of coping with and continuing to work, but also supports well-being in other areas of life. Promoting work ability can also increase well-being and happiness, as well as the employment rate (Gould et al., 2008). In 2018, the Abilitator program was renewed and opened as a web service for free use by all social and health service providers (THL, 2019). It is in the form of a questionnaire that provides an indicative evaluation of the respondent's perceived work ability and functioning, social inclusion, and well-being.

Since the ILONA project is still ongoing at the time of writing, its final results are not yet available. However, the project aims at creating a cost-effective and carefully assessed structural solution to enhance the employment of partially disabled people that can be implemented at the national level. The methodology highlights innovative group-based experiments in bringing capacity to action and in targeted training. Projected outcomes include concrete results, such as the provisioning of a material package on an employment model that supports the employment of the most

[13] The Reuse Centre is a social firm that employs people with partial work ability.

challenged people; a prescription of legislative changes that may be required to further enhance the employability of the disabled; the provisioning of communication material and publications on best practices written in cooperation with international partners, and employment creation in sectors with labour shortages (Ilonahanke, 2020b). According to an interview with Munther (2020), the material package will be either a printed publication or, more likely, an electronic publication that will have been distributed to relevant agencies in October 2021 when the project ends. The publication will most likely be in two parts: (1) an investigation into the employment situation of people with partial work ability in Finland (i.e., the current "ecosystem" in this field) and (2) examples of practical experiments in improving the situation to support the employment of such people. The material package will be disseminated to decision-makers (e.g., the Ministry of Employment and the Economy), to the media, and to the organizations in the third sector (i.e., the associations and NGOs) that provide the training and carry out the practical experiments.

5 Conclusion

This chapter has compared the employment and HRD of people with disabilities in Japan and Finland. The aim has been to explore the current employment situation as well as to look at the measures taken in Japan and Finland for enhancing the inclusion of disabled people in working life. These measures are regarded as best practices in supporting diversity, inclusion, and decent work in the two countries. The findings indicate some differences between the two countries both in the current employment situation and in the best practices to support the employment and HRD of people with disabilities.

Although there is the quota system for the employment of people with disabilities in Japan, their employment rate in Japan is low, at 23% in comparison with 61% in Finland (WHO, 2011). Thus, the best practices in Finland look like a suitable model for enhancing the employment and HRD of people with disabilities in Japan.

The project *Leap to Labour!* is a cooperation network between Finnish disability organizations and companies. This network shares information and offers consulting services and face-to-face meetings for employers and job seekers with disabilities. Thus, it promotes positive perceptions and attitudes toward disabilities and leads to diversity, inclusion, and decent work in the workplace. This network plays a big role as an employment and HRD support cluster for people with disabilities.

The *ILONA* project is a collaborative consortium or network of social firms, disability organizations, universities, and government. This consortium provides disabled people with lists of recruiting events, vocational education, and training programs in order to develop their potential and future employability. Thus, the company-university-government collaboration network also plays a big role as an employment and HRD support cluster for people with disabilities.

What is common to both projects in Finland is, first, the central role of disability organizations—which are NGOs—that may initiate the projects and collaborate with companies, government agencies, and other service providers in raising funding and executing the projects. Second, the projects are mostly funded by the EU, the main source of funding being the European Social Fund, which emphasizes the role of the EU in supporting the inclusion of disabled people in Europe, including Finland.

In Japan there is a consortium of companies in the ACE network providing employment assistance as previously discussed. ACE also collaborates with universities and educational institutes. The industry-university-government collaboration helps solve the employment and HRD problems of people with disabilities. ACE is like an employment and HRD support cluster. In this case, big companies in particular take initiatives in the cluster. The main difference with Finland is the emphasis on big companies and at the same time the lack of involvement of disability organizations in this process in Japan which stem from the fundamental differences in the societal systems between the two countries. Japan is characterized by a corporate-led economy and society in comparison with Finland, which has a relatively strong civil society similar to many other Western countries. There still remain many challenges in improving the employment rate of people with disabilities in Japan, and the best practices in Finland look like a suitable model for enhancing the employment and HRD of people with disabilities in Japan.

References

Barney, J. (1991). Firm resources and sustained competitive advantage. *Journal of Management, 17*(1), 99–120.

Buckingham, M., & Clifton, D. O. (2001). *Now, discover your strengths*. Simon & Schuster.

Cabinet Office, Government of Japan. (2021). *Annual Report on Government Measures for People with Disabilities 2021*.

Catalyst. (2015). *Catalyst census: Women board directors*. Catalyst.

European Commission. (2019). *Social enterprises and their ecosystems in Europe. Updated country report: Finland*. Author: Harri Kostilainen. Luxembourg: Publications Office of the European Union.

Eurostat. (2014). Situation of people with disabilities in the EU. News Release 184/2014.

Eurostat. (2015). Employment of disabled people. Statistical analysis of the 2011 Labour Force Survey ad hoc module. Statistical working papers. Retrieved March 8, 2021, from https://ec.europa.eu/eurostat/documents/3888793/6802087/KS-TC-14-007-EN-N.pdf/5c364add-6670-4ac9-87c7-9b8838473a7b?t=1429869414000

FAIDD. (n.d.). Employment. The Finnish Association on Intellectual and Developmental Disabilities (Kehitysvammaliitto). Retrieved May 4, 2021, from https://www.kehitysvammaliitto.fi/in-english/intellectual-disability/employment/

Farndale, E., Biron, M., Biscoe, D. R., & Raghuram, S. (2015). A global perspective on diversity and inclusion in work organizations. *The International Journal of Human Resource Management, 26*(6), 677–687.

FIBS. (2020). Finland's leading promoter of sustainable business. Retrieved March 26, 2020, from https://www.fibsry.fi/tietoa-meista/ (in Finnish).

Futagami, K., Futagami, S., & Futagami, T. (2017). *Employment of people with disabilities and disability management*. Chuokeizai-Publisher (in Japanese).

Futagami, S., & Muraki, A. (2017). *Future of career management: Prospects from the perspective of diversity and inclusion*. Yachiyo Publishing Company (in Japanese).

Futagami, S., & Muramoto, Y. (2017). A study on work attitudes of Japanese employees from the perspective of decent work. *Transition Studies Review, 24*(2), 21–29.
Gardenswartz, L., & Rowe, A. (2003). *Diverse teams at work: Capitalizing on the power of diversity* (2nd ed.). Society for Human Resource Management.
Ghai, D. (2002). Decent work: Concepts, models and indicators, Discussion Paper No. 139, International Institute for Labour Studies (IILS), International Labour Office (ILO).
Ghai, D. (2003). Decent work: Concept and indicators. *International Labour Review, 142*(2), 113–145.
Ghai, D. (2005). Decent work: Universality and diversity, Discussion Paper No. 159, International Institute for Labour Studies (IILS), International Labour Office (ILO).
Ghai, D. (2006). *Decent work: Objectives and strategies.* International Labour Office (ILO).
Gould, R., Ilmarinen, J., Järvisalo, J., & Koskinen, S. (2008). Dimensions of work ability: Results of the Health 2000 Survey Finnish Centre for Pensions (ETK), The Social Insurance Institution (Kela), National Public Health Institute (KTL), and Finnish Institute of Occupational Health (FIOH).
Idström, A., & Stenroos, M. (2013). Introduction. In A. Idström, M. Stenroos, & M. Uimonen (Eds.), *Decent work. Promising practices in the employment of people with disabilities from Sweden, Denmark, Estonia, and Finland* (pp. 5–19). ASPA Publications.
ILO. (2015a). *Disability inclusion strategy and action plan 2014–2017.* International Labour Office (ILO).
ILO. (2015b). *Decent work for persons with disabilities: Promoting rights in the global development agenda.* International Labour Office (ILO).
ILO. (2015c). *ILO and disability inclusion.* International Labour Office (ILO).
Ilonahanke. (2020a). Project information. Retrieved March 26, 2020, from https://www.ilonahanke.net/hankeinfo (in Finnish).
Ilonahanke. (2020b). Employment promotion experiments. Retrieved March 25, 2020, from https://www.ilonahanke.net/tyollisyyden-edistamiskokeilut/ (in Finnish).
Jonsen, K., Point, S., Kelan, E. K., & Grieble, A. (2021). Diversity and inclusion branding: A five-country comparison of corporate websites. *The International Journal of Human Resource Management, 32*(3), 616–649.
Kykyviisari. (2020). What is the Abilitator®? Retrieved March 26, 2020, from https://sivusto.kykyviisari.fi/en/about-the-abilitator/what-is-the-abilitator/
Lämsä, A.-L. (2012). *Active inclusion of young people with disabilities or health problems. National report—Finland.* Dublin.
Loden, M., & Rosener, J. B. (1991). *Workforce America: Managing employee diversity as a vital resources.* Irwin Publishing.
Mattila-Wiro, P., & Tiainen, R. (2019). Involving all in working life. Results and recommendations from the OTE key project "Career opportunities for people with partial work ability'. Ministry of Social Affairs and Health: Helsinki.
McKinsey & Company. (2012). *Women matter: An Asian perspective.*
Miller, F. A., & Katz, J. H. (2002). *The inclusion breakthrough: Unleashing the real power of diversity.* Berrett-Koehler Publishers, Inc.
Ministry of Social Affairs and Health of Finland. (2021). Services and support for people with disabilities. Retrieved May 4, 2021, from https://stm.fi/en/disability-services
Nikkei Asia. (2020, January 4). Japan's shortage of AI talent opens doors for disabled workers. By Saiji Ugajin. Retrieved August 19, 2021. https://asia.nikkei.com/Business/Business-trends/Japan-s-shortage-of-AI-talent-opens-doors-for-disabled-workers
Overcash, J. A. (2003). Narrative research: A review of methodology and relevance to clinical practice. *Critical Reviews in Oncology/Hematology, 48*(2), 179–184.
Paikka auki. (2020). What is the Vacant Job funding program. March 26, 2020, from https://www.paikka-auki.fi/mika-on-paikka-auki-ohjelma/ (in Finnish).
Roberson, Q. M. (2006). Disentangling the meanings of diversity and inclusion in organizations. *Group and Organization Management, 31*(2), 212–223.

Shore, L. M., Randel, A. E., Chung, B. G., Dean, M. A., Ehrhart, K. H., & Singh, G. (2011). Inclusion and diversity in work groups: A review and model for future research. *Journal of Management, 37*(4), 1262–1289.

Siltavalmennus. (2020). Social entrepreneurship as a path to meaningful work. Retrieved March 26, 2020, from https://www.siltavalmennus.fi/ilona-sosiaalinen-yrittajyys-vaylana-mielekkaaseen-tyohon/ (in Finnish).

Swanson, R. A., & Holton, E. F., III. (2009). *Foundations of human resource development* (2nd ed.). Berrett-Koehler Publishers.

TEM. (2020). Social enterprises. Ministry of Economic Affairs and Employment of Finland. Retrieved April 5, 2020, from https://tem.fi/en/social-enterprises

THL. (2019). The Abilitator tool becomes available for all service providers. Newsletter of the Finnish institute for health and welfare. Retrieved April 15, 2020, from https://thl.fi/fi/web/hyvinvoinnin-ja-terveyden-edistamisen-johtaminen/osallisuuden-edistaminen/heikoimmassa-asemassa-olevien-osallisuus/ajankohtaista/uutiskirje/uutiskirje-2-2018/kykyviisari-avautui-tyovalineeksi-kaikille-toimijoille (in Finnish).

UNDP. (2021). Latest human development index ranking. Human development reports. United Nations development programme. Latest Human Development Index Ranking | Human Development Reports (undp.org). Retrieved April 15, 2020.

United Nations. (2015). Transforming our world: The 2030 Agenda for Sustainable Development.

Veikkaus. (2020). How the profits of Veikkaus games are distributed. Retrieved April 24, 2020, from https://www.veikkaus.fi/fi/yritys#!/avustukset/avustuskohteet (in Finnish).

Verainen, L.-M. (2013). Socially responsible businesses recruiting professionals with disabilities in the project leap to labour! In A. Idström, M. Stenroos, & M. Uimonen (Eds.), *Decent work. Promising practices in the employment of people with disabilities from Sweden, Denmark, Estonia, and Finland* (pp. 139–145). ASPA Publications.

WHO. (2011). *World report on disability*. WHO and the World Bank.

World Bank. (2021). GDP per capita, PPP (current international USD). International Comparison Program, World Development Indicators database. Retrieved July 10, 2021, from https://data.worldbank.org/indicator/NY.GDP.PCAP.PP.CD?most_recent_value_desc=true

Yritystä. (2020). Yritystä! project. Retrieved April 5, 2020, from https://www.xn%2D%2Dyrityst-cxa.fi/ (in Finnish).

Interviews

Ando, M., Personnel Manager, ACE Accessibility consortium of enterprises, Tokyo, Japan, May 25 and December 1, 2016.

Lindberg, J., Development manager, VATES foundation, Helsinki, Finland, August 15, 2019.

Munther, R., Project Manager, ILONA project, Silta-Valmennusyhdistys, Tampere, Finland, April 20, 2020.

Verainen, L-M., Planning Officer, The Finnish Neuromuscular Disorders Association, Turku, Finland, August 19, 2019.

Hong Kong: "*Business as Usual*" Amidst Social Unrest

Lucía Morales and Bernadette Andreosso-O'Callaghan

Abstract With the signature of the Treaty of Nanjing in 1842, China was forced to forfeit many of its territorial and sovereignty rights and to cede a number of territories, in particular the island of Hong Kong, to the British in perpetuity. However, the final treaty, the Convention for the Extension of Hong Kong Territory, led China to lease the New Territories to Britain for 99 years. On July 1, 1997, the British presence ended under the terms of the Sino-British Joint Declaration signed in 1984, through the retrocession of the ex-colony to the People's Republic of China (PRC). The Joint Declaration stated that Hong Kong would retain political and social autonomy through a "*one country, two systems*" policy until 2047. During its time as a British colony, HK evolved from a scattered assortment of farming and fishing villages and shantytowns to become a port, a manufacturing centre, and a financial hub, all with a global dimension. However, its democratic nature seems to be fading away as Beijing is determined to tame political defiance in the former British colony. In 2014, Beijing declared that it would wield "*comprehensive jurisdiction*" over the territory, culminating in the introduction of a sweeping Hong Kong national security law in June 2020. While Hong Kong is historically associated with peaceful pro-democracy demonstrations, pro-democracy rallies have been repressed with increasing violence which has accentuated since the Umbrella Movement of 2014. More recently, there was an upsurge of violence triggered by the 2019/20 "*Extradition Bill*," with technology and social media emerging as key supporting tools for protest organisers that led to violent confrontations between the population and the local authorities. Beijing reacted by unleashing a myriad of actions to bring Hong Kong back into order and to impose the communist party's implacable rule over the

L. Morales (✉)
School of Accounting, Finance and Economics, Faculty of Business, Technological University Dublin, Dublin, Ireland
e-mail: lucia.morales@tudublin.ie

B. Andreosso-O'Callaghan
Department of Economics, Kemmy Business School, University of Limerick, Limerick, Ireland

Ruhr Universität Bochum, Bochum, Germany
e-mail: Bernadette.Andreosso@ul.ie

B. Andreosso-O'Callaghan et al. (eds.), *Sustainable Development in Asia*,
Contributions to Economics, https://doi.org/10.1007/978-3-030-94679-1_4

territory. As Beijing's grip stiffens, HK is moving relentlessly towards an authoritarian regime that its legal and democratic system does not seem capable of neutralising. This raises the crucial question of the sustainability of Hong Kong as a key financial centre and trade hub in the future.

Keywords Hong Kong · Mainland China · Technology · Financial hub · Social unrest · Sustainability

1 Introduction

To understand the undergoing tensions between Hong Kong and mainland China, one needs to examine their historical relationship. The First Opium War was fought between 1839–1842, resulting in a quick British victory that signalled the rise of the West and the decline of China (Bush, 2016). In the aftermath of the war, China was forced to pay a US$21 million indemnity, and Britain got one part of what is today's Hong Kong as a spoil of war, and the first five Treaty Ports were opened (Bracken, 2019; Downs, 2014). The Second Opium War, known as the Arrow War, was fought between 1856 and 1860, leading to the Treaty of Tientsin and to additional treaties that led to the second transfer of territory to Britain, who secured the lower Kowloon Peninsula and associated islands. The treaties signed between 1856 and 1860 are known in China as the "*unequal treaties*" imposed on an unwilling China that felt tarnished as it was obliged to surrender further territory to foreign powers. This period is seen by many Chinese as the lowest point in the country's history. The third territorial transfer took place in 1898, with Britain adding a northern extension from the Kowloon Peninsula and several other islands that were transferred back to China in 1997 (Bracken, 2019). China regards the nineteenth century as a period of great national humiliation, where foreign nations blighted Chinese territory at their will.

The British handed Hong Kong back to China in 1997 after over 150 years of British control, and the negotiations over the transfer conditions took place only between Britain and China as no representative from Hong Kong was invited to the negotiations table. The agreement reached stated that Hong Kong would remain a special administrative region until 2047 (Hau, 2021; Yahuda, 1993; History, 2021; Treaty Series, 1994). According to the Sino-British Joint Declaration (1984), the handover was supposed to result in a "*one country, two systems*" relationship with China, whereby Hong Kong would function within the ambit of its existing laws that were to remain unchanged (History, 2019). Before the handover, Hong Kong enjoyed a high level of autonomy and political freedom. The Joint Declaration sought to ensure that Hong Kong would remain the same for a period of 50 years, operating as a capitalist economy that preserves its citizens' historical rights. The Joint Declaration states, "*…Hong Kong Special Administrative Region will be directly under the authority of the Central People's Government of the People's Republic of China*"; "*…the laws currently in force in Hong Kong will remain basically unchanged*"; "*…the current social and economic systems in Hong Kong will remain unchanged and so will the lifestyle. Rights and freedoms, including those* *of the person, of speech, of the press, of assembly, of association, of travel, of movement, of correspondence, of strike, of choice of occupation, of academic research, and of religious belief will be ensured by law in the Hong Kong Special Administrative Region. Private property, ownership of enterprises, legitimate right of inheritance and foreign investment will be protected by law*" (Constitutional and Mainland Affairs Bureau, 2007; United Nations—Treaty Series, 1994, p. 62). However, the handover has brought significant challenges to Hong Kong as its residents are experiencing growing interference by the Chinese authorities in its affairs; as a result, concerns regarding the region's future are growing and the sustainability of its democratic system both before and after 2047 is undeniably under question.

This chapter seeks to examine the ongoing instability and the challenges in terms of economic and political sustainability in Hong Kong, by developing a dual assessment of the economic implications for its status as a financial centre and exploring how social media and communication technologies may have contributed to undermining Hong Kong's privileged position as a financial centre. The economic and financial environment in Hong Kong is rather contaminated by an ideological framework portraying the case of "*business as usual*" for Hong Kong and its financial industry. Over the past 25 years, Hong Kong has been facing significant challenges to keep its prominent status as a major Asian financial hub. The territory is today in intense competition with Shanghai as China's leading financial centre; this allows us to pose the following questions: will the "*one country, two systems*" model remain intact as frictions with mainland China continue? Will Hong Kong remain a prominent international financial hub? We aim to offer some critical insights into these vital questions as currently the economic, political and democratic future of Hong Kong looks very uncertain.

2 Hong Kong Historical Overview

When the island of Hong Kong became a British colony, it was a barren location with few prospects due to its limited population and lack of fertile land. Mainstream society in Hong Kong was mainly composed of small groups of peasants, artisans, and merchants, without any significant representation of the traditional Chinese literati or of the scholar-official aristocracy (Hung-Kay, 1998). As a result, no formal leadership or political power was exerted over the territory (Downs, 2014). Over the years, Hong Kong's governance has been defined by its non-interventionist nature. Such an approach contributed to the distinctiveness and differentiation of the island's society and culture from mainland China. The HK government's historical decision to follow a positive non-interventionist approach meant that the authorities limited their role to providing essential services while minimising other commitments and interventions. The educational system can be considered as a good example of the authorities' non-interventionist approach. The government has limited its role to allocating the required educational resources, providing support on the various aspects of the learning development process, and ensuring that schools' needs were met by adequately addressing increasing social demands. However, the curriculum content and most of the decisions involving the functioning of the school system have remained the responsibility of parents and teachers and reflected their respective preferences (Chang & Yeung, 2017; Hung-Kay, 1998; OECD, 2010). In terms of culture, policy was based on a laissez-faire approach. Over the years, HK's population enjoyed significant freedom when deciding about their cultural preferences, choices and consumption patterns, with many cultural goods imports undertaken with minimal and frugal government intervention. Before 1997, Hong Kongers experienced a greater access to cultural and artistic goods and services, which were characterised by more significant degrees of openness than any other Chinese urban dwellers. However, that freedom has continuously lessened since the 1997 handover, revealing an ongoing process that seeks to bring Hong Kong under the control of mainland China and of the ruling communist party, thereby jeopardizing the sustainability of its once open and democratic governance model.

2.1 *Hong Kong's Beginnings*

By the early twentieth century, the island's population had increased significantly. Most of the populace was primarily based on migrants from the surrounding Chinese regions that identified Hong Kong as a sojourners' society from the very beginning. At the time, the total number of inhabitants in the whole colony was about 300,000, including those in the leased New Territories (Hung-Kay, 1998). By the 1930s, Hong Kong exhibited the essential characteristics of a frontier society, as its population was predominantly male, typically of working age, with direct roots to China as they were born in Chinese towns and villages rather than in HK itself. Most male migrants moved to Hong Kong to seek employment and better economic opportunities while leaving their families behind in their Chinese home villages or towns. Since the 1840s, Hong Kong has been a meeting point between China and the international economy (Bush, 2016). Nonetheless, the economic and demographic development of Hong Kong city as is known today started in 1949, and not in 1842 at the end of the First Opium War. With the proclamation of the PRC in 1949, after the success of Mao's Chinese Communist Revolution, the nature of Hong Kong China changed substantially. Refugees from the revolution could not return to their Chinese homes, as had been the case for earlier migrants (Hambro, 1955). By then, Hong Kong faced significant challenges as the two million newcomers fleeing from the revolution did not initially identify with Hong Kong and considered themselves only as sojourners in Hong Kong. The newcomers faced significant challenges in adapting to their new reality. They felt that their true lives were left behind in their home places, and they struggled to attach themselves to their new surroundings, before gradually breaking their bonds with their provinces of origin. Eventually, in the 1960s and 1970s, these migrants realised that they did not have any other alternative but to settle down and grow their roots in Hong Kong (Hambro, 1955; Hung-Kay, 1998; Downs, 2014). Over time, Hong Kong experienced significant levels of economic and social development. Industrialisation took off, bringing substantial improvements to the region's standard of living, and allowing the enclave to become one of the "Four Asian Tigers," together with South Korea, Taiwan and Singapore. Economic prosperity started to offer new opportunities leading to growing socio-economic disparities with mainland China. Since then, Hong Kong has witnessed an extraordinary transformation. Its has evolved into a society with a distinct way of life that has blended Chinese and Western cultural traditions to form a modern urban-industrial civilisation as it is understood today (Cheng, 2008; Hung-Kay, 1998).

2.2 *Hong Kong's Economic Transformation*

In the 1950s, Hong Kong started its economic and social transformation driven by three converging forces:

(a) Cheap labour and migration (represented mainly by refugees from the southern part of the PRC). This increased Hong Kong's population to approximately three million people by 1960. Refugees constituted a low wage working force pool that were in turn pivotal in attracting foreign direct investment to the island.
(b) Closed Borders: China closed its border with Hong Kong in 1949–1950, afraid of "capitalist and *bourgeois* contamination" emerging from the territory. During this period, border controls were also introduced in Hong Kong, and Western economies led by the US imposed an economic embargo on exports to and imports from China (Bush, 2016; Chan, 1995). The trade ban meant that Hong Kong would not be used as an entrepôt for China's export and import activities.
(c) Multinational Companies (MNCs); MNCs were searching to expand their Asian presence to benefit from both low-cost raw materials and cheap labour to produce goods that met their quality control standards.

Consequently, Hong Kong emerged as a global manufacturing hub, marking the beginning of the island's regional and international development (Nichols, 2020). To support its flourishing economic activity, the HK government started to develop a public health and educational system, as well as low-rent public housing schemes for refugees; moreover, significant amounts of capital were invested in transportation infrastructure and in developing the ports for global distribution. Arrangements to ensure water supplies for the colony were made with Beijing. Ethnic Chinese firms grew alongside their British counterparts and were happy to be co-opted by the colonial administration (Bush, 2016; Chan, 1995). As a result, Hong Kong experienced rapid economic growth and it relatively quickly became a middle-class society that was only affected by occasional major disruptions. China and Hong Kong maintained a limited co-existence that was disrupted in 1967 during Mao's "*Great Proletarian Cultural Revolution*." During this period, energised left-wing activists mobilised protests that culminated in violent demonstrations and led to a variety of terrorist acts. The local authorities rapidly controlled the situation as Hong Kong's incumbent government took a firm position, resulting in the protesters and their followers being soon brought under Beijing's control.

In the 1950s, the City became a busy trading port, and its economy started to flourish, fuelled by manufacturing activity (Schenk, 2008). Since then, Hong Kong has emerged as a prosperous and democratic colony, and it became one of the most important global financial centres, manufacturing hubs and trade ports. However, at the same time, the region became very popular among migrants and political dissidents seeking to leave behind excruciating poverty, instability, curtailment of rights and persecution in mainland China. They were attracted to Hong Kong either for the opportunities that emerged for trade and employment in the colony or for its role as a place of political stability during wars, heightened conflict and rebellions on the mainland (So, 2011).

In the late 1970s, when Mao Zedong died and Deng Xiaoping started economic policy reforms, Hong Kong emerged as a valuable asset in opening up the Chinese economy to the rest of the world. The main ambition of the reforms was to stimulate and drive economic growth to improve and enhance the economic conditions of Chinese people. As China started to open up its economy, Hong Kong benefited from the emerging economic activity. The island also thrived as a manufacturing hub for the production and assembly of manufactured goods by multinational corporations.

In the 1980s, as the Chinese economy continued adjusting its economic model with its ambition of economic integration into the global economy, incremental economic reforms followed suit, leading multinationals to shift their production activities into South China. The shift rendered the need to reconsider the nature of Hong Kong's economic activity, and the island started to reconfigure its economic model towards the services sector, particularly towards financial services. Hong Kong emerged as a significant financial hub in the Asian region, but with the impact of the 1997 Asian Financial Crisis (AFC) and since 2003 in particular, it became clear that the territory had become more and more dependent on China's mainland economy to support its economic progress. Beijing also undertook a more interventionist approach to the territory by introducing a good number of policy steps aimed at sustaining Hong Kong's economic growth. Since then, the ties with and interventions from mainland China have started to grow and to consolidate.

2.3 *Rising Levels of Political Instability*

The economic opening up process started by China consolidated a period of economic buoyancy for Hong Kong that had stalled at the time the island was handed over to China on July 1, 1997. Interestingly, the AFC started just a day after the handover, on July 2, 1997. The AFC created severe economic difficulties for Hong Kong that saw its stock market plunging by as much as 60 per cent; property prices witnessed significant drops and GDP per capita declined by 7.8 per cent in 1998. The financial mayhem impacted employment levels, with a substantial number of

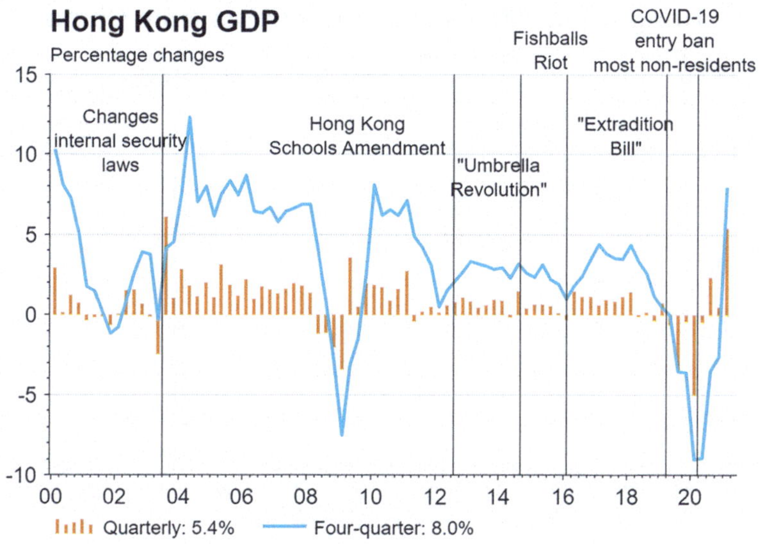

Fig. 1 Hong Kong's GDP. (Source: Refinitiv Datastream)

workers losing their jobs. This complex economic landscape was further exacerbated by the outburst of the Severe Acute Respiratory Syndrome coronavirus epidemic (SARS) that hit the region in 2003. The island authorities' slow response was a defining feature of their reaction to the SARS crisis. The mainland China origins of the virus were downplayed by the HK local authorities, so as not to cause embarrassment to the PRC. This created in turn significant discontent among Hong Kongers who started questioning the credibility of their own government, signalling the winds of change for the island, its democratic system and its society. Consequently, a number of social movements mushroomed, such as the 2014 Umbrella Movement. Figure 1 offers a clear picture of the island's economic performance and highlights critical GDP fluctuations associated with occasions when contentious policies were implemented by the HK government and the associated follow-on protests.

3 Hong Kong Pro-Democracy Protests

Historically, the relationship between mainland China and Hong Kong has been surrounded by complexity and ongoing conflicts. Currently, Hong Kong still enjoys freedoms that are not known to mainland China's citizens even though they have already been significantly slashed, particularly since the outburst of the 2020 Global Health Crisis, in line with trends at the global level. The diminution of these freedoms has become a source of concern, and it raises questions over Hong

Fig. 2 Hong Kong pro-democracy protests. (Source: Refinitiv Datastream)

Kong's economic/financial and political sustainability. China's continuous attempts to undermine Hong Kong's democratic system have been met by public social gatherings, pro-democracy movements and peaceful demonstrations. However, the protests have been disrupted by the authorities as the latest protests have intensified in terms of confrontation (Shek, 2020; Martin, 2019). Figure 2 highlights some of the most important pro-democracy demonstrations since the 1960s, showing how they have intensified since the 1997 handover and how the 2014 Umbrella Revolution marked a shift point in terms of their intensification and with connotations of more aggressive protests.

On July 1, 2003, Hong Kongers came out onto the streets to protest against Article 23 of the Basic law, fearing it would threaten freedom of association, freedom of information, the free press, and endanger freedom of speech and religion (The Financial Times, 2020). While mass protests were not unknown in the territory, the demonstrations that erupted in late September 2014 signalled a dramatic shift from previous protests. Under the 2014 Umbrella Movement, citizens called for a more transparent election process for the territory's chief executive. One of the critical points of the 1984 Joint Declaration states: "*...the Government of Hong Kong Special Administrative Region will be composed of local inhabitants ... The chief executive will be appointed by the Central People's Government on the basis of the results of elections or consultations to be held locally*."

Local observers were aware that things were different in 2014 and that trouble was looming (Bush, 2016). The breakout of the Umbrella Movement in the fall of 2014 can be considered as a cut-off point, where the police fired volleys of tear gas to scatter the crowds. The violent nature of the police actions raised the first cries of alarm in respect of their crowd-control tactics (The Washington Post, 2019; Baigorri, 2019). In the aftermath of the Umbrella protests, the Chinese government has exerted greater control in the fields of academia, media, civil society, and politics, and there is greater divisiveness between locals and mainland Chinese in Hong Kong and within Hong Kong society itself regarding the reach of Beijing's intervention in the territory's affairs (Ming Hui, 2015).

The Umbrella Movement marked a breakpoint regarding pro-democracy protests and their peaceful nature. It has revealed significant cracks and divisiveness between the Hong Kong and Chinese governments, between residents, between local and wealthy businesses, between the middle and the most affluent classes, and how younger generations perceive their freedoms compared to their elders. Different social classes and generations having distinct understandings of their economic and political interests and the importance of citizens' participation and involvement in the territory's political affairs emerged as a defining factor during the recent demonstrations. According to Bush (2016), the Umbrella Movement marked one of the most contentious episodes in a three-decade struggle by proponents of a more democratic system.

There are similarities between how the peaceful protests in Hong Kong have been violently repressed and China's own violent response to peaceful protests in the mainland. Until 2020, Hong Kong remained the only place in Greater China where people could commemorate the June 1989 Tiananmen Square protests in Beijing—coyly referred to in China as the June Fourth Incident—through a symbolic candle-light vigil in Victoria Park. In June 1989, the Tiananmen "incident" saw many unarmed peaceful pro-democracy protesters calling for political and economic reform and demanding a democratic government in China. A peaceful, friendly and gentle nature characterised the protests, but in return, the Chinese authorities responded with overwhelming force to repress the demonstrations. The response of the Communist Party was implacable, and the protests were declared illegal and subversive in nature; the government sent in the army supported by tanks to suppress the students' protests, resulting in bloodshed and casualties (So, 2011; Amnesty International UK, 2019). According to Amnesty International UK (2019), tens of thousands of demonstrators were arrested in cities across China. The final death toll from Tiananmen that night is still unknown to the public today, as the Chinese authorities have never disclosed the total number of casualties and people detained. The Tiananmen Square massacre remains a contentious topic in China as the Chinese authorities have never officially acknowledged what happened, and as there is no clarity regarding the true nature of the events and the human loss. Until now, the authorities have banned all mention of the protest; however, the "incident" still vividly resonates through Hong Kong society; at the time, the Tiananmen event triggered another crisis of confidence leading to massive demonstrations and emigration waves from Hong Kong during the 1990s due to the lack of trust in Beijing's "*One Country, Two Systems*" policy. While Hong Kong remained the only Greater China territory that could commemorate the Tiananmen massacre, the situation changed in June 2020, when the residents across the region, gathered to commemorate the victims of China's 1989 crackdown, had to defy a police ban due to restrictions on social gatherings imposed as a result of the SARS 2 COVID-19 pandemic. The opportune 2020 Global Health Crisis has enabled and has helped justify the introduction of significant limitations to further public freedoms that might have severe and lasting effects, judging by the trends followed by the prolonged COVID-19 restrictions.

In February 2019, the Government of the Special Administrative Region, Hong Kong, sought to introduce significant legislative changes through the Fugitive Offenders and Mutual Legal Assistance in Criminal Matters Legislation (Amendment) Ordinance 2019—Bill (The Legislative Council, 2019). The purported primary purpose of the "*Extradition Bill*" was to regulate the transfer of criminal fugitives wanted in different parts of China, including Taiwan, mainland China and Macau. According to the government of the Hong Kong Special Administrative Region, 2019 press release:

> *The objectives of the Bill are to address the Taiwan homicide case and to plug the loopholes in Hong Kong's overall mechanism in juridical assistance.* (Press Release, 2019)

The proposed changes by the Bill led to a powerful reaction among Hong Kongers. They represented a dramatic change to the existing laws and extradition procedures, and the Bill was perceived as a direct attack on Hong Kong's democratic system. The reform would have allowed extradition from Hong Kong to mainland China. The protests against the reform have led to more comprehensive demands for democratic reform and an inquiry into alleged police brutality (B.B.C 2019). As China is continuously tightening its grip on Hong Kong, Beijing keeps developing new proposals on amending the national security law, raising serious concerns regarding human rights, with direct implications for political activists. Before the handover in July 1997 to mainland China, extraditions were prohibited, and as a result, protests against the Bill started with numerous demonstrations against the Chinese authorities' continual interventions (Shek, 2020). Initially, demonstrations were peaceful and were perceived as a "*social event.*" However, the situation quickly evolved into violent protests, acts of vandalism, and the occupation of the Hong Kong Polytechnic University and the Chinese University of Hong Kong. People from different social classes, sectors, and with differing ideologies joined the protests, including medical doctors, teachers, information and communication professionals, and social workers. However, a defining characteristic of the protests was the heavy presence of students who mainly dominated the demonstrations. Many students were involved in the protests, and they became associated with the possession of petrol bombs and violent artefacts. Mainland China has made significant progress in silencing the pre-existing socio-political movement that emerged as a response to the Extradition Bill that is now withdrawn. However, Beijing continues to enhance its interventions in the territory, and it has now approved a plan that seeks to impose national security laws that aim to prevent and punish acts and activities that are viewed as a threat to national security (The New York Times, 2020; The Guardian, 2020).

The violent dimension was a defining factor of the demonstrations, and the lack of accountability and responsibility for organising the events was another significant feature. There are claims that the protests and strikes were organised using social media channels and that there was no evidence of well-structured organisations being part of the revolt. Some consider that the whole movement was entirely voluntary and orchestrated by amateurs (Purbrick, 2019). However, the high numbers of people arrested due to significant levels of violence that emerged because of the police's alleged excessive use of force have led some to question the idea that the demonstrations were not organised. Within the outlined context, the 2020 Health Crisis acted as a cut-off point, which contributed to diverting public attention away from protests and towards the epidemic. Social distancing and economic lockdown measures entered the scene, acting as a neutraliser of rallies and of unwelcome social gatherings. Therefore, the 2020 Health Crisis acted somehow as a timely tool to help justify the intervention by the police forces to counteract protesters' acts. And as such, SARS 2 COVID-19 might be the launch pad of a potential ban on the Tiananmen vigil commemoration in the years to come and it may lead to the introduction of further curtailments on the freedoms and democratic rights of Hong Kongers.

Hong Kong experienced serious rioting between May and July 1967, after the Cultural Revolution began in China. The riots which were instigated by leftists with Beijing's knowledge and approval led to 60 casualties (The New York Times, 2016). In September 1983, there was a protest at Victoria Park, as protesters were unhappy with high levels of inflation that were allegedly worsening the standards of living of Hong Kongers. The government's seeming indifference to the protests led to a violent riot involving looting, arson, and the ransacking of a police station in January 1984. Social unrest stiffened as taxi drivers and metro rails workers engaged in strikes, resulting in the police force using tear gas and nightsticks to control protesters. The demonstrations were characterised by the involvement of thousands of young people who engaged in looting, arson, and other vandalism in a densely populated area near the southwestern coast of the Kowloon peninsula. The Police Commissioner at the time indicated that criminal acts would not be tolerated and responded with force (The New York Times, 1984). Figure 3 identifies some of the most notorious protests that have taken place in Hong Kong since the 1960s, showing an intensification of pro-democracy protests since the 1997 handover.

As Hong Kong seeks to protect its democratic rights and liberal values, Beijing tries to further control and subjugate the territory to the rulings of the communist party. To fight back, a sequence of protests have taken place since Hong Kong was handed over to China as Hong Kong people are concerned about their liberties and their freedoms and how mainland China is trying to curtail them. For example, the introduction of changes to internal security legislation led to fierce protests in Hong Kong in 2003; the proposed amendments to the curriculum of the Hong Kong Schools (Moral and National Education in 2012) were viewed as attempts to brainwash Hong Kong's youth; the reshaping of Hong Kong's electoral system (Umbrella Movement, 2014) was interpreted as an attempt to attack the region's democratic system directly; its way of life was claimed to be under attack (Fishball Riots, 2016) with for example, the proposed legislation that changes extradition laws

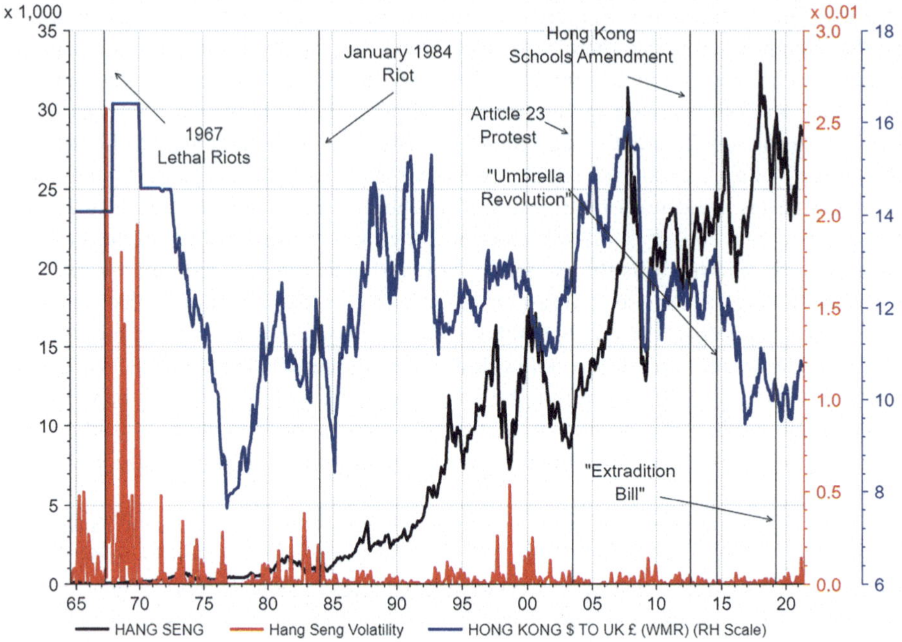

Fig. 3 Hong Kong historical protests. (Source: Refinitiv Datastream)

allowing criminal suspects to be sent to mainland China for trial (Extradition Bill, 2019).

4 Technology, Media and Social Media to Fuel Social Unrest

Technology, media and social media can play a significant role in the context of contentious politics. According to Lee (2020), the use of falsified news and rumours can be used by governments—through mainstream media—to delegitimise protest movements. They can also be used by protest movements to pressurise political power and serve to sustain themselves. Social media has led to the emergence of a new type of protest that Castells (2012) has conceptualised as a "*networked social movement*" characterised for being decentralised, leaderless and spontaneous. Over the past decade, researchers have offered evidence and insights on how social media might have contributed to protests' organisation, mobilisation and coordination (Lee et al., 2020; Chu, 2018). Research findings suggest that the early stages of protests are characterised by the orderliness and politeness of the protesters that are frequently remarked upon in media reports (Buckley & Ramzy, 2014; Dissanayake, 2014). The role of Facebook, WhatsApp and later Firechat have been highlighted as playing an active role in organising protesters (Chu, 2018; Anthony, 2014). Valenzuela (2013) points to social media playing three major distinctive roles in social movements through: (1) information sharing, (2) political expression and (3) mobilisation. However, researchers like Smidi and Shahin (2017) offer alternative views that question the role of social media, suggesting that it has played a limited or secondary role in terms of protest mobilisation. Furthermore, researchers like Poell and van Dijck (2015) offer cautionary remarks regarding the potential overestimation of the power of social media, as the fast-paced approach of information sharing could affect how activists shape their content (Lee, 2020). Another line of discussion proposes that social media channels are more likely to become "*echo chambers*" than fora for democratic debate (Sustein, 2001), with Stein (2017) concluding that the role of ICTs in the organisation and mobilisation of protesters remains inconclusive. Protest potential events at times when social mobilisation is generally weak can help maintain the potential of protest and could contribute to enhancing radical positions. Lee (2018) suggests that after the Umbrella Movement, many supporters of the pro-democracy movement have turned to support more radical tactics and ideologies. Furthermore, Santoro and Fitzpatrick (2015) suggest that radicalisation is usually associated with dissatisfaction with movements' outcomes.

In the context of Hong Kong's social unrest, the connection to social media has been identified as a significant factor in respect of the 2014 Umbrella Revolution by contributing to the spread of political consciousness among younger people, some of whom were previously politically apathetic, and by facilitating the rapid mobilisation and continuous communication between protesters. The Umbrella Movement was reported on television and social media, with the latter playing a defining role in how the protests were carried out. Students used umbrellas to protect themselves against the tear gas and pepper spray used by the police, and they rapidly became a symbol for the protests. The shadow of a violent crackdown that mirrored Chinese authorities' response to the 1989 protests emerged during the initially peaceful demonstrations in 2014. Additionally, there are growing concerns that the central government is slowly exerting control over newspapers. Increasing fears of how younger generations are taking social media as the primary source of information are growing due to the spread of sensationalist and un-journalistic "*conspiracy-type*" news.

The organisation of protests is not new in the territory, but there is no doubt that worrying trends are developing. As discussed above, the events in 2016 and 2019 showed a significant variation in the tone of the protests which have shifted from peaceful events towards violent clashes between street protesters and the police. But what kind of role has social media played in the organisation of these protests? and what role has the media and social media played in their transformation from peaceful to confrontational? The role played by social media, the official media and technology need to be considered carefully. Technology might play a crucial role as it allows individuals to hide and manipulate information. Lee (2020) argues that the considerable protests against the Extradition Bill in Hong Kong were marked by the widespread circulation of a wide range of rumours and so-called fake news. During the recent protests (Lee, 2018), there was a surge in the number of images of police and protesters' brutality that sought to fulfil different agendas. As such, social media seems to play a leading role in the increasing difficulty in differentiating between truthful and manipulated information and the implications for potential confrontation between protesters, the government and the police forces. Furthermore, the media might also be helping to hide the identities of those organising the protests, making it very difficult to know the real drivers of the protests. As such, technology can be identified as a contributing factor that helps justify the need to use emergency powers to control violence and social unrest, leading to the introduction of legislation that further undermines democratic rights. The extent to which social media can be identified as a culprit for intensifying violent protests is an issue that requires further analysis. For example, the violent nature that defined the 1967 protests cannot be attributed to the impact of social media. From an economic perspective, the increasing levels of confrontation and violence associated with the most recent events raise significant concerns regarding the territory's political stability and the implications for the sustainability of its economic and financial model.

5 The Future of Hong Kong's Economic and Social Model

Hong Kong's population amounts to 7474.2 million, 45.7 per cent male and 54.3 per cent female and a negative population growth rate of –0.3 per cent. Unemployment was 6.4 per cent as per 2020 data (see Figs. 4 and 5), and the year on year GDP Q1 change was 7.9 per cent. Hong Kong is composed of a total area of 1110.18km^2

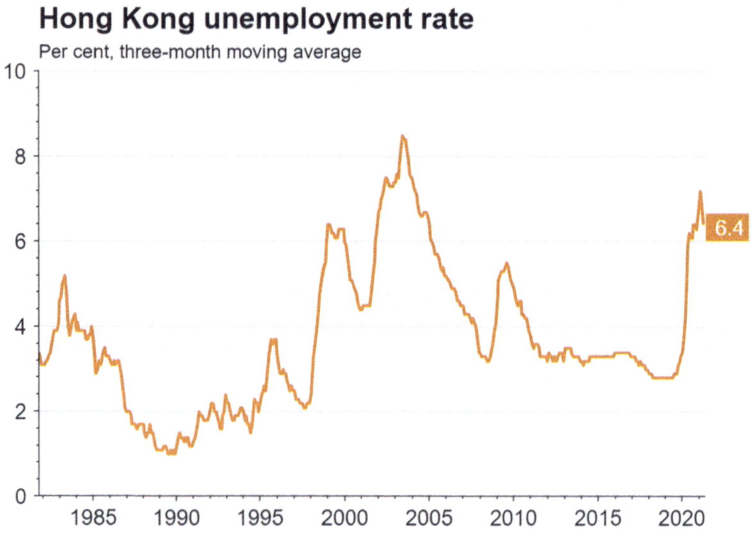

Fig. 4 Unemployment rate (Hong Kong, 1982–2021). (Source: Refinitiv Datastream)

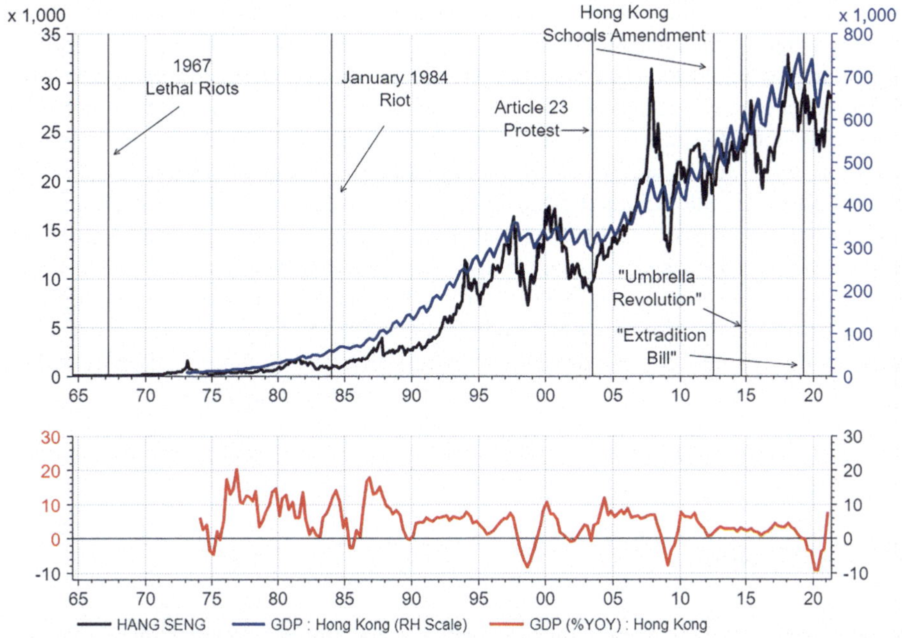

Fig. 5 Hong Kong economic indicators. (Source: Refinitiv Datastream)

covering Hong Kong Island, Kowloon, and the New Territories and Islands (Hong Kong Census and Statistics Department, 2021). The problems with its economic model mirror the problems exhibited by the world's most developed economies. Economic development and progress have improved the population's living standards, but it has also contributed to widening income inequality. In the context of Hong Kong, income distribution is more skewed than the trends exhibited by other developed economies. As a result, the economic model has created grievances against the government among those who feel left behind, with significant implications concerning imbalanced economic development, rising economic inequality levels and an impoverished middle-class. On the other hand, macroeconomic fundamentals remain relatively strong for the region, as its economy has expanded year on year in real terms. Quite remarkably, the disruptive nature of the 2014 protests did not seem to create significant problems regarding Hong Kong's position as a regional and global financial hub and a centre for services and investments, at least not in the short term (Morales & Andreosso-O'Callaghan, 2018).

According to Ching (2009), during the first decade of Hong Kong's SAR history, Beijing adopted a hands-off policy, opting for non-interference in Hong Kong affairs. However, Cao (2008) argues that, in fact, Hong Kong is defined as having two governing teams: one is the establishment team of the Hong Kong government, and the second consists of Chinese government authorities responsible for Hong Kong issues on the mainland. However, Hong Kong developed a separate identity, lifestyle, society, culture, and economic system over the years due to its separation from mainland China that started in the 1950s after the proclamation of the People's Republic of China (PRC) in 1949. As 2047 approaches, economists and investors are raising concerns regarding the erosion of the territory's freedoms and the growing intervention of Beijing in the territory's affairs; these changes are calling into question the future viability of its unique financial market (Hung, 2021). The promulgation of the National Security Law was a landmark moment effectively ending Hong Kong's civil liberties and a warning of the potential threat to Hong Kong's status as a global financial capital as the enacted changes are more draconian than those intended in the original extradition bill. International investors are looking at the territory's developments with concern and are increasingly using other locations as destinations for investment and diversification purposes. This will undermine the territory's position as a prominent international financial hub.

6 Conclusions

In conclusion, it can be argued that the historical separation between Hong Kong and mainland China can be summarised as a two-stage process:

(a) 1840s–1940s: Hong Kong was ceded to Great Britain in 1842 due to China's defeat in the First Opium War. The outcome was Hong Kong's transformation into a British colony, with the primary purpose of promoting trade and investment in China. During this period, Hong Kong remained closely connected to China from the economic and social viewpoints. The Hong Kong population was based on migrants from South China who viewed Hong Kong as a transit location whereas their feelings and identity remained tied to their Chinese hometowns (Chan, 1995). British policy had a clearly defined purpose and its main objective was to open up the Chinese economy to trade with Western nations so as to enable the projection of British power into East-Asia during the first half of the nineteenth century (Downs, 2014, p. 108). However, China itself had ambitions to define the rules of trade. At the time, China was severely affected by an internal crisis derived from large imports of opium from India. This gave rise to significant outflows of silver (China's currency of exchange at the time), with significant destabilising implications. China and Britain entered into direct confrontation, as the Chinese authorities were prepared to use coercion to preserve relative autarchy. In addition, Britain was just as determined to gain access to the Asian market, and was ready to use force to get its way into implementing what is now known and understood as the globalisation process (Bush, 2016). Undeniably, Hong Kong roots are strongly connected with the economic motives that have served the British and Chinese interests at different stages of their history, and the territory's future may be defined solely in terms of its mere economic existence.

(b) Post 1949: The Chinese Communist Revolution led to an exodus of refugees from China to Hong Kong who could not go back to China, and the colonial state introduced measures aimed at stopping the flow of refugees. In addition, the communist government introduced strict border controls, being afraid of "colonial capitalism." This process resulted in the economic transformation of Hong Kong. The City moved from being an entrepôt, oriented towards China, to becoming an export-led industrialised economy oriented towards the global market that subsequently transformed into a thriving regional and international financial hub. From the 1950s onwards, Hong Kong started to develop a separate identity, lifestyle, and culture that emerged as a blended model that shared some commonalities with mainland China and also integrated elements from Western societies.

The post 1997 handover unification process between China and Hong Kong has not been an easy and smooth transition. Hong Kong's sustainability in terms of remaining a global business region has been fundamentally challenged, as China's economy continues to grow more robust. In particular, Hong Kong's financial status is increasingly challenged by the rising competition of Shanghai and Shenzhen's financial centres. Undoubtedly, the global economy is changing, and, at the time of writing this chapter, Hong Kong needs to navigate an international landscape characterised by the Western powers' relative decline compensated by the growing influence of Communist China at both regional and global levels.

Beijing's reaction to the Hong Kong protests has been a source of major concern contributing to jeopardising the territory's status as an international financial hub and business centre due to growing levels of political instability and the curtailment of its population's freedoms and rights (Zenglein, 2020; Cantoni et al., 2018). While the region's economic fundamentals remain strong, prolonged political instability and Beijing's increasing intervention in the territory's affairs seem to severely impact the potential for future economic development. As the communist party intensifies its control, the competitiveness and sustainability of Hong Kong's economic model and financial centre are being destabilised and weakened compared to other locations. As a result, the territory's uniqueness, essence and identity are under threat as Beijing intensifies its grip on the territory.

Hong Kong's future relies on truly implementing the "*one country, two systems*" model that seems to be right now in a shambles. The future of Hong Kong as a prominent international financial hub is questionable due to a highly uncertain political environment as Beijing continues to redesign Hong Kong's economic and financial model in a time of global fundamental rights curtailment.

References

Amnesty International U.K. (2019). 1989 Tiananmen Square protests. https://www.amnesty.org.uk/china-1989-tiananmen-square-protests-demonstration-massacre

Anthony, S. (2014). Hong Kong protesters turn to mesh networks to evade China's censorship. https://www.extremetech.com/extreme/191118-hong-kong-protesters-turn-to-mesh-networks-to-evade-chinas-censorship
B.B.C. (2019). The Hong Kong protests explained in 100 and 500 words. https://www.bbc.com/news/world-asia-china-49317695
Baigorri, M. (2019). Hong Kong unrest rages on as police clash with protesters. https://www.bloomberg.com/news/articles/2019-12-01/police-clash-with-protesters-as-hong-kong-unrest-rages-on
Bracken, G. (2019). Treaty ports in China: Their genesis, development and influence. *Journal of Urban History, 45*(1), 168–176.
Buckley, C., & Ramzy, A. (2014). Hong Kong protest are leaderless but orderly. *The New York Times*. https://www.nytimes.com/2014/10/01/world/asia/in-hong-kong-clean-and-polite-but-a-protest-nonetheless.html
Bush, R. C. (2016, October). *Hong Kong in the shadow of China: Living with the Leviathan*. Bookings Institution Press, Political Science.
Cantoni, D., Yang, D. Y., Yuchtman, N., & Zhang, Y. J. (2018). Protests as strategic games: Experimental evidence from Hong Kong's anti-authoritarian movement. https://faculty.haas.berkeley.edu/yuchtman/Noam_Yuchtman_files/hk_protests.pdf
Cao, E. (2008). Governing forces under the condition of 'one country, two systems.' https://assets.publishing.service.gov.uk/government/uploads/system/uploads/attachment_data/file/32941/hk-report-jan-jun-2009.pdf
Castells, M. (2012). *Networks of outrage and hope*. Polity.
Census and Statistics Department. (2021). Hong Kong in figures. https://www.censtatd.gov.hk/en/EIndexbySubject.html?scode=460&pcode=B1010006
Chan, M. (1995). All in the family: The Hong Kong-Guangdnog link in historical perspective. In R. Kwok & A. So (Eds.), *The Hong Kong-Guangdong link: Partnership in Flux* (pp. 31–63). M.E. Sharpe.
Chang, C. K. Y., & Yeung, N. C. J. (2017). *Parental preference on primary school selection in Hong Kong*. The University of Hong Kong. http://tlerg.cetl.hku.hk/wp-content/uploads/2017/04/2017Apr20Primary-school-choices_report-to-schools.pdf
Cheng, J. Y. S. (2008). Political modernisation in Hong Kong. *The Journal of Commonwealth and Comparative Politics, 27*(3), 294–320.
Ching, F. (2009). How Beijng plays its hands: As seen from Kong. *Hong Kong Journal*, no. 15. http://www.hkbasiclaw.com/Hong%20Kong%20Journal/Frank%20Ching%20on%20How%20Beijing%20Plays%20its%20Hand.htm
Chu, D. S. C. (2018). Media use and protest mobilization: A case study of the Umbrella Movement within Hong Kong schools. *Media+Society, 4*(1). https://journals.sagepub.com/doi/full/10.1177/2056305118763350
Constitutional and Mainland Affairs Bureau. (2007). The Joint Declaration. https://www.cmab.gov.hk/en/issues/jd2.htm
Dissanayake, S. (2014). Things that could only happen in a Hong Kong protest. *B.B.C. News*. https://www.bbc.com/news/world-asia-china-29423147
Downs, J. M. (2014). *The Golden Ghetto: The American Commercial Community at Canton and the shaping of American China policy, 1784–1844*. Hong Kong University Press. 496pp.
Hambro, E. (1955). *The problem of Chinese refugees in Hong Kong*. A.W. Sijthoff.
Hau, M. (2021). The official mind of British post-imperialism: Influencing parliamentary opinions during the Anglo-Chinese negotiations on the future of Hong Kong, 1982–1984. *The International History Review*, pp. 1–19. https://doi.org/10.1080/07075332.2021.1876135
History. (2019). How Hong Kong came under 'one country, two systems' rule. https://www.history.com/news/hong-kong-china-great-britain
History. (2021). Hong Kong returned to China. https://www.history.com/this-day-in-history/hong-kong-returned-to-china

Hung, H.-F. (2021). *Hong Kong's economic future. A China file conversation*. Available at: https://www.chinafile.com/conversation/hong-kongs-economic-future

Hung-Kay, L. (1998). Hong Kong history and culture. *Chinese Sociology and Anthropology, 30*(3), 13–24.

Lee, F. L. F. (2018). Internet alternative media, movement experience, and radicalism: The case of post-Umbrella Movement Hong Kong. *Social Movement Studies, 17*(2), 219–233.

Lee, F. L. F. (2020). Social media and the spread of fake news during a social movement: The 2019 anti-ELAB protests in Hong Kong. *Communications and the Public, 5*(3–4), 122–125.

Lee, F. L. F., Chan, M., & Chen, H.-T. (2020). Social media protest attitudes during movement abeyance: A study of Hong Kong university students. *International Journal of Communication, 14*, 4933–4951.

Martin, M. F. (2019). *Hong Kong's protests of 2019*. Congressional Research Service. https://fas.org/sgp/crs/row/IF11295.pdf

Ming Hui, D. L. (2015). *Hong Kong's political future after the 'Umbrella Revolution' policy report*. S. Rajaratnam School of International Studies. https://www.jstor.org/stable/pdf/resrep05859.pdf?refreqid=excelsior%3Afff49377871 9e94d3ff6fb7c1df5f332

Morales, L., & Andreosso-O'Callaghan, B. (2018). Hong Kong unrest and implications for the Hang Seng Index. *Journal of the Asia Pacific Economy, 24*(1), 82–96.

Nichols, R. (2020). From 4 to June 9: The Chinese Communist Party's response to Tiananmen Square '89 and Hong Kong '19. In *The Alpha Kappa Phi Review. Annual Journal of Undergraduate Research in the Humanities*, I (Spring). https://www.lindsey.edu/academics/majors-and-programs/English/img/AKO-Review20.pdf

OECD. (2010). Shanghai and Hong Kong: Two distinct examples of education reform in China. https://www.oecd.org/countries/hongkongchina/46581016.pdf

Poell, T., & van Dijck, J. (2015). Social media and activist communication. In C. Atton (Ed.), *The Routledge companion to alternative and community media* (pp. 527–537). Routledge.

Purbrick, M. (2019). A report of the 2019 Hong Kong protests. *Journal of Asian Affairs, 50*(5), 465–487.

Santoro, W. A., & Fitzpatrick, M. (2015). 'The ballot or the bullet': The crisis of victory and the institutionalisation and radicalisation of the civil rights movement. *Mobilisation, 20*(2), 207–229.

Schenk, C. (2008, March 16). 'Economic history of Hong Kong.' EH.Net encyclopedia (R. Whaples, Ed.). http://eh.net/encyclopedia/economic-history-of-hong-kong/

Shek, D. T. L. (2020). Protests in Hong Kong (2019–2020): A perspective based on quality of life and well-being. *Applied Research in Quality of Life, 15*, 619–635. https://doi.org/10.1007/s11482-020-09825-2

Smidi, A., & Shahin, S. (2017). Social media and social mobilisation in the Middle East: A survey of research on the Arab spring. *India Quarterly, 73*, 196–209.

So, A. Y. (2011). 'One country, two systems' and Hong Kong-China National Integration: A crisis-transformation perspective. *Journal of Contemporary Asia, 41*(1), 99–111.

Stein, E. A. (2017). Are ICTs democratizing dictatorships? New media and mass mobilization. *Social Science Quaterly. Special Issue: The New World of Comparative Political Communication*, September 2017, 914–941. https://doi.org/10.1111/ssqu.12439

Sustein, C. (2001). *Republic.com*. Princeton University Press.

The Financial Times. (2020). Hong Kong law threatens freedom of information. https://www.ft.com/content/a9dcd620-b51e-4a68-bd95-dc387aeec3e7

The Government of the Hong Kong Special Administrative Region. (2019). Press releases. Fugitive Offenders and Mutual Legal Assistance in Criminal Matters Legislation (Amendment) Bill 2019. https://www.info.gov.hk/gia/general/201903/26/P2019032600708.htm

The Guardian. (2020). Hong Kong protesters hold banned Tiananmen vigil as anthem law is passed. https://www.theguardian.com/world/2020/jun/04/hong-kong-tiananmen-vigil-ban-china-national-anthem-bill-protest

The Legislative Council. (2019). Fugitive Offenders and Mutual Legal Assistance in Criminal Matters Legislation (Amendment) Bill 2019. https://www.legco.gov.hk/yr18-19/english/bills/b201903291.pdf

The New York Times. (1984). Hong Kong shaken by a night of rioting and looting. https://www.nytimes.com/1984/01/15/world/hong-kong-shaken-by-a-night-of-rioting-and-looting.html

The New York Times. (2016). China's cultural revolution explained. https://www.nytimes.com/2016/05/15/world/asia/china-cultural-revolution-explainer.html

The New York Times. (2020). Defying Beijing, thousands in Hong Kong hold Tiananmen vigil. https://www.nytimes.com/2020/06/04/world/asia/tiananmen-hong-kong-china.html

The Washington Post. (2019). The evolution of Hong Kong's protests. https://www.washingtonpost.com/world/2019/09/27/evolution-hong-kongs-protests/

Treaty Series. (1994). Treaties and international agreements registered or files and recorded with the Secretariat of the United Nations. Volume 1399. United Nations, 1994. Available at: https://treaties.un.org/Pages/showDetails.aspx?objid=08000002800d4d6e

United Nations. (1994). Treaty series. Treaties and International Agreements Registered or Filed and Recorded with the Secretariat of the United Nations. https://treaties.un.org/doc/Publication/UNTS/Volume%201399/v1399.pdf

Valenzuela, S. (2013). Unpacking the use of social media for protest behavior. The roles of information, opinion, expression and activism. *The American Behavioral Scientist, 57*, 920–942.

Yahuda, M. (1993). Hong Kong's future: Sino-British negotiations, perceptions, organization and political cultural. *International Affairs, 69*, 245–266.

Zenglein, M. J. (2020). Financial hub at risk. https://merics.org/en/report/financial-hub-risk

China's Rise in the Middle East: Fuelling a Tired Dragon?

Intesar Madi, Lucía Morales, and Bernadette Andreosso-O'Callaghan

Abstract China's hunger for natural resources is growing as the Chinese authorities try to fuel an economy in need of sustainable economic growth while it adjusts to its "*new normal*" growth trajectory. There is a need to reactivate an economic model that is not meeting growth level targets and remains heavily reliant on fossil fuels. The country's energy model needs to change amidst the challenges and significant costs posed by environmental degradation. Over the last decade, the Middle East's connections have become of paramount importance to China, but these links are quite fragile as they are fundamentally affected by significant uncertainty. The Chinese authorities face paramount challenges as they engage with a very conflicting region characterised by increasing political frictions, armed conflicts, and escalating instability. These difficulties suggest the need for a highly cautious strategy as the Chinese authorities keep progressing with the redefinition of their energy model centered on stability and security as having a paramount importance to a country that needs to fuel its economic model. However, coal dependency, environmental concerns and lower economic growth levels have pushed the country to reconsider its energy model towards more sustainable approaches. As the government seeks energy sustainability, the research findings suggest that the country's new energy model is shifting towards oil; this raises concerns regarding China's national security interests and sustainable economic growth goals.

Keywords China's energy model · The Middle East · Oil price war · Environmental sustainability · COVID-19

I. Madi (✉) · L. Morales
School of Accounting, Economics and Finance, Faculty of Business, Technological University Dublin, Dublin, Ireland
e-mail: intesar.madi@tudublin.ie; lucia.morales@tudublin.ie

B. Andreosso-O'Callaghan
Department of Economics, Kemmy Business School, University of Limerick, Limerick, Ireland

Ruhr Universität Bochum, Bochum, Germany
e-mail: Bernadette.Andreosso@ul.ie

B. Andreosso-O'Callaghan et al. (eds.), *Sustainable Development in Asia*, Contributions to Economics, https://doi.org/10.1007/978-3-030-94679-1_5

1 Introduction

China's hunger for natural resources is growing as the Chinese authorities try to fuel an economy in need of sustainable economic growth while it adjusts to its "*new normal*" growth trajectory. Since the 2008 Global Financial Crisis (GFC), the Chinese economy has slowed down significantly. Currently, the government is in dire need of reactivating a draconian economic model that does meet growth targets and that would remain less reliant on fossil fuels. The country's energy model needs to be reconsidered amidst the challenges and significant costs posed by both environmental degradation and climate change. Greater awareness of the negative impact of environmental externalities on the population's health and natural resources requires more sustainable approaches in terms of the country's economic and energy models. China's environment has deteriorated at a fast pace, and global demands to deal with the threat of environmental degradation (and climate change) are on the rise. According to China's National Petroleum Corporation annual report (CNPC, 2016), China's dependence on imported oil reached a historic high of 60.6 percent in 2015. The country's increasing reliance on imported oil is further aggravated by the lack of reliable sources and of safe routes that ensure a continuous and steady oil supply. Also, the volatile nature of oil prices is an area of concern as China seeks support from Russia and Saudi Arabia that are identified as its top oil-producing allies (Aidoo et al., 2017). In this context, it is essential to consider that the Middle-East connections have become of paramount importance to China, with significant ties developing over the last decade. But, rather worryingly, these new connections are quite fragile as they are affected by substantial uncertainty levels with origins in the economic and political domains.

The 2020 health crisis has caused significant economic disruptions with spillover effects to the energy sector, adding further complexities and challenges to China's and global economies. The country has embarked upon a transitioning process affected by its "*new economic normal*" and a need to reconsider its draconian energy model. With the spread of the SARS Cov2 pathogen (Covid-19),[1] the global economy has been facing considerable challenges as most economic activities were halted to mitigate its effects worldwide. China was source of the coronavirus outbreak—with the first cases registered in Wuhan, Hubei province's capital. China has become the world's manufacturing centre, and contentious measures to deal with the SARS Cov2 pathogen led to global supply chain disruptions with global implications. According to China's National Bureau of Statistics (2020), the Chinese economy shrunk by 6.8 percent due to the outbreak of Covid-19, representing the worst downturn since 1992. In the last two decades, China's economy had grown significantly, albeit with moderate population growth, but with large changes in the structure of aggregate demand driving its energy resources hunger. However, to deal with energy demands that sustain its economic model, the Chinese authorities have

[1] SARS Cov2 (Severe Acute Respiratory Syndrome Coronavirus 2) is the cause of the disease that has commonly been named Covid-19.

been engaging in and developing their international relationships with rich oil regions like Central-Asia, Southeast-Asia, Latin-America, West-Africa, and the Middle-East in particular (Soligo & Jaffe, 2010; Huandong & Mouyuan, 2017; Downs, 2019). The Middle-East has emerged as the primary oil source for China. However, it is a very conflicting region characterised by political frictions, armed conflicts, and potentially escalating instability levels. The outlined challenges suggest the need for an overly cautious strategy as China keeps progressing with the redefinition of its energy model, with stability and security being of utmost importance to a country that needs to secure high rates of economic growth (Fulton, 2019). At the same time, the Chinese authorities are trying to find their way to a transition towards a more sustainable economic model in order to fuel the country's economic development. The shift towards oil raises concerns regarding sustainability and the possibility to move towards a green economic model.

It is essential to consider that China has been quite active on the oil front. It has applied an equity ownership strategy to gain more control over oil flows as a shield against price fluctuations thereby reducing the potential of supply interruption; however, civil unrest and conflicts in the Middle-East threaten to disrupt China's energy supply channels. Besada (2018) suggests that China should work harder for regional peace to achieve a sustainable energy supply. According to Duchâtel et al. (2014, p. 1) "*...as China's energy demand continues to increase quickly, Chinese oil companies often engage with politically unstable countries and face increasing political and security risks.*" In addition to this, China is facing severe obstacles concerning energy security. Its overseas energy interests are increasing, but due to its non-intervention policy approach in other countries, further challenges emerge as China's national oil companies (NOCs) lack overseas experience.

This chapter examines China's dependency on fossil fuels to support its economic growth within the outlined context. The implications of oil price instability and China's energy connection to the Middle-Eastern region are also explored. The study offers insights into China's vulnerability regarding its oil imports from this region, while identifying significant challenges that can deter its need to secure its energy supply. In this regard, this study explores two main issues. A key first question is as follows: how does China's dependency on fossil fuels support its vision for sustainable economic growth? A second question relates to the main challenges associated with China's energy connection to the Middle-Eastern region. This study engages with the extant literature, shedding light on the Middle-East's role as China seeks to fuel its transition towards a more diversified energy model. The central research question is examined by qualitative information gathered on China's energy dilemma as the country seems to be transitioning to oil and gas, both fossil fuels. This raises therefore a number of concerns regarding the government's ability to develop a green energy and growth model. Section 1 discusses China's energy dilemma whereas Sect. 2 offers a critical assessment of China's efforts to transition towards renewable energy resources to promote its economy in the context of the new challenges posed by Covid-19. Section 3 discusses China's energy model. Section 4 presents some insights examining China's connection to the

Middle-East. Section 5 offers some reflections on China's economic sustainability and its greener energy model, and Sect. 6 concludes the paper.

2 China's Energy Dilemma

The People's Republic of China (PRC) became the world's second-largest economy for the first time in the modern era overtaking Japan's economy in 2010 (Fukumoto & Muto, 2011). With a 1.44 billion population, the people's Republic of China is the largest country in the world and the second-largest oil consumer following the United States (US) (Mortazavi et al., 2019). China's total oil consumption amounted to 13.5 million barrels per day in 2019, with projections indicating that a peak of 720 million tons would be reached by 2025. Thus, China has a strong and growing need for access to energy and to natural resources, and alternatives to fossil fuels do not seem to be developing at a speed paralleled to the country's needs.

As illustrated in Fig. 1, China's coal consumption has decreased gradually since the 1960s; it almost dropped by half its levels in the early 1960s. Since then, China's coal consumption remained stable until the mid-1990s when China's started shifting from coal to oil. The country's GDP growth has increased during this period; however, it dropped significantly after the Global Economic and Financial Crisis

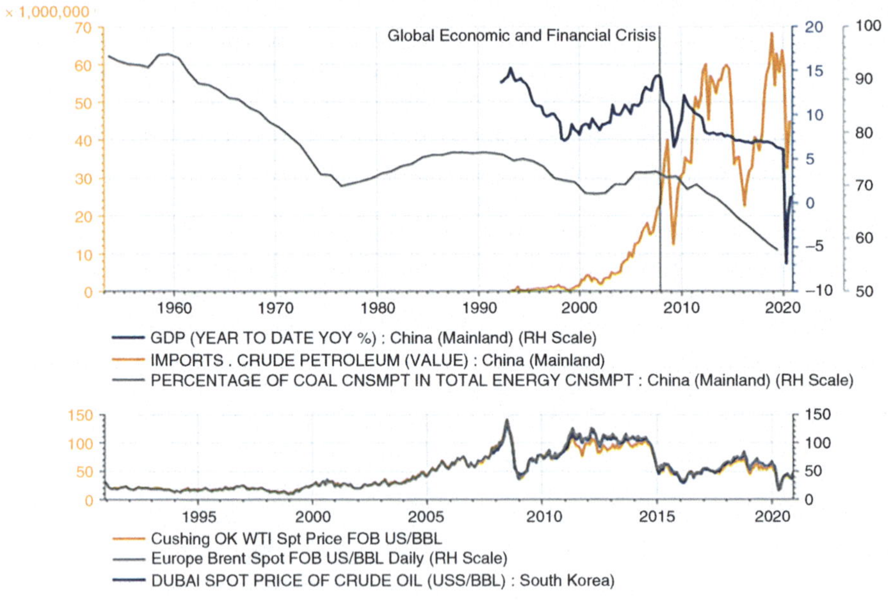

Fig. 1 China's GDP, oil imports, & oil price. (Source: Authors' elaboration using data from DataStream International (2021))

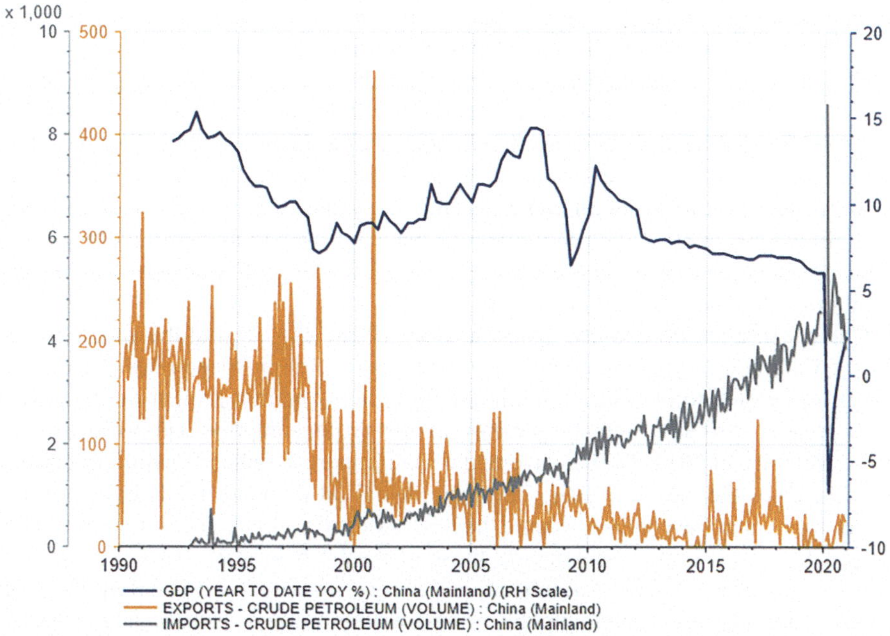

Fig. 2 China's GDP & crude oil imports & exports. (Source: Authors' elaboration using Data from DataStream International (2021))

(GFC) falling to 7.7 percent between 2011 and 2015, after registering an average growth rate of 10 percent for the period 1981 through 2010 (EIA, 2020). China's real GDP increased by 6.8 percent in 2017, but it slowed down to 6.6 percent in 2018, and it then suddenly dropped by −6.8 percent as a result of the Covid19 crisis (Morrison, 2019; EIA, 2020). The country's dependence on foreign energy sources and its economic growth rates have continued their upward trend until the GFC hit the global economy (Fig. 2), a crisis that acted as an inflection point that led to significant economic and social challenges worldwide. Additionally, the development of renewable energies requires paramount levels of investment. Therefore, the Chinese authorities face substantial challenges, as the country needs to find a balance between growth sustainability and its new economic reality that has been coined as "*its new economic normal*" (Nishimura, 2020).

China's old-growth model caused a widespread overcapacity in its energy sector, constraints on natural resources, environmental deterioration, and rising dependency on imported energy, which increasingly undermined China's economic performance. However, *the "new economic normal" provides an extraordinary opportunity to ensure that China's growth is not only strong and sustained, but also low-carbon, more energy secure, and less polluting* (The World Bank, 2014; Green & Stern, 2015, p. 43; Nishimura, 2020). But, is the country able to move towards an energy model that is more environmentally friendly? The country's energy consumption patterns suggest that this might not be the case as a shift towards oil will enhance the country's dependency on fossil fuels.

The current situation appears as a vital dilemma, and the following question arises: are renewable energies an alternative for short- and medium-term growth? Some challenges need to be considered, such as the increased cost of renewable energy, required access to remote areas in the county, climate change conditions, and good management to maintain and repair the renewable energy systems (Causevic, 2012; Mortazavi et al., 2019). Moreover, China has started to diversify fuel types by reducing energy imports and increasing its domestic energy to minimise the impact of oil price fluctuations on its economy.

China was a net oil exporter until the early 1990s (Fig. 2), but the situation has changed dramatically as the country started to grow at high-speed rates (Causevic, 2012). According to (Mortazavi et al., 2019), rapid economic growth over the past three decades caused a dramatic increase in energy consumption and power generation. Notably, in 2014, China's average net oil imports reached 6.1 million barrels per day. Over the past few years, the incremental oil demand trends have pushed China ahead, and the country became the most extensive global net oil importer; this led to China's oil imports overtaking those of the USA in 2017 (EIA, 2018). The Chinese government seeks to enhance its energy security by diversifying global supply sources by investing in pipeline infrastructure, storage infrastructure projects, and by increasing its strategic petroleum reserve at times of lower oil prices. These strategies would improve China's energy security, reduce its vulnerability to supply disruptions and presumably ease Chinese concerns about the growing reliance on oil imports, in general, and Middle-Eastern oil imports, in particular (Rioux et al., 2019).

As outlined in Table 1, throughout the 1970s and 1980s, the Chinese economy opened up to the rest of the world; its economic model started to change and new energy resources were needed to fuel the economy. China adhered to an energy policy grounded on the self-sufficiency principle. Despite this policy's main goals, China's reliance on crude oil imports increased sharply due to its rapid economic growth. By the mid-1980s, China's oil production had slowed down, and oil demand growth had exceeded domestic production. The country's demand for crude oil increased significantly from about 11.36 million tons in 1992, reaching about 335.49 million tons in 2015, which accounted for approximately 59.5 percent of global incremental oil demand growth between 1990 and 2015. Thus, the Chinese government decided to change somewhat its oil self-sufficiency principle, which was based on trade flows, and it started with its "going global" strategy in 2000 implying systematic outward direct investment by mostly SOEs (State-Owned Enterprises) in the energy sector.[2] The heavy dependence on foreign energy creates significant levels of stress on China's economy due to the intensification of trade disputes

[2]This "going global" strategy in the area of energy ought to be understood as a strategy of securing affordable energy from abroad while keeping oil and other energy reserves intact at home. It follows that the self-sufficiency principle is far from being undermined.

Table 1 History of China's oil industry development (1970–present)

Phase	Year	Development of China's oil industry
Phase 1	The 1970s	China opened to the rest of the world. Its economic model started to change—energy resources are needed to fuel the economy.
Phase 2	The 1980s	Self-sufficiency emerges as an energy policy critical objective.
Phase 3	The 1990s	Domestic oil production can no longer match the increase in crude oil demand. As a result, it becomes a net oil importing country since 1993. China promoted outward investment in the energy sector, a policy that culminated subsequently with the 2000 "*going global*" strategy for firms.
Phase 4	2000–2008	As China's oil imports doubled in 2000, energy security has become an important issue that aroused China's public concerns.
Phase 5	2009–2014	China's oil import increases rapidly. The Chinese government encourages Chinese National Oil Companies (NOCs) to expand their overseas activities by providing financial and policy support.
Phase 6	2015–Present	The CNOCs took advantage of the nation's "One Belt, One Road" ("OBOR" renamed subsequently the "Belt and Road Initiative") initiative and continued to push forward their cooperation with "OBOR" countries. The oil import dependency outstripped 72 percent in 2018.

Source: Huandong and Mouyuan (2017), and author's elaboration

with some countries such as the USA; it also weakens its economy by making it more vulnerable to any global oil price fluctuations (Shichor, 1998; Wu, 2014; Liao & Wang, 2019). In 2000, energy security, particularly oil security, has been raised as a critical issue that caused some public concern (Wu, 2014). China became a major importer of crude oil in the last two decades. Figure 3 shows how China's rapid economic growth has pushed the country to expand its crude oil consumption; its domestic crude oil production has increased slowly in recent years. This implies that China's crude oil needs have been mainly met by imports. This reliance on crude oil imports is expected to double over the next 20 years, gradually increasing to account for around 80 percent of its total oil consumption by 2035 (Zhang et al., 2020; Shao et al., 2017; Odgaard & Delman, 2014). According to the US Energy Information Administration (EIA), China became in 2007 the world's largest crude oil buyer. Its average crude oil imports rose almost 10 percent from 2018 to 2019, which increased to 10.1 million barells/day (b/d) from 9.2 million b/d in 2018.

3 Challenges to China's Energy Model

With its "going out" or "going global" strategy, China started purchasing oil and gas assets through its domestic oil companies such as China National Offshore Oil Company (CNOOC), China National Petroleum Corporation (CNPC), China's largest state-owned oil and gas firm and Sinopec (China National Petrochemical Corporation). Major Chinese oil companies had begun oil investments in overseas

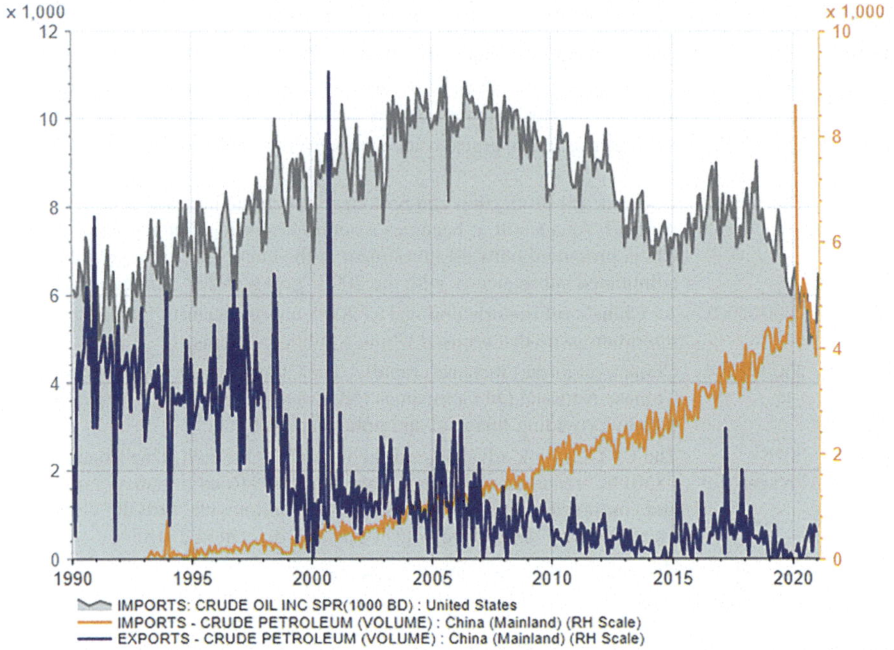

Fig. 3 China's crude oil exports & imports. & US crude oil imports. (Source: Authors own elaboration using data from DataStream International (2021))

countries such as Sudan, Peru, Venezuela, and Kazakhstan in 1996 (Bambawale & Sovacool, 2010 ; Soligo & Jaffe, 2010; Leung et al., 2011; Fulton, 2019).Thus, the availability, affordability, and accessibility of petroleum fuel from global energy markets encouraged China to invest in CNPC-owned overseas fields in order to reduce its reliance on foreign oil imports. Since 2004, CNPC has outbid India's ONGC in Angola, Kazakhstan, Ecuador, Nigeria, and Myanmar showing China's strong interest to develop its presence on less developed economies with a pool of natural resources that it can access (Janardhanan, 2010; Bambawale & Sovacool, 2010; Fulton, 2019). Notably, NOCs played an active role in persuading the central government to support their massive investments in overseas oil and gas resources (Andrews-Speed & Dannreuther, 2011). According to Zweig and Hao (2015), CNPC lent the Russian energy company Rosneft, a US$ 6 billion stake in return for 350 million oil barrels between 2005 and 2010. A few years later, CNPC provided Rosneft an additional loan of US$ 15 billion with US$ 10 billion in return for a guarantee to complete an oil pipeline to China by 2011. After more than 20 years of foreign investments, Chinese NOCs had a stake in more than 200 projects and about 50 countries in five oil and gas cooperation regions (Zweig & Hao, 2015). Furthermore, China has also begun a massive global campaign searching for energy, especially for petroleum. Therefore, China has established energy partners all across

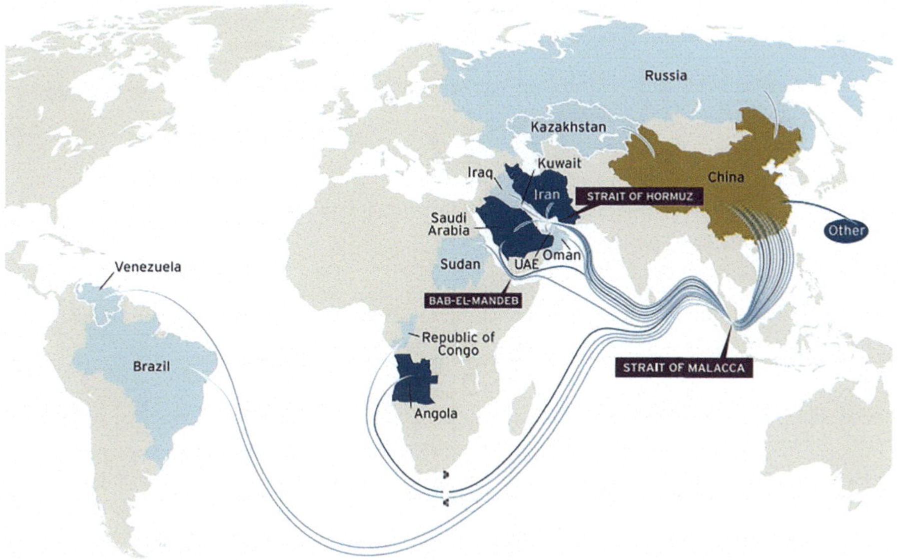

Fig. 4 China's top providers of imported crude oil. (Source: Jones et al. (2014))

the Middle East,[3] Southeast-Asia, Russia, Central-Asia, Africa, and Latin-America (Cole, 2003; Lons et al., 2019).

China has shifted its focus towards the Middle-Eastern region because of its predominant role in energy markets and of the strategic location for trade routes and sea-lanes that link Asia to Europe and Africa. The Middle-East has emerged as vital to the BRI's future, which is designed to place China at the centre of global trade networks (Lons et al., 2019). The Middle-East has a considerable amount of energy resources and plays an essential role in China's demand for crude oil; thus, this region is considered as being China's largest energy supplier (Shao et al., 2017). It is important to note that almost 17 percent of total China's crude oil imports from this region come from Saudi Arabia alone.

Figure 4 offers some insights into China's global approach to secure oil resources, and it provides an interactive visualization of China's global energy ties. China imports at least 44 percent of its oil from the Middle-East. This oil has to pass through the Strait of Hormuz and Bab al-Mandab. Other Chinese oil imports, approximately 56 percent, must pass through the Strait of Malacca.

As shown in Table 2, which provides a breakdown of the top countries supplying crude oil to China in 2019, the overwhelming share of Middle-Eastern countries appears clearly. In particular, Saudi Arabia is today China's top source of crude oil

[3]This group encompasses the following countries: Saudi Arabia, Iraq, Oman, Kuwait, United Arab Emirates, and Iran.

Table 2 The top 15 countries that supplied 90.1 percent of the crude oil imported into China during 2019

Country	Saudi Arabia	Russia	Iraq	Angola	Brazil	Oman	Kuwait	UAE	Iran	Others
Percentage of imports	16.8%	15.3%	9.9%	9.5%	7.8%	6.9%	4.5%	3.1%	3%	12.6%

Source: EIA (2019) and Hao et al. (2019)

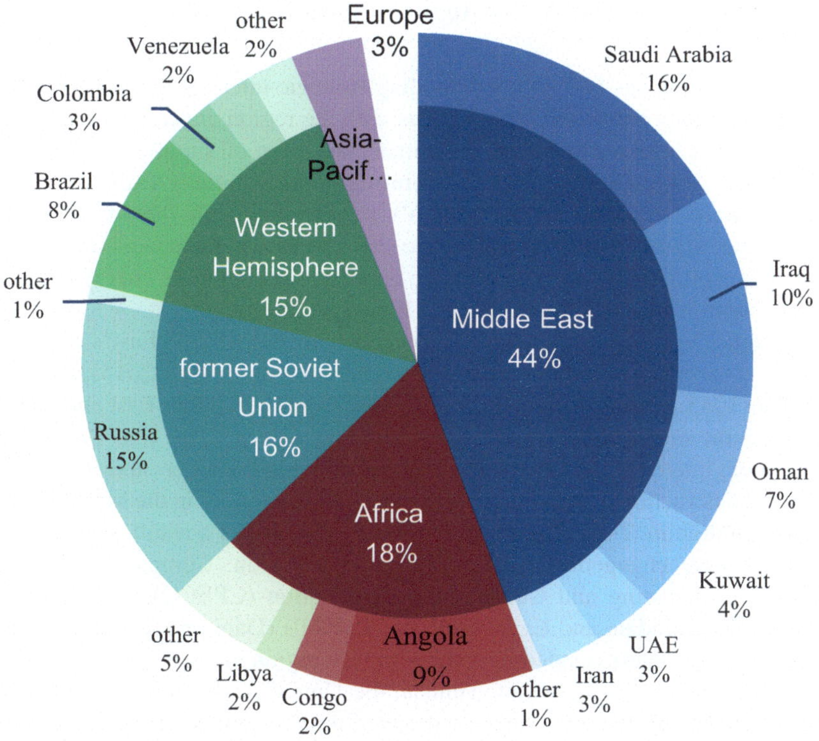

Fig. 5 China's crude oil imports by source, 2019. (Source: FACTS Global Energy Services, *China Oil Monthly*, February 2020)

imports with a 16.8 percent share, followed by Russia with a 15.3 percent share. China's imports from the United Kingdom, Brazil, and Libya have increased notably since 2017 (Fig. 5); supply from Iran fell to 3 percent of China's imports in 2018 and 2019 compared with 8 percent in 2016 due to the US sanctions on Iran's crude oil. China reported that oil imports from Iran fell to about 100,000 b/d at the end of 2019, Saudi Arabia offset most of this loss (EIA, 2020). Vasquez (2019) mentioned that a few years earlier (in 2014), Chinese oil imports had reached 6.2 million barrels per day while domestic production had reached only 4.8 million. The Middle-Eastern Countries[4] were already identified at the time as China's largest importers of crude oil with 44 percent of the total Chinese oil imports in 2019; these supplying countries were followed by Africa (22 percent) and Russia, the former states of the Soviet Union with a 13 percent share and Latin America (11 percent). Note that Saudi Arabia and Angola were China's largest imported oil sources in 2014, representing 29 percent of the total (Vasquez, 2019; EIA, 2020).

[4]This group encompasses the following countries: Saudi Arabia, Iraq, Oman, Kuwait, United Arab Emirates, and Iran.

4 The Middle-East: A Strategic Region for China

Historically, China has had no long-standing strategic interests in the Middle-East; however, the relationship and interlinkages with the region are strengthening as the Middle-East has been positioned as the primary source of oil supplies for the country (Luft, 2006). Although the Middle-Eastern region was initially excluded from its strategy toward Asia and Africa, China's relationship with the Middle-Eastern countries has significantly changed since 2011. China's rapid economic growth and thirst for oil demanded an aggressive approach to pursue its energy needs and to engage with a very conflicting region (Elnaggar, 2020).

Although China has a nascent relationship with the Middle-East's top energy suppliers, it is not a newcomer to the region (Daojiong & Meidan, 2015). During the Cold War (1945–1991), China disengaged itself from the Middle-East and had little presence in the region (Scobell & Nader, 2016). However, in the mid-1980s, China became more interested in the area and allowed individual workers and companies to engage in construction projects and offer consultation services in the Middle-Eastern markets (Zhongmin, 2008; Daojiong & Meidan, 2015). As a result, many Chinese companies were engaged and established in the region. Companies like China Petroleum Engineering and Construction Corporation (CPECC) started activities in Kuwait, Iraq, Sudan, and Egypt early in the 1980s (Daojiong & Meidan, 2015). Since then, CNPC has extended its activities in the region in countries such as Egypt, Iran, Libya, Oman, Qatar, Sudan, Tunisia, the United Arab Emirates, and Yemen (Shichor, 1998). By the end of the cold war, China's approach toward the Middle East had developed significantly. The country had established diplomatic relations with all countries in the region and deepened its economic ties to support its rapid economic growth (Lyall, 2019). It is worth pointing out that the Middle-East has become the most critical region for China due to its strategic location. It links Asia to Europe and Africa, a crucial source of much-needed energy resources and an area of expanding economic ties (Wormuth, 2019).

In 2019, China was the world's top crude oil importer, with annual crude oil imports reaching 10.1 million barrels per day (EIA, 2020). During the same year, more than half of China's crude oil imports were from the Organization of the Petroleum Exporting Countries (OPEC). Over 30 percent of total China's crude oil imports came from Saudi Arabia and Russia. On the whole, in this region, China's relationship with Saudi Arabia emerges indeed as crucial. China's oil imports from Saudi Arabia reached 1,802,788 barrels per day in July 2019 compared to the same period in 2018, when it accounted for 921,811 barrels per day. However, China's growing reliance on oil imports from Saudi Arabia and Russia has increased over time. This heavy reliance on oil is likely to directly influence China's national security interests and economic growth goals. In other words, China's economic growth will be more sensitive to the fluctuation of oil prices, and this will further affect the country's economic stability. Moreover, the reality of increasing oil imports mainly from one region could put China's economy under unwanted foreign pressure, and it does not help much in terms of its greener vision that seeks to align with an energy model that is less reliant on fossil fuels.

4.1 Challenges to Oil Dependency

As it is well known, the most easily reachable petroleum reserves easily accessible to China are located in the turbulent and volatile Middle East. Elnaggar (2020) mentioned that many countries in the MiddleEast struggle with the aftermath of the Arab Spring Revolution, such as high political and economic instability and slow growth due to falling oil prices. China's challenges are exacerbated by energy price volatility that emerges as an area of concern combined with energy security worries. With the country focusing on importing oil from countries that face significant disruptions and uncertainty due to due to severe conflicts such as wars, strikes, and sanctions—aspects that are quite common in the Middle-Eastern region—security in terms of energy supplies is under jeopardy (Jarrett et al., 2019); there are significant concerns regarding trade and energy accessibility, like the turmoil in Iraq and the ongoing conflict between Palestinians and Israelis, and other tensions in Afghanistan, Syria, and other parts of this region (Jing, 2019). However, China's dependency on imported oil has motivated active Chinese involvement in the conflict-ridden regions in Africa, making it difficult for the PRC to follow its traditional non-intervention principle (Causevic, 2012). China's consumption of petroleum and other liquids has declined in the first quarter of 2020 because of the oil price war between Russia and Saudi Arabia and because of the outbreak of the Covid-19, which worsened the situation and caused an enormous decline in oil demand (EIA, 2020; Ozili & Arun, 2020).

Early in 2020, the Covid-19 outbreak led to a collapse in oil demand. Crude oil prices fell sharply following a significant decline in oil demand caused by a Russia and Saudi Arabia oil price war that significantly hit the global energy markets. The dramatic decline in oil demand caused by repeated and prolonged quarantines in countries, affecting mostly travel restrictions as the commonly followed steps worldwide to contain the Covid19, has resulted in a drop in global oil consumption (Aloui et al., 2020). Albulescu (2020, p. 2) mentions that "*Saudi Arabia starts an oil price war on March 09, 2020, and floods the market with oil. In one single day, the crude oil price plunges more than 20 percent.*" In April 2020, oil price frictions started when Saudi Arabia intended to slash its oil production to around 4.8 million barrels per day "*from the April production levels*" to keep oil prices at moderate levels. Although the OPEC members agreed on this level, Russia refused this more profound decline in oil production. As a result of the dramatic reduction in global oil consumption, Saudi Arabia dropped production further by one million barrels per day and causes prices to fall lower than Russia's willing levels (Gebhard-koenigstein, 2020). This economic conflict resulted in a sheer drop in oil prices, with the price of oil imploding by 65 percent in the first weeks of March, registering the most significant oil price drop since the Gulf War in 1991 (OPEC, 2020).

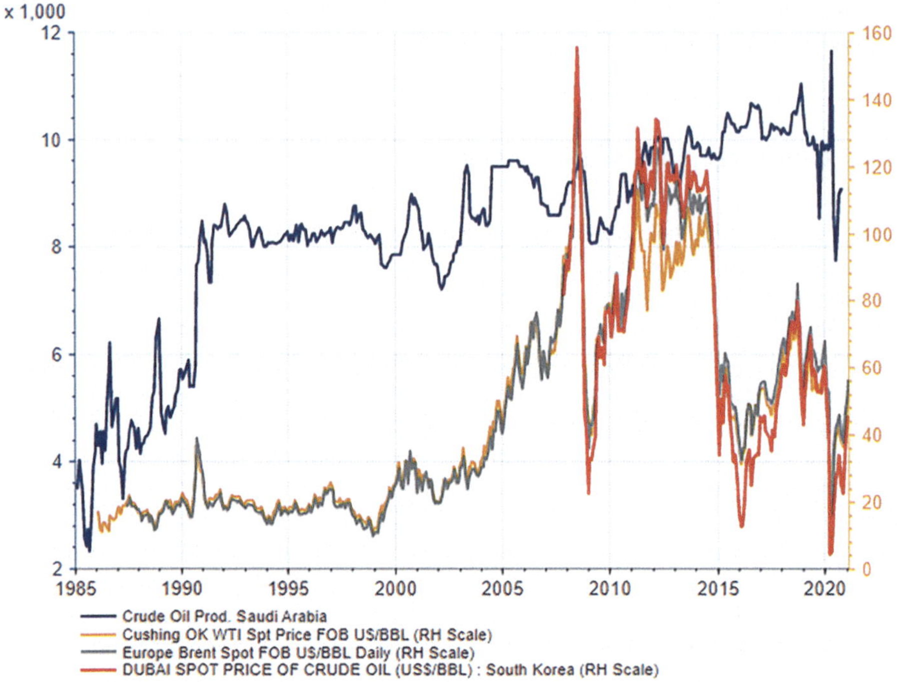

Fig. 6 Change in Saudi Arabia crude oil production & crude oil price. (Source: Author elaboration using data from DataStream International (2021))

Furthermore, to fight the spread of Covid-19, several countries have implemented the closure of many workplaces. This has resulted in global oil demand falling from 100 to 73 million barrels of oil per day in April (Fig. 6), "*Supply glut has filled up 76 percent of crude storage facilities in the USA. Lack of storage space and pipeline transmission capacity has pushed up storage costs forcing contract holders to sell WTI contracts at negative prices. Reducing supply by temporarily plugging off wells is a complex job with high degree of impact on reservoir health and is also expensive and a tedious process. So operators continue to operate wells at losses*" (Beh & Lin, 2021, p. 3).

Ozili (2020) states that the Covid-19 crisis worsened this situation and has affected global energy markets such as coal, gas, and renewable energy markets. However, the impact on oil markets was more severe. The measures taken to contain the Covid19 have resulted in a decline in global energy demands (Ozili, 2020). Figure 7 offers a comparison of global oil market disruptions in the context of past oil prices slumps or recessions. According to the World Bank (2020), the Brent Spot's oil price index fell by 85 percent between January 22 and April 21, which is more than the drop-in prices registered during the global economic and financial crisis. At the time, the price index fell by 70 percent from the end-August to

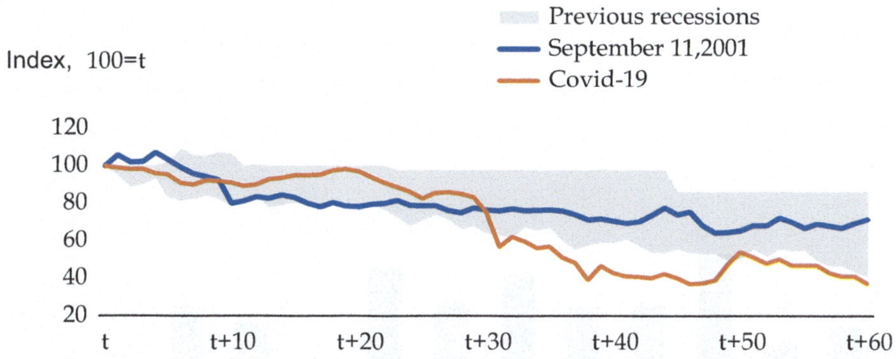

Fig. 7 Oil markets during current and past oil price recessions. (Source: Bloomberg (2020), World Bank (2020). Note: The y-axis is a price index, with "100 = *t*" indicating prices at the start of the events. The x-axis shows the passage of time (in days). Start dates for the two events are the first trading day before a major event occurred: September 10, 2001, for 9/11; and January 22, 2020, for COVID-19. Swath shows the four global recessions: 1974–1975, 1981–1982, 1990–1991, and 2008–2009. For the first two recessions, daily data were unavailable, so monthly percent changes were taken (assuming each month lasts 22 working days))

late-December 2008, more than the price implosion throughout end-June 2014 to mid-January 2016 (77 percent).

5 China's Economic Sustainability and Green Energy Model Under Question

These preliminary findings offer some evidence on current oil price dynamics (Fig. 8) and their importance to China's oil market and its economic sustainability. In other words, the fluctuations in oil prices will have an impact on China's economic growth at a greater level. According to Zhang Qianqian (2011), oil price volatility may influence the whole economy, production, consumption, cost, price, trade, and investment. On the other hand, low oil prices will support economic growth in oil-importing countries. Downs et al. (2020) mentioned that the collapse in oil prices during 2014–2015 intensified China's economic growth. Since then, China's oil imports have increased considerably. In 2018, China's conventional oil reserves reached 25.62 billion barrels, the 13th largest in the world (EIA, 2018). However, China has experienced many environmental problems, a widespread overcapacity in its energy sector, constraints on natural resources, and rising dependence on imported energy; all these factors increasingly undermined China's economic performance. As a result, the country has been pushed to change its energy model towards more sustainable approaches that meet its energy needs. Overall, it seems that China is making substantial efforts to reduce its coal consumption. China has now turned to oil and is becoming a net importer of oil since 1993; this is a

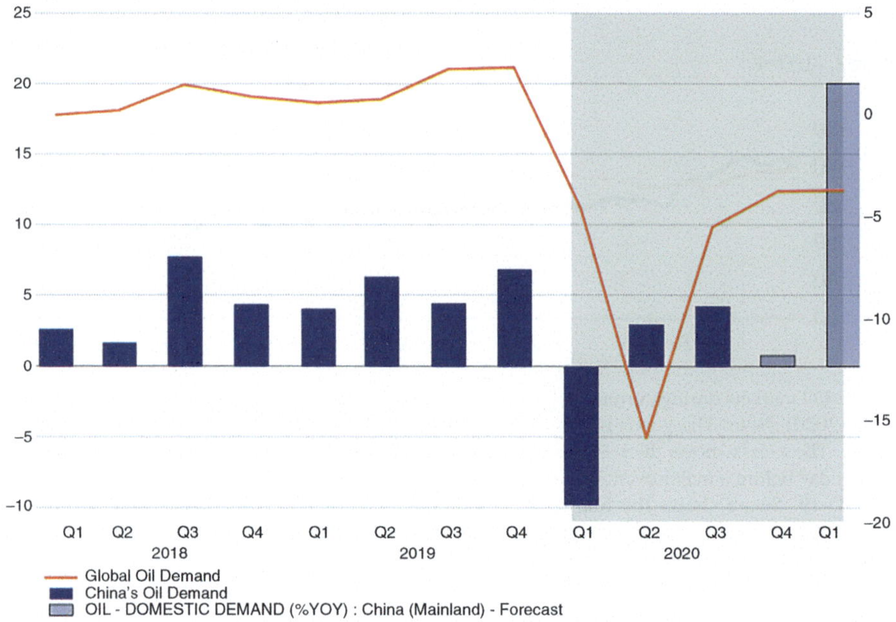

Fig. 8 Global oil demand growth. (Source: Authors elaboration using data from DataStream International (2021))

source of concern in so far as it keeps reinforcing its over-reliance on fossil fuels. This heavy reliance on oil does not seem to align with the Chinese government's vision of a greener economy and energy model. The current energy trends are expected to directly impact China's national security interests and economic growth goals. In other words, China's economic growth will be more sensitive to the fluctuation of oil prices; and this will further affect the country's economic stability.

5.1 The PRC Changing Role to Secure Oil

The PRC's thirst for petroleum could result in China's changing roles to secure overseas energy supplies and diplomatic efforts to ensure oil resources. The Chinese authorities might need to work harder in terms of regional peace, security, and stability to achieve sustainable energy supply, as flagged by Besada and Salam (2017). Although most oil and gas imports come from countries of the Middle-East (Saudi Arabia, Iraq, Kuwait, Oman, United Arab Emirates, and Iran), energy security, especially oil security, is a critical issue faced by the Chinese government. China's annual crude oil imports from countries along the Belt and Road Initiative reached 10.1 million barrels per day (b/d) in 2019, with just over 4 million barrels per day of that total coming from the Middle East in 2018 (EIA, 2020; Meidan, 2020).

In 2018, China's dependency on oil imports reached 72 percent; thus, after this significant increase in oil demand, China's energy security has become a top priority for its authorities since 2018. China is engaging with affluent oil countries and is strengthening energy and economic security, which raises questions about how it would be able to maintain stable energy trade relationships with these countries. Research studies suggest that in order to enhance its degree of energy security, China should diversify its oil import sources (Ge & Fan, 2013). Chen (2011) and Shi and Cai (2020) argue that increasing overseas energy investments may indirectly promote oil security through several channels. For example, establishing long-term relationships with oil-producing countries and investing in infrastructural projects that favor China's energy interests, it would be possible for the country to enhance its international oil supply.

5.2 China's Energy Model and the Environment

With the challenge of environmental degradation and climate change, China is aiming to change its energy model and to build a clean, low carbon, safe and efficient energy system for the future (Guo et al., 2020; Ji et al., 2019; Xu et al., 2019; Ji & Zhang, 2019; CNREC, 2019). But it seems quite unlikely that China will decrease its reliance on oil and natural gas imports in the foreseeable future. Despite goals to increase self-sufficiency, China's dependency on crude oil and natural gas imports will likely remain strong. Key strategic factors such as inventory stockpiling, declining domestic oil production, and China's challenging geology need to be carefully evaluated (Rioux et al., 2019). China's consumption of energy and carbon emissions has increased considerably since 1978 (Mortazavi et al., 2019). Oil consumption reached 639 million tonnes and increased by 6.5 percent from 2018; coal consumption reached 3.84 billion tonnes; natural gas consumption increased by 18 percent in 2018 (CNREC, 2019).

Although China is aiming to diversify its energy sources by supporting renewable resources and reducing energy dependency, it remains the largest importer of oil and natural gas in the world (Zavadska et al., 2020). As shown in Table 3, as the country's economy continues to grow, its demand for all energy sources (notably oil and natural gas) keep increasing. However, the share of oil in China's primary energy consumption remains around 20 percent. In contrast, the percentage of coal in China's primary energy mix declined from 60 percent in 2017 to 58 percent in 2018, while oil and gas consumption has increased to 20 percent and 8 percent respectively in 2019. partly because of the Chinese government's efforts to expand natural gas production and consumption (B.P. Statistical Review, 2019). China's demand for natural gas is growing more rapidly than that for other energy resources, showing once more how the country's energy model remains tied to fossil fuels. Increased natural gas consumption is mostly responsible for the projected decline in coal use from 73 percent to 65 percent of energy consumption between 1996 and 2020 (Downs, 2019). Moreover, in terms of fuel consumption, the CNPC (2018) reported

Table 3 China's energy market in 2018

Units in Mtoe unless otherwise stated	Level			Growth rate per annum % (Mtoe)				Share (%)		
	2008	2017	2018	2007–2017	2018	2007–2017	2018	2008	2017	2018
Consumption										
Primary energy	2230	3139	3273	3.9	4.3	99	134	100	100	100
Oil	385	611	641	4.9	5.0	23	31	17	19	20
Natural gas	70	207	243	13	18	15	37	3.2	6.6	7.4
Coal	1609	1890	1907	1.8	0.9	31	16	72	60	58
Nuclear	15	56	67	15	19	4.2	10	0.7	1.8	2.0
Hydro	144	264	272	9.2	3.2	15	8.5	6.5	8.4	8.3
Renewables (in power)	6.4	111	144	41	29	11	32	0.3	3.5	4.4
Wind	3.0	67	83	49	24	6.6	16	0.1	2.1	2.5
Solar	0.0	27	40	100	51	2.7	14	0.0	0.8	1.2
Biomass & geothermal	3.4	18	21	23	14	1.6	2.5	0.2	0.6	0.6
Production										
Oil (Mb/d)	3.8	3.8	3.8	0.3	−1.3	0.0	0.0	n/a	n/a	n/a
Biofuels (Mb/d)	28	40	58	5.9	44	1.8	18	n/a	n/a	n/a
Natural gas (Bcm)	81	149	162	7.9	8.3	7.9	12	n/a	n/a	n/a
Coal	1492	1747	1829	2.0	4.7	31	82	n/a	n/a	n/a
Carbon										
CO2 emissions (million tonnes)	7379	9230	9429	2.5	2.2	199	199	n/a	n/a	n/a

Source: B.P. Statistical Review of World Energy (2019)

that coal consumption would decrease significantly after 2020 and that it would reach 21.7 percent by 2035. On the other hand, it is estimated that gas and electricity consumption will continue to rise. The report forecasts that by 2050, electricity consumption as a percentage of final energy consumption would reach 38.4 percent, whereas the consumption of coal would decrease to 16.7 percent by 2050.

Finally, the way China's energy consumption patterns have changed over time are visible in Fig. 9; this new trend of consumption—oil and gas—is associated with high levels of pollution.

According to Tang et al. (2016), China's economic growth has mostly come at the cost of its environment with implications for global climate change concerns, as China is the world's first polluter. Energy production and consumption are considered as one of the main reasons that harm China's environment. Despite the profound implications of an increase in coal consumption on the environment, China's coal consumption remains relatively high. It follows an upward trend, a trend which is in direct conflict with the predictions indicating that the country will reduce coal consumption dramatically by 2035, as outlined in Fig. 9. Furthermore,

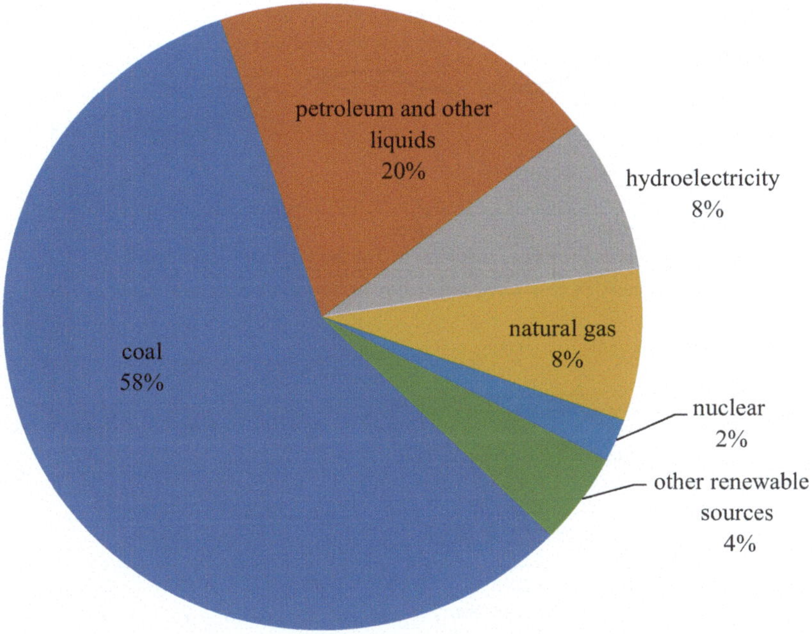

Fig. 9 China total primary energy consumption by fuel type, 2019. (Source: BP Statistical Review of World Energy 2020)

most air pollution in China is related to coal combustion, which is the source of 90 percent of SO2 emissions, 70 percent of dust emissions, 67 percent of NOx emissions, and 70 percent of the CO_2 emissions (EIA, 2019). Thus, China faces a challenging situation. As noted in the last Five-Year Plan, for China to reduce CO2 emissions, the Chinese authorities have developed new strategies to restructure China's energy mix (Zavadska et al., 2020). According to China's National Renewable Energy Centre (CNREC, 2019), for China, to support the Paris Agreement goals (limiting global temperature rise to below 2 °C to reduce CO2 emissions), the primary energy demand level in 2050 would need to fall below 2017 levels. However, coal usage in power generation continues to be quite high in contrast with the country's reality (CNREC, 2019). Therefore, the extent to which China would be able to move towards renewable energy resources to promote its economy and align its vision of a "*beautiful China*" remains a big dilemma. China has no other option but to import more oil to meet its energy demands. In 2018, China's dependence on oil imports exceeded 70 percent, and it can be expected that the reliance on oil imports will continue to increase (Zhang, 2019). It is predicted that China's dependency on fossil fuels will decrease by 2035. With coal and oil consumption dropping by 22 percent and 24 percent, respectively (Fig. 10).

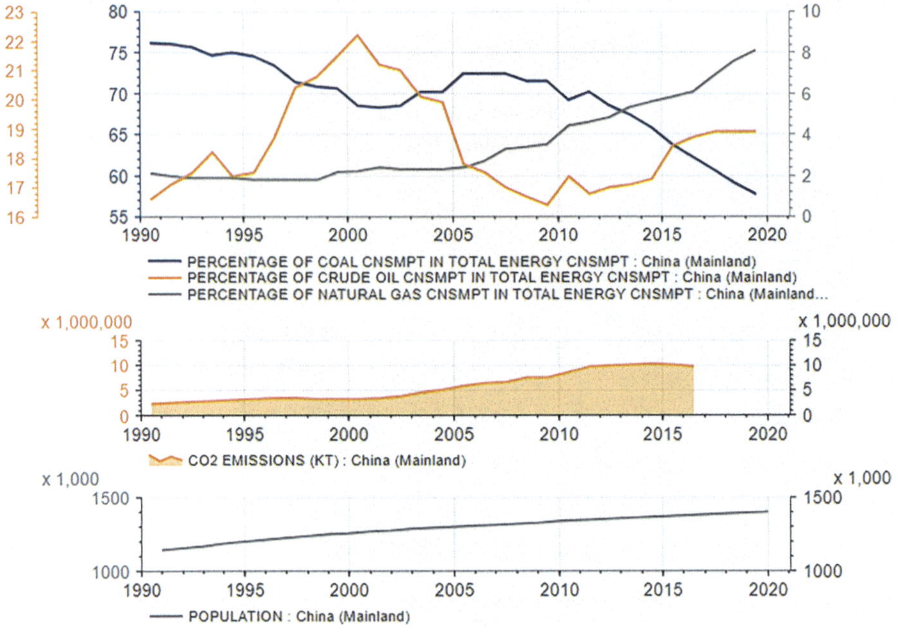

Fig. 10 Energy consumption and environmental impact. (Source: Authors elaboration using data from DataStream International (2021))

6 Conclusion

In less than 20 years, China became the world's second-largest economy for the first time in the modern era. Its rapid economic growth has been heavily connected with the consumption of fossil fuels and in particular with coal. The Chinese economy has accounted for over 90 percent of coal consumption worldwide, showing that coal is heavily ingrained as part of its history. This makes the transition to alternative energy resources quite challenging. Over the years, China has faced significant criticisms due to its heavy reliance on coal. The international community has put considerable pressure on China to reconsider its energy model, combined with rising domestic awareness levels on the connection between coal consumption, environmental damage, and health problems. Another point to be considered is that the GFC has acted as an inflection point, and that the Chinese growth rates started to slow down significantly. The combination of coal dependency, environmental concerns, and lower economic growth levels has pushed the country to reconsider its energy model towards more sustainable approaches. As the government seeks energy sustainability, this research suggest that the country's new energy model is shifting towards oil. This raises concerns regarding China's national security interests and sustainable economic growth goals. Moreover, the Middle-East has emerged as a critical player in China's quest to diversify its energy model, with over 45 percent of total energy imports in China coming from this region. China's energy consumption will continue to grow as the country is shifting from coal to oil and gas, flagging further its fossil fuel dependency. This heavy dependence on one primary energy source will have a considerable impact on China's economy, and it will put to question the sustainability of its energy model, on two accounts: first, a sizeable share of fossil fuels come from the Middle-East, a region characterized by high levels of instability; second, the shift from one type of fossil fuels (coal) to another type (oil and gas) clashes with China's ambition to be seen as an environmentally concerned global actor.

References

Aidoo, R., et al. (2017). *Footprints of the dragon: China's oil diplomacy and its impacts on sustainable development policy in Ecuador and Ghana.* 8.1. http://journals.openedition.org/poldev. https://doi.org/10.4000/POLDEV.2408.

Albulescu, C. (2020). *Coronavirus and oil price crash.* HAL Id: hal-02507184. pp. 1–14.

Aloui, D., et al. (2020). *COVID 19's impact on crude oil and natural gas S & P GS indexes.* HAL Id: halshs-02613280.

Andrews-Speed, P., & Dannreuther, R. (2011). China, oil and global politics, Routledge. *Journal of World Energy Law & Business*, 62–69. https://doi.org/10.1002/wilm.10463

Bambawale, M. J., & Sovacool, B. K. (2010). China's energy security: The perspective of energy users. *Applied Energy, 88*(5), 1949–1956. https://doi.org/10.1016/j.apenergy.2010.12.016

Beh, L. S., & Lin, W. L. (2021). Impact of COVID-19 on ASEAN tourism industry. *Journal of Asian Public Policy*, 1–21. https://doi.org/10.1080/17516234.2020.1871180

Besada, H. (2018). China' s energy strategy in the MENA region. *China Quarterly of International Strategic Studies, 3*(February). https://doi.org/10.1142/S2377740017500269

Besada, H., & Salam, J. (2017). *The new silk road: China' energy policy and strategy in the Mena region.* College of Business and Economics, Qatar University.

Bloomberg. (2020). *China oil demand has plunged 20% because of the virus, Bloomberg Green.* [Online] Available: Bloomberg Subscription Service. Accessed: 19 Nov 2020.

B. P. Statistical Review. (2019). *Statistical review of world energy.* http://www.bp.com/statisticalreview

B. P. Statistical Review. (2020). *Statistical review of world energy* (Vol. 67, pp. 1–56). http//www.bp.com/statisticalreview

Causevic, A. (2012). Rising Chinese crude oil demand and prospects. *Peace Research Institute Frankfurt (PRIF)*, (116).

Chen, J. (2011). The emergence of minorities in the Middle East. *Strategic Forum National Defense University, 271*, 1–8.

CNPC. (2016). *China National Petroleum Corporation Annual report of CNPC in 2016, CNPC International Department.*

CNPC. (2018). *China National Petroleum Corporation annual report.*

CNREC. (2019). *China National Renewable Energy Centre.*

Cole, B. D. (2003). *"Oil for the Lamps of China" – Beijing' s 21st-century search for energy.* Institute for National Strategic Studies National Defense University.

Daojiong, Z., & Meidan, M. (2015). China and the Middle East in a new energy landscape. *Chatham House Paper, 3*(October), 1–13.

DataStream International. (2021). *In international financial statistics* [online]. Available: Refinitiv Workspace/Economics.

Downs, E. (2019). High anxiety: The trade war and China' S oil and gas supply security. *COLUMBIA/SIPA. Center on Global Energy Policy, November*, 1–27.

Downs, E., et al. (2020). China and the Oil Price War: A Mixed Blessing. *Columbia Center on Global Energy Policy, March*, 1–17. https://www.energypolicy.columbia.edu/sites/default/files/file-uploads/China commentary, final design, 3.24.20.pdf

Duchâtel, M., Bräuner, O., & Hang, Z. (2014, June). *Protecting China' S overseas interests the slow shift away mathieu duchâtel, oliver bräuner*. Stockholm International Peace Research Institute.

EIA. (2018, July). *Energy implications of China's transition toward consumption-led growth*. U.S. Energy Information Administration. www.eia.gov

EIA. (2019). *Country analysis executive summary: China*. U.S: Energy Information Administration www.eia.gov/international/analysis/country/MEX

EIA. (2020). *Country analysis executive summary: China, U.S. energy information administration, independent statistic & analysis*. www.eia.gov/international/analysis/country/MEX

Elnaggar, Y. (2020). *China's growing role in the Middle East*. Middle East Institute. Retrieved October 11, 2021, from https://www.mei.edu/publications/chinas-growing-role-middle-east

FGE. (2020). *Crude oil data*. FGE, Facts Global Energy. Retrieved October 11, 2021, from https://www.fgenergy.com/data/crude-oil-data.aspx

Fukumoto, T., & Muto, I. (2011). *Rebalancing China' s economic growth: Some insights from Japan' s experience*. Bank of Japan Working Paper Series.

Fulton, J. (2019). *China's changing role in the Middle East* (pp. 1689–1699). Atlantic Council, Rafik Hariri Center for Middle East.

Ge, F., & Fan, Y. (2013). Quantifying the risk to crude oil imports in China: An improved portfolio approach. *Energy Economics, 40*, 72–80. https://doi.org/10.1016/j.eneco.2013.06.009

Gebhard-koenigstein, A. (2020). *Coronavirus: Economic impacts and policy responses Roadmap*. National Journal Presentation Center.

Green, F., & Stern, N. (2015, June). *China's "new normal": Structural change, better growth, and peak emissions* (p. 64). The Centre for Climate Change Economics and Policy & The Grantham Research Institute on Climate Change.

Guo, Z., et al. (2020). The impacts of reducing renewable energy subsidies on China's energy transition by using a hybrid dynamic computable general equilibrium model. *Frontiers in Energy Research, 8*(March). https://doi.org/10.3389/fenrg.2020.00025

Hao, Y., & Zhao, M. (2019). *China country report* (pp. 115–130). Beijing Institute of Technology, China: Center for Energy and Environmental Policy Research.

Huandong, J., & Mouyuan, W. (2017). History and achievements of Chinese oil companies' foreign cooperation. *China Oil & Gas, 3*, 58–63.

Janardhanan, N. (2010). Global energy geopolitics and the strategy of Chinese oil corporates. In V. R. Raghavan (Ed.), *Emerging challenges to energy security in the Asia Pacific* (pp. 70–86). Centre for Security Analysis.

Jarrett, U., Mohaddes, K., & Mohtadi, H. (2019). Oil price volatility, financial institutions and economic growth. *Energy Policy, 126*(August), 131–144. https://doi.org/10.1016/j.enpol.2018.10.068

Ji, Q., & Zhang, D. (2019). How much does financial development contribute to renewable energy growth and upgrading of energy structure in China? *Energy Policy, 128*(71573214), 114–124. https://doi.org/10.1016/j.enpol.2018.12.047

Ji, Q., Li, J., & Sun, X. (2019). New challenge and research development in global energy financialization. *Emerging Markets Finance and Trade, 55*(12), 2669–2672. https://doi.org/10.1080/1540496X.2019.1636588

Jing, Z. (2019). Oil and gas trade between China and countries and regions along the 'belt and road': A panoramic perspective. *Energy Policy, 129*, 1111–1120. https://doi.org/10.1016/j.enpol.2019.03.020

Jones, B., Steven, D., & Brien, E. O. (2014, March). *Fueling a new order? of energy*. BROOKINGs Institution.

Jones, B., Steven, D., & Brien, E. O. (2014). *Fueling a new order? of energy*. BROOKINGs Institution.

Leung, G., Li, R., & Low, M. (2011). Transitions in China's oil economy, 1990–2010. *Eurasian Geography and Economics, 52*(4), 483–500. https://doi.org/10.2747/1539-7216.52.4.483

Liao, M., & Wang, Y. (2019). China's energy consumption rebound effect analysis based on the perspective of technological progress. *Sustainability (Switzerland), 11*(5). https://doi.org/10.3390/su11051461

Lons, C., et al. (2019). China's great game in the Middle East. *European Council on Foreign Relations, October*, 33.

Luft, G. (2006) *Fueling the dragon: China's race into the oil market, by Gal Luft*. Available at: http://www.iags.org/china.htm. Accessed 27 Jan 2021.

Lyall, N. (2019). *China's rise in the Middle East: Beyond economics, the diplomat*. Available at: https://thediplomat.com/2019/02/chinas-rise-in-the-middle-east-beyond-economics/. Accessed 11 Oct 2021.

Meidan, M. (2020, January). *China: Key themes for 2020* (pp. 1–12). The Oxford Institute for Energy Studies.

Morrison, W. M. (2019). *China ' s economic rise: History, trends, challenges, and implications for the United States*. Congressional Research Service.

Mortazavi, S. M., Maleki, A., & Yousefi, H. (2019). Analysis of robustness of the Chinese economy and energy supply / demand fluctuations. *International Journal of Low-Carbon Technologies, February*, 147–159. https://doi.org/10.1093/ijlct/cty051

NBSC. (2020). *The national economy sustained steady recovery in October*. National Bureau of Statistics of China. Retrieved October 11, 2021, from http://www.stats.gov.cn/english/PressRelease/202011/t20201116_1803044.html

Nishimura, Y. (2020). New normal and new economy: A new growth engine for China. *International Journal of Economic Policy Studies, 14*(2), 301–312. https://doi.org/10.1007/s42495-020-00037-y

Odgaard, O., & Delman, J. (2014). China's energy security and its challenges towards 2035. *Energy Policy, 71*, 107–117. https://doi.org/10.1016/j.enpol.2014.03.040

OPEC. (2020). *Annual report*. Organization of the Petroleum Exporting Countries.

Ozili, P. K. (2020). *Causes, COVID-19 pandemic and economic crisis: The Nigerian experience and structural causes*. SSRN.

Ozili, P. K., & Arun, T. (2020, April). Spillover of COVID-19: Impact on the global economy. *SSRN Electronic Journal*. https://doi.org/10.2139/ssrn.3562570

Rioux, B., Galkin, P., & Wu, K. (2019). An economic analysis of China's domestic crude oil supply policies. *Chinese Journal of Population Resources and Environment, 17*(3), 217–228. https://doi.org/10.1080/10042857.2019.1650247

Scobell, A., & Nader, A. (2016). *China in the Middle East: The wary dragon*. RAND Corporation. https://doi.org/10.7249/rr1229

Shao, Y., Qiao, H., & Wang, S. (2017). What determines China's crude oil importing trade patterns? Empirical evidences from 55 countries between 1992 and 2015. *Energy Policy, 109*(May), 854–862. https://doi.org/10.1016/j.enpol.2017.05.063

Shi, B., & Cai, T. (2020). Has China's oil investment in belt and road initiative countries helped its oil import? *Energies, 13*(12). https://doi.org/10.3390/en13123176

Shichor, Y. (1998). *China's economic relations with the Middle East: New dimensions*. China Report. Sage. https://doi.org/10.1177/000944559803400310

Soligo, R., & Jaffe, A. (2010). *China's growing energy dependence: The costs and policy implications of supply alternatives* (pp. 1–19). Baker Institute Working Papers. papers3://publication/uuid/3F1EE664-0854-41B3-9382-4A2CA5F6E42A.

Tang, X., et al. (2016). China's coal consumption declining: Impermanent or permanent? *Resources, Conservation and Recycling, 129*(2018), 307–313. https://doi.org/10.1016/j.resconrec.2016.07.018

The World Bank. (2014, May). *China economic update* (p. 1). The World Bank.

The World Bank. (2020). *China economic update*. Washington, DC.

Vasquez, P. I. (2019). *China's oil and gas footprint in Latin America and Africa*. 11.1. http://journals.openedition.org/poldev. https://doi.org/10.4000/POLDEV.3174.

Wormuth, C. (2019). *Russia and China in the Middle East: Implications for the United States in an era of strategic competition*. https://doi.org/10.7249/ct511

Wu, K. (2014). China's energy security: Oil and gas. *Energy Policy, 73*, 4–11. https://doi.org/10.1016/j.enpol.2014.05.040

Xu, X., et al. (2019). Global renewable energy development: Influencing factors, trend predictions and countermeasures. *Resources Policy, 63*(June). https://doi.org/10.1016/j.resourpol.2019.101470

Zavadska, M., Morales, L., & Andreosso O'Callaghan, B. (2020). Is China's dependency on coal a threat to its economic.

Zhang, Q. (2011). The impact of international oil price fluctuation on China's economy. *Energy Procedia, 5*, 1360–1364. https://doi.org/10.1016/j.egypro.2011.03.235

Zhang, W., Wei, R., & Peng, S. (2020). The oil-slick trade: An analysis of embodied crude oil in China's trade and consumption. *Energy Economics, 88*, 104763. https://doi.org/10.1016/j.eneco.2020.104763

Zhongmin, L. (2008). *Thirty years of China's diplomacy in the Middle East (Part 1). Social Sciences in*. Ningxia, No.5.

Zweig, D., & Hao, Y. (2015). *Sino–US energy triangles resource diplomacy under hegemony*.

The Macroeconomic Impact of Government Debt: An Empirical Analysis of Thailand

Utai Uprasen

Abstract The issue of rising public debt is an important topic of increased focal point in the developing world. Especially, since the COVID-19 outbreak, governments in many countries create debts to relieve the effects of the pandemic. Thailand is no exception. The public debt is estimated at 58.60 per cent of the GDP in 2021. This raises the concern on the potential macroeconomic impact of public debt, especially the effect on economic growth. The connection between public debt and economic growth is ongoing controversial matter. The existing theories and empirical findings exhibit ambiguous effects of public debt on economic growth. Accordingly, this chapter scrutinizes the impact of government debt on economic growth of Thailand. An autoregressive distributed lag (ARDL) model is adopted for empirical estimations, based on endogenous growth theory, using quarterly data between 2002Q1 and 2019Q4. The Toda-Yamamoto approach on Granger causality test is employed to increase the robustness of the study. The findings indicate that a rise in total public debt, especially from domestic public debt, contributes to economic growth in general. However, the findings should be interpreted cautiously in terms of policy implications for the debt's effect in COVID-19 context. This is because most of the money is used to support consumption rather than to contribute on productive sectors.

Keywords Government debt · Economic growth · Thailand

1 Introduction

Thailand is an upper middle-income country in Southeast Asia. The government encourages economic growth through various channels, including creation of public debt. The COVID-19 pandemic raises the public debt of Thailand significantly. The Thai authorities raised the debt ceiling from 60 to 70 per cent of GDP in September

U. Uprasen (✉)
Pukyong National University, Busan, Korea
e-mail: utai_uprasen@pknu.ac.kr

B. Andreosso-O'Callaghan et al. (eds.), *Sustainable Development in Asia*, Contributions to Economics, https://doi.org/10.1007/978-3-030-94679-1_6

2021. Therefore, the issue of the effect of public debt on economic growth is crucial to not only scholars but also to the policymakers. There is no consensus among the existing theories regarding the impact of public debt on economic growth. While the Keynesian hypothesis predicts the positive impact, the debt overhang hypothesis and the Ricardian equivalence hypothesis anticipate the negative and insignificant effects, respectively. The current empirical findings also exhibit ambiguous effects of public debt on economic growth. Accordingly, this chapter contributes to the existing literature by investigating the case of Thailand. An autoregressive distributed lag (ARDL) model is employed for empirical estimation, using quarterly data between 2002Q1 and 2019Q4. The Toda-Yamamoto approach on Granger causality test is also conducted to increase the robustness of the study.

The study is arranged as follows. While Sect. 1 is the introduction, Sect. 2 describes the public debt and economic growth of Thailand after the financial crisis in 1997 to date. Section 3 presents the related literature review, and the research methodology is elaborated in Sect. 4. While the estimation results are discussed in Sect. 5, the conclusion of study and policy implication are drawn in Sect. 6.

2 Thailand's Government Debt

The overview of Thailand's public debt is described as following. Figure 1 shows that since the Asian financial crisis in 1997, Thailand has performed moderate economic growth, approximately 5 per cent annually. The growth was dropped down by 7 per cent in 2020 due to the unprecedented COVID-19 pandemic.

The government of Thailand has created public debt in order to stimulate economic growth over time. For the past decade, the authorities showed high discipline to manage the public debt at around 40 per cent of GDP. It was

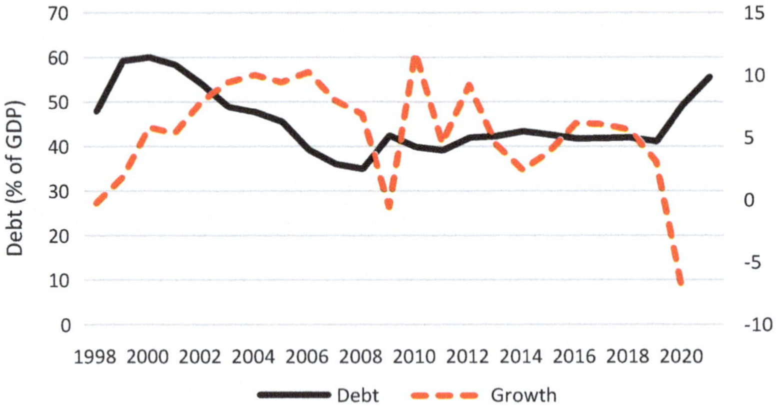

Fig. 1 Thailand's nominal GDP growth and public debt, as of July 2021. (*Source*: Author's calculation using data from Bank of Thailand and Public Debt Management Office)

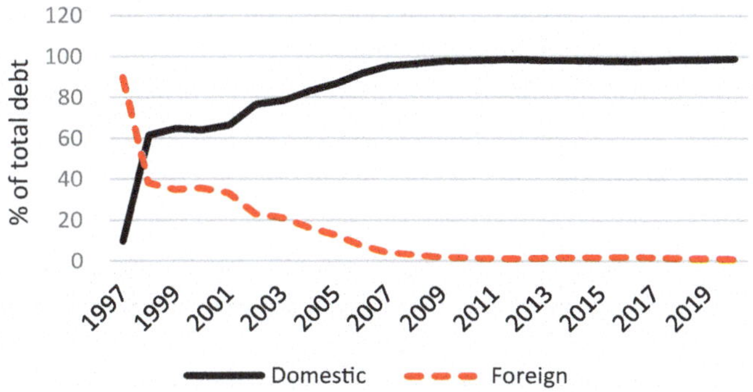

Fig. 2 Domestic and external debt, 1997–2020. (*Source*: Author's calculation using data from Bank of Thailand)

Table 1 Public debt components, as of July 2021

Debt components	Million baht	%	% of GDP
1. Direct government debt	7,836,723.70	87.96	48.90
2. State enterprise debt	781,052.43	8.77	4.87
3. Financial institutions guaranteed debt	284,141.61	3.19	1.77
4. Financial Institutions Development Fund (FIDF) debt	0.00	0.00	0.00
5. Government agency debt	7146.04	0.08	0.04
Total debt	8,909,063.78	100.00	55.59
Estimated GDP	16,027,047.59	0.00	0.00

Source: Public Debt Management Office, Thailand

6,901,801 million baht (41 per cent of GDP in 2019). Figure 2 illustrates that the debt elements have switched from external debt to domestic debt after the financial crisis in 1997. The domestic debt made up 98 per cent of total government debt in 2020.

In 2020, the government of Thailand borrowed money for 1 trillion baht to mitigate the consequences from COVID-19 outbreak. The 600 billion baht was used as financial aid to individuals and the related health plans. The other 400 billion baht was for economic and social rehabilitation through community infrastructure. The total public debt was increased to 7,848,155 million baht (49 per cent of GDP) by July 2020. In May 2021, the Thai government borrowed another 500 billion baht for COVID-19 relief measures. The majority of money, 300 billion baht, was spent as financial support to the people. Another 30 billion baht was spent on related medical activities. The rest of money, 170 billion baht, was managed to promote investment and consumption. As of July 2021, the public debt was 8,909,063 million baht, which accounted for 56 per cent of GDP.

Table 1 shows the public debt structure of Thailand. The main component of public debt is direct government debt, which constitutes 87.96 per cent of total debt. The other important debt components are state enterprise debt (8.77 per cent) and financial institutions guaranteed debt (3.19 per cent). In September 2021, the government of Thailand raised the debt ceiling from 60 to 70 per cent of GDP to relieve the effect from COVID-19 pandemic.

3 Literature Review

The existing literature pertaining the effect of public debt on economic growth might be elaborated in four groups, based on the theoretical argument and empirical finding, as the followings.

First, positive effect, the Keynesian point of view posits the effect of government debt on economic growth through fiscal multiplier effect. Productive public spending from public debt encourages economic growth. In addition, the impact from deficit-financed spending on growth is higher than tax-financed spending (Holtfrerich, 2013). The empirical findings from Uzun et al. (2012) revealed that foreign public debt has positive effect on growth rate of GDP per capita in 19 transitional economies from 1991 to 2009. Owusu-Nantwi and Erickson (2016) also postulated that a 1 per cent rise in government debt promotes GDP growth of Ghana by 2.80 per cent between 1970 and 2012. However, using data from 118 countries, Eberhardt and Presbitero (2015) found that while public debt contributes to economic growth in the long run, it has no impact in the short run.

Second, negative effect, the debt overhang hypothesis (Myers, 1977; Reinhart et al., 2012) asserts that public debt decreases economic growth through certain mechanisms. The negative impact of debt can occur through crowding-out effect. The government borrowing induces substantial increase in real interest rate. This injures investment of private sector which leads to economic downturn (Huang et al., 2018). Another potential mechanism is the effect of fiscal illusion (Patinkin, 1965; Pereira & Rodrigues, 2001). The short-sighted taxpayers just enjoy their current consumptions and not realize their future tax burdens. The rise in current consumption at the cost of saving lowers investment. As a result, it lowers the long-term economic growth. Pattillo et al. (2004) asserted that a double of debt lowers economic growth by 1 per cent in the highly indebted countries. The empirical estimation by Szabó (2013) showed that a 1 per cent rise in debt-to-GDP ratio reduces GDP growth rate of 27 European Union members by 0.03 per cent from 2008 to 2014. The negative effect was also reported by Gómez-Puig and Sosvilla-Rivero (2018) for the case of the Euro area countries. The negative impacts were also discovered in Latin American and Asian countries (Sen et al., 2007). For the Asian countries, using panel data between 1980 and 2012, Asteriou et al. (2021) found that the negative consequence exists in both short and long run. When the case of Malaysia was examined, Yoong et al. (2020) demonstrated that the nominal GDP per capita reduces by 0.42 per cent, when the debt-to-GDP ratio increases by 1 per cent. Moreover, the same effects were found when 111 countries from developing countries and OECD nations were scrutinized during 1970 to 2010 (Ahlborn & Schweickert, 2018), and the case of large panel data of developed and developing countries (Woo & Kumar, 2015).

Third, nonlinear effect, the level of threshold debt determines its impact on economic growth. The threshold theory rests on the integration of debt overhang concept and crowding-in and crowding-out effects of the public debt. The positive effect of public debt on growth can be anticipated if its level is lower than the threshold value, whereas the negative impact can be the case if the public debt is higher than the threshold level (Mupunga & Le Roux, 2015; Reinhart & Rogoff, 2010). The explanations are as follows. The crowding-in effect emanating from government spending dominates the crowding-out effect arising from decrease in private investment, when the public debt is smaller than the threshold. Nevertheless, the crowding-out effect dominates the crowding-in effect, if the level of public debt is greater than the threshold (Sachs, 1989; Krugman, 1988). The empirical works (Reinhart & Rogoff, 2010; Herndon et al., 2014) revealed that the threshold of public debt is 90 per cent of the country's GDP for the case of developed countries. However, the level of threshold can also vary from 90 to 115 per cent (Minea & Parent, 2012). Besides, for emerging countries, the threshold level is lower than the developed countries. The percentage of public debt to GDP should below 60 (Reinhart & Rogoff, 2010). Nonetheless, Presbitero (2012) asserted that the threshold was above 90 per cent for the developing countries from 1990 to 2007, based on his empirical findings. In contrast, Chudik et al. (2017) investigated the case of 40 developed and developing economies from 1965 to 2010. The findings indicated that public debt only reduces economic growth. The threshold level does not exist.

Fourth, no effect, the insignificant impact of government debt on economic growth can be explained through the Ricardian equivalence hypothesis, REH (Ricardo, 1951). The debt-financed government spending has no effect on economy since the taxpayers realize that the future tax will be collected in order to pay for the debt. Barro (1989) describes that debt-financed government spending is just money movement between economic agents. The empirical work showed that public debt has no effect on GDP growth of OECD countries (Panizza & Presbitero, 2014). The same outcome was also found when 82 developed countries were examined from 1980 to 2009 (Kourtellos et al., 2013).

Based on the above literature review, it is worth mentioning that there is no consensus on the effect of government debt on economic growth in both theoretical and empirical perspectives. The empirical findings can vary depending on the certain cases, studied periods, and research methodologies. The case of Thailand has never been investigated. Consequently, this chapter aims at examining the effect of public debt on economic growth of Thailand.

4 Methodology

4.1 The Model

The endogenous growth model (Romer, 1986) is adopted as our theoretical framework. It is a growth model which allows more realistic assumption, compared to neoclassical growth model (Solow, 1956, 1957), such as the production function exhibits constant returns to capital. Accordingly, the production function is specified as Eq. (1).

$$Y = AK \tag{1}$$

where *Y* and *K* represent output of the economy and stock of capital, respectively. Term A is a positive constant. The public debt is incorporated into a model through capital stock. Moreover, to mitigate the omitted variables bias in the estimations, the other three related variables are included in the study, as follows.

$$Y = f(INV, OPE, MON, DEB) \tag{2}$$

Consequently, output of the economy is a function of investment (*INV*), trade openness (*OPE*), broad money (*MON*) and government debt (*DEB*). Equation (2) is specified in a logarithmic form as Eq. (3).

$$ln\, Y_t = \beta_0 + \beta_1\, ln\, INV_t + \beta_2\, ln\, OPE_t + \beta_3\, ln\, MON_t + \beta_4\, ln\, DEB_t + \varepsilon_t \tag{3}$$

For the purpose of convenience, let $x_t = ln\ X_t$. Equation (3) is transformed into Eq. (4) as below.

$$gdp_t = \beta_0 + \beta_1 inv_t + \beta_2 ope_t + \beta_3 mon_t + \beta_4 deb_t + \varepsilon_t \tag{4}$$

The expected signs of β_1, β_2 and β_3 are positive. Nevertheless, the anticipated sign of β_4 is undetermined. It can be positive, negative or insignificant, as argued by the Keynesian hypothesis, the debt overhang hypothesis and the Ricardian equivalence hypothesis, respectively. Equation (4) is rearranged into the autoregressive distributed lag (ARDL) model (Pesaran et al., 2001) for the purpose of empirical estimations, as model I, as the following.

$$
\begin{aligned}
\text{Model I}: \Delta gdp_t &= \alpha + \sum_{i=1}^{a} \beta_i \Delta gdp_{t-i} + \sum_{i=0}^{b} \gamma_i \Delta inv_{t-i} + \sum_{i=0}^{c} \delta_i \Delta ope_{t-i} \\
&+ \sum_{i=0}^{d} \omega_i \Delta mon_{t-i} + \sum_{i=0}^{e} \varphi_i \Delta deb_{t-i} + \tau gdp_{t-1} + \sigma inv_{t-1} + \rho ope_{t-1} \\
&+ \pi mon_{t-1} + \mu deb_{t-1} + \varepsilon_t \qquad (5)
\end{aligned}
$$

The ARDL model is employed for empirical estimation, because our studied variables are combinations of integrated of order 0 and 1 variables, I(0) and I (1) variables, according to the results from ADF unit root test in Sect. 5. In addition, the ARDL technique yields reliable estimation results with limited number of observations (Toda, 1994). The Δ is the first difference. It implies short-run elements of the model, and a to e represent optimal lag lengths. The coefficients of one lag variables (τ, σ, ρ, π, μ) indicate the long run aspect of the model. Equation (5) is used to scrutinize the effect of total government debt (*deb*) on the economic growth. The connection between short-run aspect and the long-run aspect of the model is presented by the error correction form, as the following.

$$
\begin{aligned}
\Delta gdp_t &= \alpha + \sum_{i=1}^{a} \beta_i \Delta gdp_{t-i} + \sum_{i=0}^{b} \gamma_i \Delta inv_{t-i} + \sum_{i=0}^{c} \delta_i \Delta ope_{t-i} \\
&+ \sum_{i=0}^{d} \omega_i \Delta mon_{t-i} + \sum_{i=0}^{e} \varphi_i \Delta deb_{t-i} + \vartheta ECM_{t-1} + \varepsilon_t \qquad (6)
\end{aligned}
$$

where ECM_{t-1} is an error correction term. It indicates adjustment speed of the short-run disequilibrium of the model towards the long-run equilibrium.

In addition, the total government debt (*deb*) is disaggregated into domestic debt (*dom*) and external debt (*ext*) in our study in order to observe the impact of specific type of government debt. Therefore, Eq. (5) is transformed into Eq. (7), model II, as follows.

$$
\begin{aligned}
\text{Model II}: \Delta gdp_t &= \alpha + \sum_{i=1}^{a} \beta_i \Delta gdp_{t-i} + \sum_{i=0}^{b} \gamma_i \Delta inv_{t-i} + \sum_{i=0}^{c} \delta_i \Delta ope_{t-i} \\
&+ \sum_{i=0}^{d} \omega_i \Delta mon_{t-i} + \sum_{i=0}^{e} \varphi_i \Delta dom_{t-i} + \sum_{i=0}^{f} \vartheta_i \Delta ext_{t-i} + \tau gdp_{t-1} \\
&+ \sigma inv_{t-1} + \rho ope_{t-1} + \pi mon_{t-1} + \mu dom_{t-1} + \theta ext_{t-1} + \varepsilon_t \qquad (7)
\end{aligned}
$$

Accordingly, model I and II, which are specified as Eqs. (5) and (7), are estimated to investigate the effect of the total government debt (*deb*), domestic government debt (*dom*) and external government debt (*ext*) respectively. The empirical results are reported in Sect. 5.

4.2 Data

The quarterly data (2002Q1–2019Q4) are used in our estimations. The economic growth (*gdp*) is measured through real gross domestic product (GDP) per capita (USD at 2010 constant prices). The gross fixed capital formation (% of GDP) is used to represent investment (*inv*). The broad money (*mon*) is specified as per cent of GDP. All three variables (*gdp*, *inv*, *mon*) are acquired from the International Financial Statistics (IFS), the International Monetary Fund (IMF) databases. Trade openness (*ope*) is defined as the summation of total imports and total exports, as per cent of GDP. The data are collected from the World Integrated Trade Solution (WITS). The total public debt (*deb*), domestic public debt (*dom*) and external public debt (*ext*) are expressed as per cent of GDP. The data are derived from the Public Debt Management Office of Thailand.

5 Empirical Results

5.1 Unit Root Test

The studied variables of model I and model II are tested for unit root, using Augmented Dickey-Fuller (ADF) test. The test results are presented in Table 2.

The degree of cointegration of variable from the ADF test indicates that the studied variables are combination between I(0) and I(1) variables. These results

Table 2 Augmented Dickey-Fuller unit root test

	Level form		First different form		I(n)
Variable	t-stat	Prob.	t-stat	Prob.	
gdp	−2.127	0.522	−3.477**	0.050	I(1)
inv	−3.746**	0.026			I(0)
ope	−1.316	0.876	−10.843***	0.000	I(1)
mon	−2.943	0.155	−8.791***	0.000	I(1)
deb	−1.106	0.921	−7.297***	0.000	I(1)
dom	−3.275	0.078			I(0)
ext	−0.543	0.979	−6.325***	0.000	I(1)

Note: The ***, **, * indicate level of significance at 1%, 5% and 10%, respectively. I(n) stands for integrated of order n variable imply that the ARDL model is applicable for the estimation of model I and II, since there is no I(2) variable in our work.

5.2 *The Bounds Test*

There are two estimations in our work. The first estimation (model I) is conducted in order to scrutinize the effect of total government debt (*deb*) on economic growth, whereas the second estimation (model II) aims to investigate the effect of domestic (*dom*) and external (*ext*) government debts, using Eqs. (5) and (6) respectively. Consequently, the ARDL bounds test is employed for each model to examine the long-run cointegration properties of the studied variables. The test results are displayed in Table 3.

Based on the bounds test, the long-run cointegration properties among studied variables will exist if the calculated F-statistic is greater than the upper bound critical value. The calculated F-statistics of model I and II are 7.837 and 5.822, respectively. Both of them are higher than the upper bound critical value at 1 per cent significance level. Hence, there exist the long-run cointegration relationships among studied variables in both models.

5.3 *The Estimating Coefficients*

The existence of cointegration properties of studied variables enables us to conduct the empirical estimation in both long-run and short-run aspects, using the ARDL model. The effects of total, domestic and external government debt on economic growth are displayed in Table 4.

According to model I, the total debt shows positive impact on economic growth of Thailand. A 1 per cent increase in total public debt (*deb*) leads to an increase in real GDP per capita by 0.233 per cent in the long run. The empirical outcomes in model II, when the total public debt is disaggregated into domestic and external debt, indicate that the positive contribution on economic growth of the government debt comes from domestic debt (*dom*), rather than the external debt (*ext*). An increase in

Table 3 The bounds test

	Model I: Total debt		Model II: Disaggregated debt	
Level of significance	Lower bound	Upper bound	Lower bound	Upper bound
10%	2.320	3.232	2.193	3.161
5%	2.725	3.718	2.564	3.650
1%	3.608	4.860	3.373	4.717
Calculated F-statistic	7.837***		5.822***	

Note: The ***, **, * indicate level of significance at 1%, 5% and 10%, respectively

Table 4 The long-run coefficients

	Model I: Total debt		Model II: Disaggregated debt	
Variable	Coefficient	t-Statistic	Coefficient	t-Statistic
inv	0.296**	2.076	0.052	0.228
ope	0.404***	2.688	0.017	0.731
mon	0.225**	2.218	0.054*	1.860
deb	0.233***	3.192		
dom			0.118***	5.507
ext			0.029	0.962
c	−4.666	−1.140	−2.397	−1.621

Note: The ***, **, * indicate level of significance at 1%, 5% and 10%, respectively

1 per cent of domestic government debt encourages economic growth by 0.118 per cent in the long run. Our empirical outcomes indicate that the government debt affects economic growth of Thailand through the fiscal multiplier effect, based on the Keynesian point of view. Our findings on positive effect of government debt on economic growth are in line with Uzun et al. (2012) in the case of 19 transitional economies and Owusu-Nantwi and Erickson (2016) for the case of Ghana. However, while a rise in 1 per cent of the government debt promotes economic growth of Ghana by 2.800 per cent, it is only 0.233 per cent for Thailand. The positive contribution of government debt on economic growth is also found in the USA (Bohn, 1998; Greiner, 2011), Malaysia (Daud & Podivinsky, 2014) and 93 low-income countries (Abbas & Christensen, 2010).

Besides the role of public debt, the other related variables affect the economic growth of Thailand in the long term, as anticipated. A 1 per cent rise in investment, trade openness and broad money leads to the increase in Thailand's economic growth by 0.296, 0.404 and 0.225 per cent, respectively.

The short-run effects of the government debt are presented in Table 5. The results reveal that total government debt (*deb*) does not affect economic growth in the short term. However, the domestic debt (*dom*) shows positive impact (0.019) on economic growth, whereas the external debt (*ext*) has negative impact on economic growth (−0.102) in the short run. Accordingly, the insignificant impact of total government debt in the short run might be explained through the counteraction between domestic debt and external government debt. Our findings are consistent with Eberhardt and Presbitero (2015), which found that while public debt contributes to economic growth in the long run, it has no impact in the short run from the study using the samples from 118 countries.

5.4 Diagnostic Tests of the Model

The certain diagnostic tests are conducted in order to check the validity of our estimating models, as presented in Table 6. The absolute values of ECM_{t-1} are

Table 5 The short-run coefficients

	Model I: Total debt		Model II: Disaggregated debt	
Variable	Coefficient	t-Statistic	Coefficient	t-Statistic
Δgdp_{t-1}	0.436***	3.371	0.198*	1.925
Δgdp_{t-2}	−0.735***	−6.447	−0.722***	−8.017
Δgdp_{t-3}	−0.280*	−1.856	−0.253*	−1.888
Δinv_t	−0.000	−0.042	0.128**	2.187
Δinv_{t-1}	0.016*	1.798	−0.062	−0.943
Δinv_{t-2}			−0.205***	−3.525
Δinv_{t-3}			−0.104*	−1.987
Δope_t	−0.005	−0.558	0.005	0.736
Δope_{t-1}	0.023**	2.087		
Δope_{t-2}	−0.026**	−2.622		
Δope_{t-3}	−0.025**	−2.364		
Δmon_t	0.029**	2.072	0.019*	1.698
Δmon_{t-1}	0.037***	2.779	0.057***	5.696
Δmon_{t-2}	−0.016	−1.095	−0.027**	−2.051
Δmon_{t-3}	0.022**	2.101	0.029***	2.836
Δdeb_t	−0.007	−0.549		
Δdeb_{t-1}	−0.005	−0.495		
Δdeb_{t-2}	0.022**	2.038		
Δdom_t			−0.003	−0.288
Δdom_{t-1}			−0.010	−1.193
Δdom_{t-2}			0.019**	2.394
Δext_t			−0.026	−0.829
Δext_{t-1}			0.042	1.263
Δext_{t-2}			−0.102***	−3.168

Note: The ***, **, * indicate level of significance at 1%, 5% and 10%, respectively

Table 6 Diagnostic statistics of the ARDL model

Test	Model I: Total debt	Model II: Disaggregated debt
ECM_{t-1}	−0.083*** (0.000)	−0.285*** (0.000)
LM test	0.579 (0.450)	0.359 (0.552)
RESET test	1.332 (0.254)	0.051 (0.823)
R^2	0.717	0.744

Note: The ***, **, * indicate level of significance at 1%, 5% and 10%, respectively. P-values are provided in parentheses

lower than one, together with negative signs (−0.083 and −0.285) reveal that the disequilibrium in the short run is adjusted towards long-run equilibrium in both models, with the adjustment speed at 8.30 and 28.50 per cent, respectively. The Breusch-Godfrey LM tests show insignificant testing results at one degree of freedom. As a result, the autocorrelation problem does not exist in both models. The Ramsey's RESET tests show the insignificant chi-square statistics. It indicates

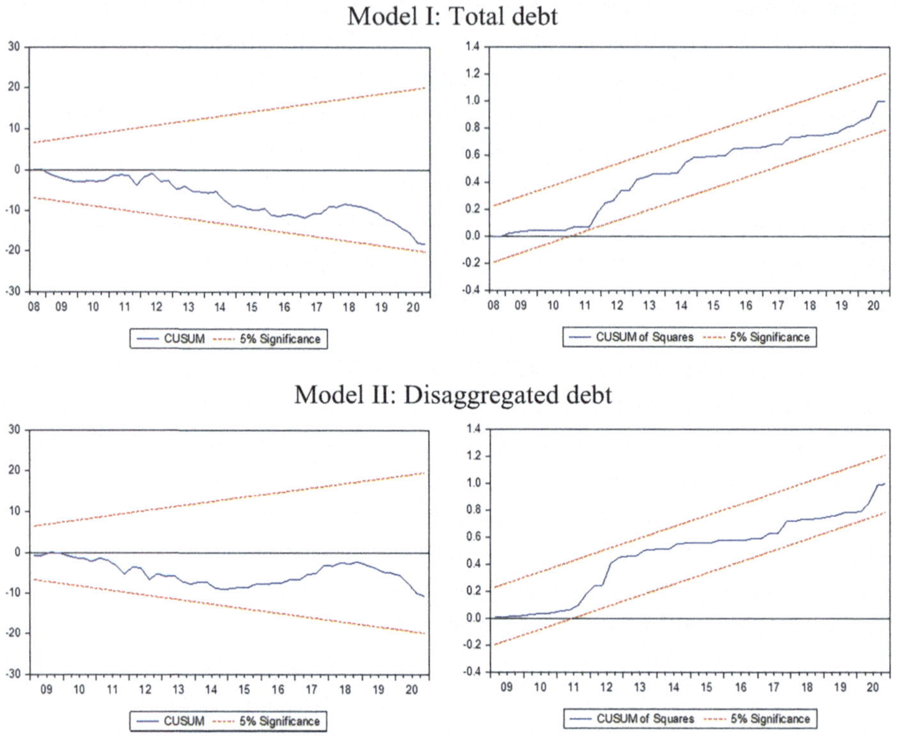

Fig. 3 Stability of coefficients. Model I: Total debt; Model II: Disaggregated debt

that model I and II are correctly specified. The goodness of fit of model I is 0.717 and it is 0.744 for model II.

Finally, the results from the cumulative sum of recursive residuals (CUSUM) and cumulative sum of squares of recursive residual (CUSUM of Squares) in Fig. 3 confirm the stability of estimating coefficients over time

5.5 *Toda-Yamamoto Causality Test*

Besides the ARDL model estimation, we conduct causality test, based on Toda-Yamamoto method, to increase the robustness of the study. The outcomes from causality tests are presented in Table 7.

Accordingly, although the causality from total government debt (*deb*) to economic growth (*gdp*) is not confirmed, there is a unidirectional causality from domestic public debt (*dom*) to economic growth. The Toda-Yamamoto causality test also reveals that economic growth of Thailand is caused by investment (*inv*) and broad money (*mon*).

Table 7 Toda-Yamamoto approach on Granger causality test

Variable	Wald-statistic	P-value	Causality
Model I: Total debt			
inv → *gdp*	8.564*	0.073	Unidirectional
ope → *gdp*	4.752	0.314	
mon → *gdp*	15.938***	0.003	Bidirectional
deb → *gdp*	6.837	0.145	
gdp → *deb*	11.067**	0.026	Unidirectional
inv → *deb*	7.948*	0.094	Unidirectional
ope → *deb*	2.080	0.721	
mon → *deb*	6.959	0.138	
Model II: Disaggregated debt			
inv → *gdp*	8.860*	0.065	Bidirectional
ope → *gdp*	5.120	0.275	
mon → *gdp*	10.734**	0.030	Bidirectional
dom → *gdp*	12.372**	0.015	Unidirectional
ext → *gdp*	6.837	0.145	
gdp → *dom*	7.068	0.132	
inv → *dom*	4.174	0.383	
ope → *dom*	0.287	0.991	
mon → *dom*	1.722	0.787	
ext → *dom*	1.269	0.867	
gdp → *ext*	13.900***	0.008	Unidirectional
inv → *ext*	2.862	0.581	
ope → *ext*	9.414*	0.052	Bidirectional
mon → *ext*	2.949	0.566	
dom → *ext*	2.187	0.702	

Note: The ***, **, * indicate level of significance at 1%, 5% and 10%, respectively

6 Conclusion

The issue of the effect of public debt on economic growth is important for both scholars and policymakers. The impact of public debt on economic growth is ongoing controversial matter. The existing theories predict the positive, negative and insignificant effects of public debt on economic growth, based on the argument of the Keynesian hypothesis, the debt overhang hypothesis and the Ricardian equivalence hypothesis, respectively. The current empirical findings also exhibit ambiguous effects of public debt on economic growth. This chapter contributes to the existing public debt and economic growth literature by focusing on Thailand, where it is prone to increase public debt to 70 per cent of GDP. Accordingly, an autoregressive distributed lag (ARDL) model is adopted for empirical estimations, using quarterly data between 2002Q1 and 2019Q4. The Toda-Yamamoto approach on Granger causality test is also employed to increase the robustness of the study. The findings indicate that a rise in total public debt, especially from domestic public debt, contributes to economic growth in general. A 1 per cent rise in total public debt contributes to the growth of real GDP per capita by 0.233 per cent. Our empirical findings indicate that the public debt affects economic growth of Thailand through the fiscal multiplier effect, based on the Keynesian point of view.

However, our findings should be interpreted cautiously in terms of policy implications regarding the debt's effect in COVID-19 context and the future debt creation. This is because most of the money, which the government borrowed in order to relieve the consequence from the COVID-19 pandemic, was used as financial aid to support consumption of the people rather than to contribute on productive sectors. Moreover, the average debt-to-GDP ratio in our studied period (40 per cent of GDP) does not exceed the general threshold level (60 per cent of GDP) of the developing countries. Since the government of Thailand raised the ceiling of public debt from 60 to 70 per cent of GDP, an additional debt may raise the debt-to-GDP ratio exceeding the general standard threshold of 60 per cent substantially. Consequently, the argument of the debt overhang hypothesis might be valid in the future.

References

Abbas, A. S. M., & Christensen, J. E. (2010). The role of domestic debt markets in economic growth: An empirical investigation for low-income countries and emerging markets. *IMF Economic Review, 57*, 209–255.

Ahlborn, M., & Schweickert, R. (2018). Public debt and economic growth—Economic systems matter. *International Economics and Economic Policy, 15*(2), 373–403.

Asteriou, D., Keith Pilbeam, K., & Pratiwi, C. E. (2021). Public debt and economic growth: Panel data evidence for Asian countries. *Journal of Economics and Finance, 45*(2), 270–287.

Barro, R. J. (1989). The Ricardian approach to budget deficits. *The Journal of Economic Perspectives, 3*(2), 37–54.

Bohn, H. (1998). The behaviour of U.S. public debt and deficits. *Quarterly Journal of Economics, 113*(3), 949–963.

Chudik, A., Mohaddes, K., Pesaran, M. H., & Raissi, M. (2017). Is there a debt-threshold effect on output growth? *The Review of Economics and Statistics, 99*(1), 135–150.

Daud, S. N. M., & Podivinsky, J. (2014). Government debt and economic growth in Malaysia: The role of institutional quality. *Applied Economics Letters, 21*(17), 1179–1183.

Eberhardt, M., & Presbitero, A. F. (2015). Public debt and growth: Heterogeneity and non-linearity. *Journal of International Economics, 97*(1), 45–58.

Gómez-Puig, M., & Sosvilla-Rivero, S. (2018). Public debt and economic growth: Further evidence for the Euro area. *Acta Oeconomica, 68*(2), 209–229.

Greiner, A. (2011). Economic growth, public debt and welfare: Comparing three budgetary rules. *German Economic Review, 12*(2), 205–222.

Herndon, T., Ash, M., & Pollin, R. (2014). Does high public debt consistently stifle economic growth? A critique of Reinhart and Rogoff. *Cambridge Journal of Economics, 38*(2), 257–279.

Holtfrerich, C. L. (2013). Government debt in economic thought of the long 19th century. *Discussion Papers 2013/4*. Free University Berlin, School of Business & Economics, Germany.

Huang, Y., Panizza, U., & Varghese, R. (2018). Does public debt crowd out corporate investment? International evidence. *CEPR Discussion Paper No. DP12931*. Centre for Economic Policy Research, London, UK.

Kourtellos, A., Stengos, T., & Tan, C. M. (2013). The effect of public debt on growth in multiple regimes. *Journal of Macroeconomics, 38*(Part A), 35–43.

Krugman, P. (1988). Financing vs. forgiving a debt overhang. *Journal of Development Economics, 29*(3), 253–268.

Minea, A., & Parent, A. (2012). Is high public debt always harmful to economic growth? Reinhart and Rogoff and some complex nonlinearities. *CERDI Working Papers No. 201218*. Etudes et Documents.

Mupunga, N., & Le Roux, P. (2015). Estimating the optimal growth-maximising public debt threshold for Zimbabwe. *Southern African Business Review, 19*(3), 102–128.

Myers, S. C. (1977). Determinants of corporate borrowing. *Journal of Financial Economics, 5*(2), 147–175.

Owusu-Nantwi, V., & Erickson, C. (2016). Public debt and economic growth in Ghana. *African Development Review, 28*(1), 116–126.

Panizza, U., & Presbitero, A. F. (2014). Public debt and economic growth: Is there a causal effect? *Journal of Macroeconomics, 41*, 21–41.

Patinkin, D. (1965). *Money, interest and prices: An integration of monetary and value theory* (2nd ed.). Harper & Row.

Pattillo, C., Poirson, H., & Ricci, L. (2004). What are the channels through which external debt affects growth? *IMF Working Papers 2004/015*. International Monetary Fund, Washington.

Pereira, A. M., & Rodrigues, P. G. (2001). Public debt and economic performance. *DGEP Working Paper 20*. Ministério das Finanças, Portugal.

Pesaran, H. M., Shin, Y. C., & Smith, R. J. (2001). Bounds testing approaches to the analysis of level relationships. *Journal of Applied Econometrics, 6*(3), 289–326.

Presbitero, A. F. (2012). Total public debt and growth in developing countries. *European Journal of Development Research, 24*(4), 606–626.

Reinhart, C. M., Reinhart, V. R., & Rogoff, K. S. (2012). Public debt overhangs: Advanced economy episodes since 1800. *Journal of Economic Perspectives, 26*(3), 69–86.

Reinhart, C. M., & Rogoff, K. S. (2010). Growth in a time of debt. *American Economic Review, 100*(2), 573–578.

Ricardo, D. (1951). On the principles of political economy and taxation. In P. Sraffa (Ed.), *The works and correspondence of David Ricardo* (Vol. 1). Cambridge University Press.

Romer, P. M. (1986). Increasing returns and long-run growth. *Journal of Political Economy, 94*(5), 1002–1037.

Sachs, J. D. (1989). The debt overhang of developing countries. In G. A. Calvo, R. Findlay, P. Kouri, & J. B. de Macedo (Eds.), *Debt stabilization and development*. Basil Blackwell.

Sen, S., Kasibhatla, K. M., & Stewart, D. B. (2007). Debt overhang and economic growth—The Asian and the Latin American experiences. *Economic Systems, 31*(1), 3–11.

Solow, R. M. (1956). A contribution to the theory of economic growth. *Quarterly Journal of Economics, 70*(1), 65–94.

Solow, R. M. (1957). Technical change and the aggregate productions. *Reviews of Economic and Statistics, 39*(3), 312–320.

Szabó, Z. (2013). The effect of sovereign debt on economic growth and economic development. *Public Finance Quarterly, 58*(3), 251–270.

Toda, H. Y. (1994). Finite sample properties of likelihood ratio tests for cointegrating ranks when linear trends are present. *Review of Economics & Statistics, 76*(1), 66–79.

Uzun, A., Kabadayi, B., & Emsen, O. S. (2012). The impacts of external debt on economic growth in transition economies. *Chinese Business Review, 11*(5), 491–499.

Woo, J., & Kumar, M. S. (2015). Public debt and growth. *Economica, 82*(328), 705–739.

Yoong, F. T., Latip, A. R. A., Sanusi, N. A., & Kusairi, S. (2020). Public debt and economic growth nexus in Malaysia: An ARDL approach. *Journal of Asian Finance Economics and Business, 7*(11), 137–145.

The World's Top Five Financial Centers: Geopolitical Uncertainties

Lucía Morales and Bernadette Andreosso-O'Callaghan

Abstract The evolution of the world's international financial centers is an ongoing process of reallocation with a recent marked shift in economic and financial activity towards Asia. The global financial landscape has always been an integral part of the power distribution system worldwide, as financial centers have helped redefine global economic and political dynamics. Accordingly, there is a pressing need to rethink and redesign the global financial architecture so that it can better serve the geoeconomics and geopolitical interests of countries. A number of institutions assess the need to update and improve the existing international and multilateral financial framework in order to accommodate the changing dynamics. Furthermore, there are pressing demands to enable emerging and developing economies to engage in this competitive process, a process that has been constructed by the world's major economic powers guided by the USA, in line with their interests, with some recent inputs from countries such as China.

Developing a broader context to help understand if the undergoing events contribute to reconceptualise the financial transactions and if they are showing signs of a fundamental shift from the "West" to the "East" is thus of paramount importance. Therefore, the analysis of financial centers and their dynamics emerges as a critical area of research, as they will be vital players in how economic and political power is going to be redefined over the next few decades.

Keywords World top financial centers · Social unrest · Geopolitics · Geoeconomics · Uncertainty · Sustainability

L. Morales (✉)
School of Accounting, Finance and Economics, Faculty of Business, Technological University Dublin, Dublin, Ireland
e-mail: lucia.morales@tudublin.ie

B. Andreosso-O'Callaghan
Department of Economics, Kemmy Business School, University of Limerick, Limerick, Ireland

Ruhr Universität Bochum, Bochum, Germany
e-mail: Bernadette.Andreosso@ul.ie

B. Andreosso-O'Callaghan et al. (eds.), *Sustainable Development in Asia*, Contributions to Economics, https://doi.org/10.1007/978-3-030-94679-1_7

1 Introduction

The changing nature of the world economy and the threats posed by economic sustainability emerge as significant challenges to the functioning of the global economic and financial system. The Global Financial Report (IMF, 2021) reflects on the ongoing policy support measures needed to aid the global economy to rebound from the COVID-19 health crisis, and it stresses the need for a sustainable financial system that enables the transition towards a more sustainable global economy (Calò & Herzberg, 2019). However, some initial worries emerge as the transition, and changing process might lead to a disorderly sequence of changes that can materialize into new risks with potential destabilizing power. The lack of an adequate regulatory framework could easily lead to increasing economic and financial instability levels that could expand into systemic risks (IMF, 2021). Over the past decade, and particularly since the 2008 global financial crisis (GFC), the world economy has been affected by rising global tensions. More recently, challenges such as the enduring global health crisis, the US–China trade war, and the "awkward" 2020 US presidential election (Ullah et al., 2020) have emerged. The world's first economic power is facing unprecedented challenging times due to the consolidation of its ongoing domestic problems that are contributing to question the country's international leadership, fuelling thereby the debate around the USA as being a declining economic and political power (The Economist, 2021b; Reuters, 2020; Kitchen & Cox, 2019; Cox, 2012; Quah, 2011). In line with McTague (2020), countries worldwide were used to admiring, loathing, and fearing America, but pitying America is today a new variant that poses significant concerns regarding the US role as a point of reference for global leadership. Further challenges can be found in the dynamics exhibited by cryptocurrencies and by the continuous political frictions between the UK and the European Union leading to Brexit. To add to the mêlée, one must include the threats posed by environmental degradation.

The world has entered a worrying phase of growing economic imbalances and inequalities fuelled by domestic and international conflicts of a very diverse nature. The GFC represented an inflexion point in the world economic trajectory and it showed clearly how the financial system is strongly intertwined with the dynamics of the global economy and with its political system. Moreover, the geographical shift in the world economy from *"West"* to *"East"* is acting as a significant catalyst for more substantial geoeconomic change (Csomós & Derudder, 2013; PCW, 2017a, b). The rise of emerging economies is challenging the status quo by pushing an agenda that requires redesigning the global economic and political architecture (EC, 2021a; PCW, 2017a, b). According to the European Commission (EC), by 2040, the economic power of the E7 economies (China, India, Indonesia, Brazil, Russia, Mexico, and Turkey) could be double the size of the G7 economies (USA, UK, France, Germany, Japan, Canada, and Italy).

Within the outlined context, Global Financial Centers (GFCs) emerge as critical players. They provide a broad range of financial services extending from banking, insurance, and foreign exchange trading activities that are vital in enabling the smooth functioning of the global economic system. Therefore, financial services need to be up to speed regarding the reallocation of global economic activity and regarding technological change, in order to facilitate more flexible transactions and to ensure that liquidity flows throughout the economy in a stable, orderly, and secure manner (Derudder et al., 2011; Calò & Herzberg, 2019). In this chapter, we offer some critical insights into the importance of GFCs to understand geopolitical dynamics and their spillover effects on the global economy. The remainder of the chapter is structured as follows. The section that ensues provides a brief overview examining the global economic and financial landscape. Section 3 provides some details that will introduce the world's top financial centers. Economic imbalances and inequalities are discussed in Sect. 4, and insights into the global financial cycle are offered in Sect. 5. Section 6 introduces financial innovation and the digital economy. Section 7 engages with the geopolitical debate, and Sect. 8 provides some concluding remarks.

2 Global Insights

The evolution of the international financial centers is an ongoing process involving the reallocation of financial activities as the world faces a shift in economic and financial activity towards Asia, and more particularly East-Asia (Cheung et al., 2018). The global financial landscape has always been an integral part of the power distribution system worldwide, as financial centers have helped redefine the dynamics of geoeconomic and geopolitical forces (Kurecic, 2015). Cassis (2006) and Spufford (2006) reflect on the historical patterns of international financial centers concluding that the power of a center is built on the economic and political power of the underlying economy and that it can last for a long time after the economic and political power fades away. In her seminal work, Strange (1970) offered ground-breaking views on the unequal pace of change that characterizes the international political system and its strong connection to the international economic system. Strange (1970) emphasized the effects of this unequal rate of change on the international society, and how they affect the relations of states one with another, and the implications for future relationships. In the global financial system context, it is of interest to acknowledge the polarization of financial activity that has enabled the concentration of economic and financial power in a few developed economies. However, significant mistakes were made when trying to decouple the functioning of the financial system from economic dynamics, leading to a substantial misunderstanding of the growing connections between the financial and economic systems. The connection between the economy and the financial sector has been further enhanced by a new wave of globalization and by the liberalization process taking place since the 1990s. According to Jednak (2018), financial integration emerges as a critical element of economic integration due to the association between capital movements and economic development. The association between financial development and economic growth appears to be positive and monotonic (Berger et al.,

2021; Popov, 2017). However, the nexus between economic growth and international financial integration is an area of ongoing debate in the discipline of economics, where a clear view on their association and causal effects has still not emerged (Schularick & Steger, 2010; WAIFC, 2020). In addition, the rise in economic interdependence and interaction between countries has contributed to growing frictions as countries' political leaders seek to guard and position their interests in the international context. The pace and dynamics of the global economic system have augmented, resulting in increasing challenges to navigate the international landscape and to understand how states engage, interact, and behave. Further areas of concern relate to how international dynamics have led to growing inequality levels and to implications in terms of political claims with a clear tendency for extremism in several countries, a trend that has intensified as a result of the GFC. The complexity of the global economy is increasing, and it is having substantial implications on how the world economies position themselves domestically and internationally, and how they are contributing to redefine the nature of financial activity.

Greater global financial integration has been associated with significant benefits to foster economic activity, but it also entails an increase in the potential of escalating levels of systemic risk. The financial system supports international trade by efficiently allocating capital, by providing opportunities for risk diversification, and by enabling the materialization of greater returns (BIS, 2017). Due to the significance of financial channels, central banks played a critical role in the global economic recovery process in the aftermath of the GFC. Central banks stepped in with unconventional policy measures such as quantitative easing that sought to rescue the global economy and, as a result, these had an impact upon the main drivers and dynamics of the financial markets. The Federal Reserve, the European Central Bank, and other central banks worldwide took on an unprecedented active role. Central banks resorted to economic and monetary stimulus programs that required the mobilization of a significant volume of financial resources and critical incentives to enable the economic recovery process (Klement, 2021). In the aftermath of the global financial turmoil, it seemed that financial centers fared surprisingly well. However, Cassis and Wójcik (2018) provide interesting insights for further reflection. They offer some words of caution regarding developments in the last decade and the need to take the term "financial resilience" with care. Governments resorted to the heavy intervention of financial centers in their quest to save big banks from failing due to their active role in absorbing the toxic debts produced and bailed out by taxpayers. The outcome has been that New York and London have recovered from the crisis relatively quickly, and that they remain as global financial centers (Lai et al., 2020). Paris and Frankfurt emerged indeed as being quite resilient, in parallel with the remarkable growth experienced by China and Singapore. In addition, Tokyo has undergone an increase in international financial activity, but it does not measure up to the scale of its economy. When connecting the dynamics of the world economy and their political and economic interests, undoubtedly GFCs are at a central stage as they are in charge of mobilizing countries' financial resources, and as such, they have a critical contribution to delimit countries' economic power.

3 The World Top Financial Centers

Over the past decades, financial markets at the global level have become more integrated, adding significant difficulties to policymakers' tasks when trying to isolate domestic economic and financial conditions from regional and international factors (Habib & Venditti, 2018). Financial globalization has emerged as a significant pillar in the development of the global economy (Ferrer, 2018). But the risks associated with increasing levels of financial integration as global markets interconnection has grown, became a substantial source of concern. International regulatory frameworks and policies are underdeveloped and insufficient in helping the control and monitoring of financial activity; they lack the necessary mechanisms that help minimize the impact of global economic and financial shocks and their spillover effects (EU, 2020; Talcott, 2010). On the other hand, Lund et al. (2017) argue that a new form of financial globalization that is characterized as being more stable is emerging. They conclude that a new form of financial globalization arose from the rubbles of the GFC that is understood to be more risk-sensitive, rational, and that it is ultimately becoming a more resilient version of global financial integration. The authors argue that the 2007/08 shock led to the retrenchment of global banking. However, we might not overlook the rapid developments in the FinTech sector as traditional banking activities face a significant transformation and a disruption phase with important risk unknowns (KPMG, 2021). Furthermore, Lund et al. (2017) argue that the global stock of foreign investment relative to GDP has not been significantly altered since 2007, and in absolute terms, foreign investments have grown. However, new risks emerge from the surge of cryptocurrencies, from the development of the FinTech sector, from the financial challenges associated with environmental concerns, and moreover, from China's growing presence in the financial system.

At the moment, a handful of advanced economies dominate the concentration of investments stocks, with some emerging changes taking place as more countries are starting to participate. However, the world's most advanced economies and their prominent international financial centers are exhibiting higher levels of integration into the global economic and financial system as they keep consolidating their dominance. Countries like the USA, Luxembourg, the UK, the Netherlands, and Germany dictate the rules of the financial landscape. In parallel, China is on the rise with a notable improvement in the country's investment portfolios that include bond investment, portfolio equity, activities in terms of foreign direct investment, and total stock of foreign bank lending. However, the Chinese financial system still has a significant amount of work to do to catch up with sophistication levels that characterize the most advanced economies (Lund et al., 2017).

According to the Global Financial Centers Index (Yen, 2021), the world's top financial centers are New York, London, Hong Kong, Singapore, San Francisco, Shanghai, Los Angeles, Beijing, and Tokyo, all depicted in Table 1. The index shows how New York has moved up to a leadership position, at the cost of London, considered as the global financial hub for decades. The status of international financial centers such as London redefine its position, and it can lead to the

Table 1 Top financial centers

Center	GFCI 30 rank	GFCI 30 rating	Rank (+/−)	Rating (+/−)	Region
New York	1	762	0	−2	North America
London	2	740	0	−3	Western Europe
Hong Kong	3	716	1	−25	Asia/Pacific
Singapore	4	715	1	−25	Asia/Pacific
San Francisco	5	714	7	−4	North America
Shanghai	6	713	−3	−29	Asia/Pacific
Los Angeles	7	712	6	−4	North America
Beijing	8	711	−2	−26	Asia/Pacific
Tokyo	9	706	−2	−30	Asia/Pacific
Paris	10	705	15	6	Western Europe
Chicago	11	704	4	−10	North America
Boston	12	703	12	0	North America
Seoul	13	702	3	−11	Asia/Pacific
Frankfurt	14	701	−5	−26	Western Europe
Washington DC	15	700	−1	−15	North America
Shenzhen	16	699	−8	−32	Asia/Pacific
Amsterdam	17	698	11	3	Western Europe
Dubai	18	694	1	−16	Middle East & Africa
Toronto	19	693	10	−1	North America
Geneva	20	692	0	−17	Western Europe

Source: Yen—Long Finance (2021)

concentration of activity in the City, or it could trigger the emergence of a multitude of smaller financial centers in Europe without forgetting the rise of Asian Financial hubs (Calò & Herzberg, 2019). Hong Kong is identified as the third financial center, but it is losing its international appeal due to ongoing political uncertainty (see chapter "Hong Kong: "*Business as Usual*" Amidst Social Unrest" in this volume). Increasing social unrest and its violent connotations derived from Beijing's growing levels of control and intervention in the Chinese special administrative region—as the one country-two systems 2047 deadline looms—are pushing international investors to reallocate capital away from Hong Kong (The Economist, 2020a). As a result, Hong Kong has experienced a loss in terms of rating points; it is now very closely followed by Singapore, San Francisco, Shanghai, Los Angeles, and Beijing, with less than one to five points difference signalling that it might soon lose its third position. International investors fear the rise of a "black swan event" with effects at the global level due to continuous uncertainty affecting the global economy and with core Asian and Western markets having shown sharp declines in transactions. In addition, Asian stock markets have experienced significant drops in retail, consumer services, and transport businesses, and Western markets have largely followed suit (McKinsey and Company, 2021).

The Global Financial Centers Index (GFCI) includes the world's top financial centers, and a closer look at its performance reveals a downward trend. In September 2021, the index registered an average fall of 12.9 points representing a 2.05 per cent drop compared to the previous year. While the change might be viewed as relatively minor, the fall—the third consecutive fall in the average rating—represents a downward trend. The rating continues to decline compared to the levels registered in 2019, suggesting an investors' potential lack of confidence in the world economy. Some critical aspects that have contributed to the index instability can be found in the impact of COVID-19 and its spillover effects on the world markets through increased levels of uncertainty (Financial Times, 2020; The Guardian, 2020a, b). International trade dynamics are also contributing to global instability as the world's leading economies have resorted to protectionism, followed by rising levels of local unrest affecting the world's top economies. In addition, geopolitical dynamics have also contributed to heightening instability levels by raising significant concerns among international investors. In particular, Chinese financial centers are the focus of attention as the country has been immersed in a sequence of financial scandals combined with increasing levels of government intervention as more regulation over technological companies has been introduced (The Economist, 2021a; Financial Times, 2021). Developments in the European Union further complicate the situation, as the UK keeps challenging the basic principles of the EU-UK Withdrawal Agreement (EC, 2021b), signalling turbulent times ahead.

4 Global Economic Imbalances

The global economy exhibits signs of a robust economic recovery reflected by rising growth levels in the post-recession months, hinting at the most vigorous comeback in eighty years (The World Bank, 2021).[1] Nevertheless, the economic bounceback will not be equal, and the world's major economies will be leading the way, with the effects of COVID-19 casting a large shadow on almost every region of the world. Across the world, there are constant warnings of viral mutations of COVID-19 that can deter the economic recovery process as countries might resort to yet more economic lockdowns (The Economist, 2020b). Unquestionably, the recovery process is paralleled with increasing levels of economic inequality and imbalances as the major economies might register more robust growth aided by massive fiscal and monetary incentives, as in the case of the USA and the European Union. In contrast, many developing economies will lag behind. The less-developed economies might keep struggling due to their limitations on introducing vital monetary and fiscal stimulus programs to counteract the effects of the ongoing global health crisis and its socioeconomic implications. Additional challenges derived from environmental degradation and the

[1] This has to be understood, obviously, as a recovery from extremely and unprecedented low levels of growth.

dynamics exhibited by a fast-moving socioeconomic system contributes to adding further challenges and complexities to the world's less-developed economies.

The situation is further aggravated by the rise of protectionist measures globally, leading to a progressive distortion of international trade relationships that contribute to widen the gap between the world's most developed economies and intensifying adverse spillover effects on global capital flows. In times of uncertainty, countries worldwide seek to protect their interests. According to Gunnella and Guaglietti (2019), by 2017, more than 50 per cent of exports from the G20 countries were subject to harmful trade measures. The shift towards protectionism has had an impact upon economic growth, leading to an extensive range of discriminatory measures and actions that decelerated growth in a number of sectors. The well-known contributing factors to the decline of global trade dynamics include Brexit, a rise in Euroscepticism coupled with questionable moves in the area of economic integration in the European context, and the curtailment of the benefits associated with the freedom of movement. Moreover, it is commonly argued that the years of the Trump Administration and its alignment to a "populist rhetoric" have caused significant harm to international relationships (Bonikowski, 2019). According to this view, actions of the US Administration have contributed to volatility, to tensions and to erratic diplomatic strategies, fuelling a lack of trust between global economic leaders and critical economic and political players. Allegations of unfair trade practices and of intellectual property theft voiced by US President Donald Trump to China have nurtured a new trade war with the reintroduction of barriers—tariffs and non-tariff barriers—to curtail international trade activities. The overall outcome has been that economic dynamics have been negatively affected, and that the harm inflicted from the trade restrictions has had a knock-on effect on the functioning of the global financial markets.

In parallel, the complexities of the intertwined international production chains show their unquestionable vulnerability to shocks and the very fragile equilibrium of the chosen model of globalization. This fragility contributes to magnifying the impact of global imbalances, inequality, and uncertainty. The erosion of confidence in terms of the benefits of globalization has led to elevated levels of uncertainty from international trade activity. As public support for the globalization process has waned, there are significant implications for financial flows. Increasing uncertainty levels can push up borrowing costs for households and firms, with a knock-on effect on investors seeking higher returns as a response to rising levels of risk (Habib & Venditti, 2018). Therefore, global trade distortions have led investors to reassess their portfolios and to reallocate their investments towards safe havens.

Clearly, the global economy is immersed in a transition process energized by the challenges posed by the global health crisis, the looming effects of a global energy crisis, and the polarization of countries' political and economic agendas. Global economies are affected by substantial levels of unrest, with fast-changing dynamics impacting international relations and the balance of economic and political power. As a result, the benefits of the globalization process are under question, and the precepts that justify the need for a sustainable global economic system are gaining supporters (ECB, 2019; Gunnella & Guaglietti, 2019).

5 The Global Financial Cycle

Over the past fifty years, financial globalization has been on the rise, aided by a flexible regulatory framework that evolved into a significant deregulation of the financial system. The introduced measures contributed to the acceleration of the development of global banking and capital markets. According to Miranda-Agrippino and Rey (2021) and Rey (2013), the degree of co-movement in risky asset prices, capital flows, leverage, and financial aggregates worldwide is known as the Global Financial Cycle. The Global Financial Cycle is understood as a comprehensive phenomenon that affects different types of financial variables and levels of risk. Rey (2015) has offered evidence of the solid global co-movement between asset prices, gross capital flows, leverage, credit, and risk premia that characterize and define the dynamics of the Global Financial Cycle. In addition, Rey (2013, 2015) highlights the existence of a close relationship between the Global Financial Cycle and the different measures of risk-aversion. According to the extant literature, the increasing levels of financial integration have led to the emergence of a Global Financial Cycle strongly influenced by the US monetary policy (Davis & van Wincoop, 2021; Habib & Venditti, 2018). Rey (2015, p. 2) offers a definition that highlights the main elements of the Global Financial Cycle as follows: *"global financial cycles are associated with surges and retrenchments in capital flows, booms, and busts in assets prices and crisis" and are characterized by large common movements in asset prices, gross flows and leverage"*. In this context, Global Financial Cycles play a critical role as they are in charge of channelling and conducting global financial flows.

Undoubtedly, the world's first economy plays a significant role in global risk dynamics that were quite visible during the GFC. The world's economic and financial systems are interconnected, and the channels for interconnection are multiple and very diverse, with major global players taking a dominant role. As such, the Global Financial Cycle is subject to prompting swings in capital flows and asset prices with a worldwide dimension. According to Miranda-Agrippino and Rey (2021), the case of the USA is quite relevant, in particular the role of the Federal Reserve, as it has become a very active player through its monetary policy that directly affects the performance of the Global Financial Cycle. While on the other hand, the People's Bank of China and the European Central Bank play a more significant role in terms of both the commodity cycle and the dynamics associated with global trade. Mathur (2020) argues that the decade that followed the GFC signified a period of significant deterioration in terms of global economic and financial performance. Davis and van Wincoop (2021) offer further insights suggesting that changes have materialized pointing to a slowing down of the globalization process and to the weakening of the global financial system. In contrast, Lund et al. (2017) offer a different viewpoint in favor of a new form of financial globalization that is characterized as being more stable. Overall, it seems that global dynamics have been defined by the increasing polarization of economic interests and by the erosion of economic multilateralism in favor of protectionism.

Early research examining international monetary spillovers shows a significant connection to the world interests as an essential factor that drives capital flows and contributes to periods of enhanced credit, leading to credit booms and subsequent busts (Calvo et al., 1996). Global risks are identified as a significant factor in explaining extreme capital flow episodes until the unfolding of the 2008 financial crisis (Fratzscher, 2012; Forbes & Warnock, 2012). A recent study by Caggiano and Castelnuovo (2021) points to the stronger effects of global financial uncertainty derived from shocks on global output as global financial conditions deteriorate. Another up-to-date study by Davis and Van Wincoop (2021) offers insights into the fluctuations in the prices of safe and risky assets and the implications for gross and net capital flows over the global financial cycle. The study confirms the extensive evidence that highlights the importance of risk and risk-aversion as drivers of the Global Financial Cycle by examining the impact of a global risk-aversion shock in a multi-country model. Their research findings indicate that investors' heterogeneity within countries accounts for the drop in gross capital flows during a downturn in the Global Financial Cycle. Furthermore, cross-country heterogeneity is needed to account for the differential in vulnerability levels exhibited by countries to a negative Global Financial Cycle shock. In addition, the authors pinpoint the importance of acknowledging vulnerabilities associated with the net foreign asset position of safe assets, as they are critical when determining leverage levels. In addition, global risk-aversion is identified as a critical driver of stock returns with significant implications for capital flows and with a lack of evidence with regard to the impact on countries' exchange rate regimes (Davis & van Wincoop, 2021; Habib & Venditti, 2018). Consequently, the connection between the GFC and the Global Financial Cycles emerges as critical due to implications for global capital flows.

6 Financial Innovation

The globalization process has induced innovation and accelerated technology transmission, and while it offers opportunities to disseminate information, it does not guarantee that all nations and organizations will benefit equally (Skare & Soriano, 2021; Central Bank of Ireland, 2017). The acceleration of financial technology that is commonly known as *FinTech*—referring to the contraction of *"financial technology"*—is leading towards a new era. Although *FinTech* is viewed as a uniquely recent marriage of financial services and information technology, the interlinkage of finance and technology has a long history, with financial and technological developments being mutually reinforcing (Lund et al., 2017; Arner et al., 2015). According to Milanesi (2021), the past few years have nevertheless witnessed a significant level of development in financial services due to the unprecedented levels of growth and development in financial technology. Some of the major innovations can be found in the context of digital currencies, the fast development of the blockchain market, and the dynamics exhibited on distributed ledger technology, peer-to-peer lending, and marketplace lending (McKinsey Global Institute, 2017).

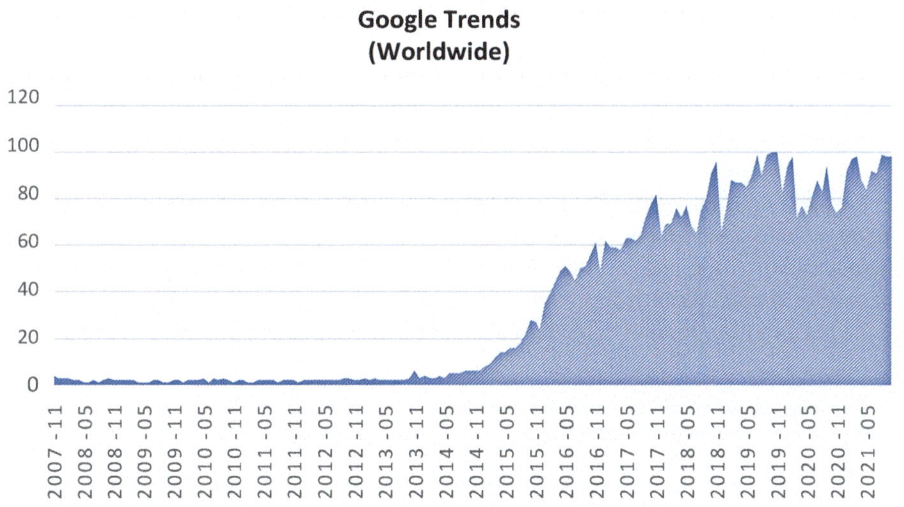

Fig. 1 FinTech google trends worldwide. (Source: Google Trends (2021))

Digital trends are having an impact on the financial sector in such a way that it has created a socioeconomic disruption of the magnitude not seen since the original Industrial Revolution, and that it is having a significant impact on how global financial centers redesign their operations (Deloitte, 2016, 2018; Milanesi, 2021).

Fast developments in the financial system by the hand of technological advances and progress represent significant challenges for regulators and markets' participants, as the balance between the potential benefits associated with innovation are considered in the context of emerging risks within a rigid regulatory context with global challenges (World Economic Forum, 2021; Arner et al., 2015). According to google trends, the *FinTech* sector has attracted significant attention only since 2014, as illustrated in Fig. 1 above.

Financial globalization, innovation, and technological advances within the digital age require greater regulatory attention to help minimize potential systemic risks. The sector is facing significant levels of uncertainty that could emerge due to the decoupling between international regulations and guidelines and the speed of development displayed by the financial system. The Asian region, particularly China and India, are witnessing a rapid emergence of new players from outside the financial sector that are making significant changes in how technology is applied to the delivery of financial services (Chan, 2015; Ji, 2020). The rapid development of *FinTech*, especially in the Asian and African regions, has prompted the need to reconsider the potential risks associated with the sector and the potential implications for the overall financial system and the activities of the global financial cycles. In the case of the African continent, the top *FinTech* hubs are located in South Africa, Nigeria, Kenya, and Egypt; these countries gather most of the *FinTech* funding and they are characterized by a more robust financial regulatory ecosystem. However, countries beyond the mentioned hubs are characterized by a significant lack of, or absence of, regulations that expose users and *FinTech* services providers to emerging risks (Lewis, 2021). The development of "regulatory technology" or *"RegTech"* appears as a much-needed framework to help understand the role played by technology within the financial system and the importance of achieving an appropriate balance that enables the development of the sector while emerging risks are kept at bay and monitored.

Former chairman of the US Federal Reserve (1979–1987), Paul Volcker, offered an interesting assessment of the global financial system. He queried the role of financial innovation and its benefits to the economy. Volcker's thoughts questioned the role of financial innovations in economic development and are a good reminder of the need to monitor and consider the emergence of financial instability. In his own words:

> I wish somebody would give me some shred of evidence linking financial innovation with a benefit to the economy. (Paul Volcker, former Chairman of the Federal Reserve, 2009)

The globalization process has contributed to improvements in technology adoption through the transfer of foreign knowledge and by enhancing international competition. However, the specific role of the globalization process in the adoption of technology and the implications for financial globalization is an area of research that requires further insights. The development of technology has contributed to the development of the financial system as a dynamic segment lying at the intersection between financial services and the technology sectors. Technology-focused-start-ups and new market entrants provide innovation (products and services) based on the currently available products and services in the traditional financial services industry (Cassis & Wójcik, 2018, p. 218; PCW, 2016, p. 3). According to Arner et al. (2015) the global financial crisis of 2007/08 can be considered as being an articulating point in the relationship between technology and financial services. Before the crisis, established financial firms dominated the introduction of new technology to financial services. Since then, new start-ups and established technology firms have started to deliver financial products and services to companies and retail consumers with a clear acceleration due to the ongoing global health crisis in 2020. The global financial crisis provided the needed conditions that contributed to the rise of *FinTech*, as the established financial sector became more vulnerable, and competition from new start-ups and technology-based firms was possible. Internet infrastructure and data science offer opportunities to mature economies in Europe, Japan, and North America to develop alternative financial services while enabling the introduction of financial services in emerging and developing economies. Economies that lack the appropriate structures to nurture traditional financial services and banking activities, as in the case of the less-developed economies, are characterized by most of the population not having a formal bank account. The outcome has been that the global adoption of *FinTech* services has moved upward from 16 per cent in 2015 to 64 per cent in 2019 of global consumer adoption, and that the global awareness of *FinTech* is also extremely high with approximately 96 per cent of consumers being aware of at least one alternative *FinTech* service (Forbes, 2020; EY, 2019). According to Wiwanto (2020), three main factors are driving the significant rise of the *FinTech* industry: (a) their focus on underserved areas of banking, (b) a lack of trust in the traditional banking industry, (c) and their sharp focus. These are significant elements that might contribute to redefining the role of global financial centers as they reconsider how technological progress is shaping financial transactions and their implications on capital flows.

According to the EY (2019) *FinTech* Adoption index, *FinTech* has become the norm. EY (2019) defines *FinTech* as organizations that combine innovative business models with technology so as to enable, enhance, and disrupt financial services. The report core findings, as already mentioned show a global consumer adoption of 64 per cent, indicating that *FinTech* is becoming mainstream in the surveyed markets, with China and India leading the way. Adoption rates have experienced dramatic growth with 16 per cent in 2015, 31 per cent in 2017, and above 60 per cent in 2019, representing an increase of almost 100 per cent almost every couple of years. Approximately 96 per cent of global consumers are aware of at least one money transfer and payment *FinTech* service, showing that consumers' awareness is at an all-time high. *FinTech* services are now commonly used by consumers globally, with most-used services, including money transfer payments being particularly prevalent in China with a rate of 95 percent. Savings and investments, budgeting and financial planning, insurance and borrowing services are other frequently used services.

In summary, the *FinTech* industry has experienced dramatic levels of growth between 2010 and 2021. The highest growth was reached in 2019, with the total value of investment in FinTech companies reaching 215.4 billion US dollars, with global investment reaching record high levels in 2021, and with the first half of the year totalling 98 billion US dollars from about 2500 investment deals (Statista, 2021). The KPMG's latest Pulse *FinTech* Report (2021) shows that the full recovery is in full swing after investments were largely stalled during the COVID-19 pandemic. The industry registered in 2020 approximately 121.5 bn invested in *FinTech* globally, with 87 bn accounting for the second half of the year. KPGM has indicated that overall investment in *FinTech* surged to a record high in the first half of 2021 as investors, particularly corporation firms and venture capitalists, made big bets on market leaders in numerous jurisdictions and across almost all subsectors (The Guardian, 2021).

7 Geopolitical Uncertainties

The global expansion of Chinese finance and the emerging trends in the *FinTech* sector are posing significant concerns to Western countries as they can contest the dominance of their traditional banking system (Hellendoorn, 2021). In 2015, Beijing's vast vision for global connectivity was supported by the launch of China's Digital Silk Road, an initiative that seeks to improve communication networks and capabilities in mobile payment systems and e-commerce, among many other Belt Road Initiatives (The Diplomat, 2021; Atlantic Council, 2021;

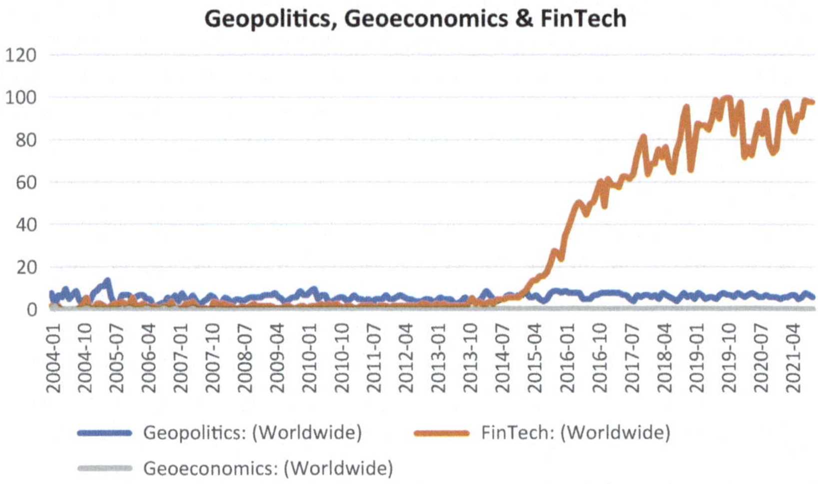

Fig. 2 Geopolitics, geoeconomics, and *FinTech* trends worldwide. (Source: Google Trends (2021))

Nedopil, 2021; Silk Road Briefing, 2019). Technological advances have contributed to the development of *FinTech*, and China is a leading force in the area. The country has been able to improve financial inclusiveness and to extend financial services to its population by reaching areas that did not have access to traditional financial services (Zhu, 2021). As a result, China has one of the most dynamic *FinTech* markets globally, with investments growing at a significant pace, bringing new dynamics and potential risks to the financial system. Therefore, the developments in the *FinTech* sector are attracting a considerable level of attention worldwide (Fig. 2 below).

The rise of the Chinese banking sector is also generating significant interest among researchers and financial analysts, as historically, banks have been central players in defining geopolitical dynamics. Therefore, the banking and financial sector activities are poised to become a central axe in the US–China strategic competition.

However, the increasing presence of China in international finance is raising concerns since—as reiterated above—tensions increase between China, the USA and the US core allies leading to the emergence of national and international security fears. History has taught quite clearly that the shifting of financial centers is interwoven with geopolitics and with wars. The conflicting nature of financial activity can be illustrated by confrontations that emerged when financial activity shifted from Venice to Florence, subsequently to Genoa, Amsterdam, London, and New York (Mosselaar, 2018). Therefore, a historical context is very important when examining the rise of Chinese banks and the vision and ambition of the Chinese Communist Party to bring Shanghai to the forefront of the financial system. The international community is not at ease regarding the future implications of a heavy representation of Chinese financial players. Some of the major concerns relate to changes that lead towards an international financial system that might become increasingly dependent on decisions made by Chinese regulators. This change could result in the Chinese Community Party having an even stronger influence on global affairs as they could take an increasing role as mediators and arbitrageurs of the international financial markets (Hellendoorn, 2021). So far, the Chinese authorities have enacted policies to help develop the digital payments systems that could enable the necessary conditions to foster the global presence of Chinese banks and financial institutions. At a time when Western banks, especially European ones, are struggling to be profitable in their home markets and beyond, and when *FinTech* is enabling the Asian financial systems to develop at a faster pace, there are significant fears that China might be able to increase its geopolitical presence (Zhu, 2021). For over a decade, the GFC followed by the Eurozone idiosyncratic economic and financial shocks and crises, in combination with very low-interest rates, growing regulatory demands and lagging economic growth, have all created the perfect conditions to undermine the competitiveness of both European and American banks. While the Chinese financial system and its banking sector have not yet reached the levels of sophistication achieved by their Western counterparts, they have been immersed in a significant reform process seeking to become more global and competitive. Therefore, if Chinese banks continue their transformation, the years ahead will unveil sizable competition that will nurture further rivalries between Asian and Western institutions; this could lead to heightening conflict. The current shifting dynamics in the structure of the international system are also linked to national security problems as the Western countries are raising concerns about the potential negative effects and implications in terms of national security.

Furthermore, the challenges associated with environmental degradation require a more transparent financial landscape as the world financial centers are critical players in enabling progress towards sustainable economic and financial development. The integration of environmental and social governance (ESG) as part of investment portfolio strategies and the expansion of the green bond market are critical aspects that will help governments to expand and develop national roadmaps for financial regulation. Global financial systems and investments require the integration of environmental risk metrics and more substantial market supervision of the banking sector. The capital markets, the *FinTech* industry, and insurance and financial services also need to align to the challenges posed by global environmental degradation, if they are to play a critical role in transforming the global economy into a more sustainable model (UNCOP26, 2021; UN, 2018; UN, 2021). Since over the centuries, shifts in financial centers have been tied to changing geopolitical dynamics, Western policymakers might need to consider how they will accommodate the rise of Chinese finance if they are to protect their national security interests (Hellendoorn, 2021). The continued development and growth of Chinese banks and its financial system could lead to a situation that facilitates the potential dominance of China's financial institutions over their Western counterparts; the ensuing fierce competition between the world's major economies will have paramount implications when defining the future balance of global economic, financial, and political power.

8 Conclusions

Over the past three decades, the world's top financial centers have been affected by substantial uncertainty derived from global political and economic events with significant implications for the stability of the international financial system. The global economic and financial landscape is changing rapidly, and the world's top financial centers need to be abreast of the needs of a more interconnected and integrated global economy that needs to be supported by a fast responding, stable, and dynamic financial system. The global economy requires appropriate policies at both the national and international levels, so as to mitigate financial stability risks, as the latter have a significant impact on the functioning of the international economic system, as painfully demonstrated by the 2007/08 global economic and financial shock. In this chapter, we have explored the most significant current global economic dynamics, intending to offer insights into the importance of the top financial centers and how they might contribute to accelerating the shift in economic and political power. Over the past two decades, significant levels of volatility have unsettled financial markets, and regional and capital flows appear to be particularly vulnerable and exposed to substantial spillover effects across core financial hubs (Kusumahadi & Permana, 2021).

In addition, the dynamics exhibited by global financial centers are showing the growing strength and increasing power of the Asian financial hubs. The Asian region is taking central stage with a growing financial sector identified among Chinese cities, with Shanghai playing a significant role in domestic banking and finance and with *FinTech* creating sizeable disruptions.

The ongoing US–China trade war, the uncertainties derived from the UK divorce from the European Union, ongoing social unrest in Hong Kong, the prolonged COVID-19 and global health crisis, and the unfolding events associated with the Russia-Ukraine war, all have economic implications that have led to global geopolitical fears with spillover effects to the world top financial centers. One of the impacts of the GFC is that it has led to an increasing role of the state-finance nexus, resulting in a significant increase in the size and power of central banks. The ECB (European Central Bank) and the Federal Reserve cases are quite remarkable due to their vigorous interventions and their vital role in trying to instil stability in their global financial centers.

All these ongoing changes are contributing to the realignment and the redefinition of geoeconomics and geopolitics that will define international economic and financial dynamics over the next decades. Therefore, the analysis of financial centers and their dynamics emerge as a critical area of research. As such, it is of paramount importance that researchers develop a broader context to help understand if the undergoing events are contributing to redefining financial transactions, and if they are showing signs of a fundamental shift of economic and financial activity from the *"West"* to the *"East"*.

References

Arner, D. W., Barberis, J., & Buckley, B. P. (2015). The evolution of FinTech: A new post-crisis paradigm? *Georgetown Journal of International Law, 47*(4), 1271–1320.

Atlantic Council. (2021). Geopolitical change and the emergence of Chinese banking. https://www.atlanticcouncil.org/blogs/geopolitical-change-and-the-emergence-of-chinese-banking/

Bank of International Settlements. (2017). *Understanding globalization*. 87th Annual Report.

Berger, E. A., Butler, A. W., Hu, E., & Zekhnini, M. (2021). Financial integration and credit democratization: Linking banking deregulation to economic growth. *Journal of Financial Intermediation, 45*, 1–14.

Bonikowski, B. (2019). Trump's populism: The mobilisation of nationalist cleavages and the future of U.S. democracy. In K. Weyland & R. Madrid (Eds.), *When democracy Trumps populism: Lessons from Europe & Latin America* (pp. 110–131). Cambridge University Press.

Caggiano, G., & Castelnuovo, E. (2021). Global uncertainty. *CESifo Working Paper No. 8885*. Available at SSRN: https://ssrn.com/abstract=3788705

Calò, S., & Herzberg, V. (2019). The future of global financial centers after Brexit: An EU perspective. *Financial Stability Notes, 2019*(9), 1–15. https://www.centralbank.ie/docs/default-source/publications/financial-stability-notes/no-9-the-future-of-global-financial-centers-after-brexit%2D%2D-an-eu-perspective-(calo-and-herzberg).pdf

Calvo, G. A., Leiderman, L., & Reinhart, C. M. (1996). Inflows of capital to developing countries in the 1990s. *Journal of Economic Perspectives, 10*(2), 123–139.

Cassis, Y. (2006). *Capitals of capital: A history of International Financial Centers, 1780–2005*. Cambridge University Press. https://doi.org/10.1017/CBO9780511607424

Cassis, Y., & Wójcik, D. (2018). *International financial centers after the global financial crisis and Brexit*. Oxford University Press. https://doi.org/10.1093/oso/9780198817314.001.0001

Central Bank of Ireland. (2017). Globalization and innovation in finance: Policy challenges—Governor Philip R. Lane. https://www.centralbank.ie/news/article/globalization-and-innovation-in-finance-policy-challenges

Chan, R. (2015). Asian regulators seek FinTech balance. *Finance Asia*. https://www.financeasia.com/article/asian-regulators-seek-FinTech-balance/401588

Cheung, L., Wong, E., NG, P., & Wong, K. (2018). Assessing the impact of globalization: Lessons from Hong Kong. *BIS papers No. 100*. https://www.bis.org/publ/bppdf/bispap100_i.pdf

Cox, M. (2012). Power shifts, economic change and the decline of the West? *International Relations, 26*(4), 369–388.

Csomós, G., & Derudder, B. (2013). European cities as command and control center, 2006–11. *European Urban and Regional Studies, 21*(3), 345–352.

Davis, J. S., & van Wincoop, E. (2021). A theory of the global financial cycle. *Technical Report*. National Bureau of Economic Research. *Working Paper 29217*. https://www.nber.org/papers/w29217

Deloitte. (2016). Finance in the digital age. https://www2.deloitte.com/content/dam/Deloitte/in/Documents/finance-transformation/in-ft-digital-age-finance-noexp.pdf

Deloitte. (2018). Deloitte Trust Index—Banking 2018. https://www2.deloitte.com/au/en/pages/financial-services/articles/deloitte-trust-index-banking-survey.html

Derudder, B., Hoyler, M., & Taylor, P. (2011). Goodbye Reykjavik: International banking centers and the global financial crisis. *Area, 43*(2), 173–182.

EC. (2021a). Economic power shifts. Competence Center on Foresight. https://knowledge4policy.ec.europa.eu/foresight/topic/expanding-influence-east-south/power-shifts_en

EC. (2021b). The EU-UK withdrawal agreement. https://ec.europa.eu/info/strategy/relations-non-eu-countries/relations-united-kingdom/eu-uk-withdrawal-agreement_en

EU. (2020). A new vision for Europe's capital markets. Final Report of the High Level Forum on the Capital Markets Union. https://ec.europa.eu/info/sites/default/files/business_economy_euro/growth_and_investment/documents/200610-cmu-high-level-forum-final-report_en.pdf

EY. (2019). *Global FinTech adoption index*. Available at https://www.ey.com/en_ie/ey-global-fintech-adoption-index

European Central Bank. (2019). Economic Bulleting. Issue3/2019. https://www.ecb.europa.eu/pub/economic-bulletin/html/eb201903.en.html

Ferrer, R. (2018). The challenges of financial globalization. CaixaBank Research. https://www.caixabankresearch.com/en/economics-markets/financial-markets/challenges-financial-globalization?792=

Financial Times. (2020). Coronavirus sends ripples through global economy. https://www.ft.com/content/e9fbbb78-4901-11ea-aeb3-955839e06441

Financial Times. (2021). Knocking dow Chinese tech walls. https://www.ft.com/content/a3c6724a-ca94-4126-92ee-0da947c1d1dc

Forbes, K. J., & Warnock, F. E. (2012). Capital flows waves: Surges, stops, flight, and retrenchment. *Journal of International Economics, 88*(2), 235–251.

Forbes. (2020). *FinTech 50 2020: The newcomers*. Available at: https://www.forbes.com/sites/jeffkauflin/2020/02/12/fintech-50-2020-the-newcomers/

Fratzscher, M. (2012). Capital flows, push versus pull factors and the global financial crisis. *Journal of International Economics, 88*(2), 341–356.

Google Trends. (2021). https://trends.google.com/trends/?geo=IE

Gunnella, V., & Guaglietti, L. (2019). The economic implications of rising protectionism: A Euro area and global perspective. Published as part of the ECB Economic Bulleting, Issue 3/2019. https://www.ecb.europa.eu/pub/economic-bulletin/articles/2019/html/ecb.ebart201903_01~e589a502e5.en.html

Habib, M. M., & Venditti, F. (2018). The global financial cycle: Implications for the global economy and the Euro area. European Central Bank. https://www.ecb.europa.eu/pub/economic-bulletin/articles/2018/html/ecb.ebart201806_01.en.html

Hellendoorn, E. (2021). Geopolitical change and the emergence of Chinese banking. Atlantick Council Blog Post. https://www.atlanticcouncil.org/blogs/geopolitical-change-and-the-emergence-of-chinese-banking/

IMF. (2021). COVID-19, crypto and climate: Navigating challenging transitions. *Global Financial Stability Report*. https://www.elibrary.imf.org/view/books/082/465808-9781513595603-en/465808-9781513595603-en-book.xml

Jednak, S. (2018). Financial integration: Crisis and economic development. In B. Sergi, F. Fidanoski, M. Ziolo, & V. Naumovski (Eds.), *Regaining global stability after the financial crisis*. IGI Global.

Ji, Y. (2020). Seeking balance between FinTech innovation and regulation in China. East Asia Forum. https://www.eastasiaforum.org/2020/12/09/seeking-balance-between-FinTech-innovation-and-regulation-in-china/

Kitchen, N., & Cox, M. (2019). Power, structural power, and American decline. *Cambridge Review of International Affairs, 32*(6), 734–752.

Klement, J. (2021). Geoeconomics: The interplay between geopolitics, economics, and investment. CFA Institute Research Foundation Monograph. https://www.cfainstitute.org/-/media/documents/book/rf-publication/2021/geo-economics-full.ashx

KPGM. (2021). Pulse of FinTech H1'21. https://home.kpmg/ie/en/home/industries/FinTech.html

Kurecic, P. (2015). Geoeconomic and geopolitical conflicts: Outcomes of the geopolitical economy in a contemporary world. *Word Review of Political Economy, 6*(4), 522–543.

Kusumahadi, T. A., & Permana, F. C. (2021). Impact of COVID-19 on global stock market volatility. *Journal of Economic Integration, 36*(1), 20–45.

Lai, K. P. Y., Pan, F., Sokol, M., & Wojcik, D. (2020). New financial geographies of Asia. *Regional Studies, 54*(2), 143–148.

Lewis, S. (2021). Report: Africa's Top FinTech Hubs are also its most regulated. *FinTech Africa*. https://FinTechnews.africa/39967/FinTech/report-africas-top-FinTech-hubs-are-also-its-most-regulated/

Lund, S., Windhagen, E., Manyika, J., Harle, P., Woetzel, J., & Goldshtein, D. (2017). The new dynamics of financial globalization. McKinsey Global Institute. https://www.mckinsey.com/industries/financial-services/our-insights/the-new-dynamics-of-financial-globalization

Mathur, A. (2020). The next decade fir geoeconomics. Observer Research Foundation. https://www.orfonline.org/expert-speak/next-decade-geoeconomics/

McKinsey and Company. (2021). Understanding Chinese consumers: Growth engine of the world. *China Consumer Report 2021*. Special edition. https://www.mckinsey.com/~/media/mckinsey/featured%20insights/china/china%20still%20the%20worlds%20growth%20engine%20after%20covid%2019/mckinsey%20china%20consumer%20report%202021.pdf

McKinsey Global Institute. (2017). The new dynamics of financial globalization. https://www.mckinsey.com/industries/financial-services/our-insights/the-new-dynamics-of-financial-globalization#part%202

McTague. (2020). *The decline of the American world*. The Atlantic. Available at https://www.theatlantic.com/international/archive/2020/06/america-image-power-trump/613228/

Milanesi, D. (2021). The rise of financial technology (FinTech) innovation and the futrue of the banking system. A comparative analysis of the FinTech legislative and regulatory frameworks in the United States, Europe, and the United Kingdom. https://law.stanford.edu/projects/the-rise-of-financial-technology-FinTech-innovation-and-the-future-of-the-banking-and-financial-system-a-comparative-analysis-of-the-FinTech-legislative-and-regulatory-frameworks-in-the-united-stat/

Miranda-Agrippino, S., & Rey, H. (2021). The global financial cycle. *NBER Working Paper w29327*. National Bureau of Economic Research. https://www.nber.org/papers/w29327; https://doi.org/10.3386/w29327

Mosselaar, J. S. (2018). A concise financial history of Europe. Robecco, Rotterdam. https://www.robeco.com/docm/docu-summer-read-a-concise-financial-history-of-europe.pdf

Nedopil, C. (2021). China's investments in the Belt and Road Initiative (BRI) in 2020—A year of COVID-19. International Institute of Green Finance. CUFE. https://greenfdc.org/wp-content/uploads/2021/01/China-BRI-Investment-Report-2020.pdf

PCW. (2016). *Traditional FInancial Services Firms fear almost a quarter of their business is at risk from FinTechs*. Available at https://www.pwc.com/ca/en/media/release/2016-03-15-fintech-blurred-lines.html

PCW. (2017a). Shift of global economic power to emerging economies set to continue in the long run with India, Indonesia and Vietnam among start performers. https://www.pwc.com/hu/en/pressroom/2017/shift_of_global_economic_power.html

PCW. (2017b). The long view. How will the global economic order change by 2020? The world in 2050—Summary Report. https://www.pwc.com/gx/en/world-2050/assets/pwc-world-in-2050-summary-report-feb-2017.pdf

Popov, A. (2017, December). Evidence on finance and economic growth. *Working Paper Series, No. 2115*. European Central Bank. https://www.ecb.europa.eu/pub/pdf/scpwps/ecb.wp2115.en.pdf

Quah, D. (2011). The global economy's shifting center of gravity. *Global Policy, 2*(1), 3–9.

Reuters. (2020). China's rise and US fears about decline. https://www.reuters.com/article/uk-global-power-kemp-idUKKBN2770Q3

Rey, H. (2013). Dilemma not trilemma: The global financial cycle and monetary policy independence. Technical Report, Proceedings—Economic Policy Symposium—Jackson Hole. (2016). International channels of transmission of monetary policy and the Mundellian trilemma. *IMF Economic Review, 64*(1), 6–35, May.

Rey, H. (2015). Dilemma not trilemma: The global financial cycle and monetary policy independence. *NBER Working Paper No. 21162*.

Schularick, M., & Steger, T. (2010). Financial integration, investment, and economic growth: Evidence from two eras of financial globalisation. *The Review of Economics and Statists, 92*(4), 756–768.

Silk Road Briefing. (2019). Who is financing the new economic Silk Road? https://www.silkroadbriefing.com/news/2019/07/10/financing-new-economic-silk-road/

Skare, M., & Soriano, D. R. (2021). How globalization is changing digital technology adoption: An international perspective. *Journal of Innovation & Knowledge, 2*(34), 1–12.

Statista. (2021). Total value of investments into FinTech companies worldwide from 2010 to 1st half 2021. https://www.statista.com/statistics/719385/investments-into-fintech-companies-globally/

Strange, S. (1970, April). International economics and international relations: A case of mutual neglect. *International Affairs* (Royal Institute of International Affairs 1944–), *46*(2), 304–315.

Spufford, P. (2006). From Antwerp and Amsterdam to London: The decline of financial centers in Europe. *De Economist, 154*, 143–175. https://doi.org/10.1007/s10645-006-9000-7

Talcott, S. (2010). Paul Volcker: Preventing another financial crash. Harvard Kennedy School, Belfer Center for Science and International Affairs. https://www.belfercenter.org/publication/paul-volcker-preventing-another-financial-crash

The Diplomat. (2021). China's Digital Silk Road and the global digital order. https://thediplomat.com/2021/04/chinas-digital-silk-road-and-the-global-digital-order/

The Economist. (2020a). Can Hong Kong remain a global financial center? https://www.economist.com/finance-and-economics/2020/06/06/can-hong-kong-remain-a-global-financial-center

The Economist. (2020b). What the coronavirus means for financial markets. https://www.economist.com/finance-and-economics/2020/02/08/what-the-coronavirus-means-for-financial-markets

The Economist. (2021a). China has become a laboratory for regulation of digital technology. https://www.economist.com/china/2021/09/11/china-has-become-a-laboratory-for-the-regulation-of-digital-technology

The Economist. (2021b). Niall Ferguson on why the end of America's empire won't be peaceful. https://www.economist.com/by-invitation/2021/08/20/niall-ferguson-on-why-the-end-of-americas-empire-wont-be-peaceful

The Guardian. (2020a). Will the coronavirus outbreak derail the global economy? https://www.theguardian.com/news/2020/feb/10/will-the-coronavirus-outbreak-derail-the-global-economy

The Guardian. (2020b). World financial markets rocked by China Coronavirus. https://www.theguardian.com/business/2020/jan/23/financial-markets-china-coronavirus-outbreak-economy

The Guardian. (2021). UK FinTech investment hits new record after £18bn buying spree. https://www.theguardian.com/business/2021/aug/10/uk-FinTech-investment-hits-new-record-after-18bn-buying-spree

The World Bank. (2021). The global economy: On track for strong but uneven growth as COVID-19 still weighs. https://www.worldbank.org/en/news/feature/2021/06/08/the-global-economy-on-track-for-strong-but-uneven-growth-as-covid-19-still-weighs

Ullah, A., Aria, A., & Akhter, M. N. (2020). EU trade policy Amid US-China trade confrontation. The Asian Institute of Research. *Journal of Social and Political Sciences, 3*(1), 90–102.

UN. (2018). Mobilising the world's financial centers is essential to make progress on climate change and sustainable development. https://www.unep.org/resources/report/mobilizing-worlds-financial-centers-essential-make-progress-climate-change-and

UN. (2021). UN Climate Change Conference UK 2021. Finance. https://ukcop26.org/cop26-goals/finance/

UNCOP26. (2021). *United the world to tackle climate change*. Available at https://ukcop26.org/

Volcker, P. (2009). Think more boldly. *The Wall Street Journal*. https://www.wsj.com/articles/SB10001424052748704825504574586330960597134

WAIFC. (2020). The role of financial centers in driving economic growth. https://waifc.finance/assets/files/waifc-role-of-financial-centers.ac23eaa8ead8569a3ae1b6034f918987.pdf

Wiwanto, F. (2020). Three factors driving the rise of FinTech and what the banking industry can learn from them. https://www.forbes.com/sites/forbesfinancecouncil/2020/04/02/three-factors-driving-the-rise-of-FinTech-and-what-the-banking-industry-can-learn-from-them/
World Economic Forum. (2021). How financial innovation is changing. https://www.weforum.org/agenda/2021/09/how-financial-innovation-is-changing/
Yen. (2021). The Global Financial Centers Index. https://www.longfinance.net/programs/financial-center-futures/global-financial-centers-index/
Zhu, V. (2021). China's FinTech: The end of the Wild West. Institut Montaigne. Policy Paper April 2021. https://www.institutmontaigne.org/ressources/pdfs/publications/china-FinTech-end-of-wild-west-note.pdf

Microfinance: A Gender Equality Tool in the Context of Vietnam

Long Bui-Thanh, Lucía Morales, and Bernadette Andreosso-O'Callaghan

Abstract Vietnam is considered one of the fastest-growing economies in the Southeast Asian region, but the country's economic development and socio-economic sustainability are marked by significant gender imbalances. As such, this chapter offers a valuable contribution to this field of study, as it engages with a quantitative analysis of microfinance tools and the role that they can play in helping to empower women in Vietnam. Women are important economic actors with unquestionable social and economic contributions. This research study is supported by a sample of 351 women microfinance-borrowers in Tra Vinh province located in the Mekong Delta in the southern region of Vietnam. The implementation of logistic regression modelling contributed to the identification of relevant factors that aided women in enhancing their economic, social, and family role. In addition, the analysis is supported by insights from interviews conducted with relevant microfinance institutions that offer further insights into the value of microfinance to address inequality barriers in Tra Vinh province. The empirical outcomes highlight that microfinance tools have enabled women borrowers to have access to the needed financial resources. Access to financial resources has enabled women to exercise some level of control over their own income and savings, but women are still heavily reliant on males due to their historical culturally dominant role. This is a small but very important achievement in a society that is dominated by its patriarchal system, and where microfinance has contributed to facilitating women's access to financial resources that are mainly used to look after their children, family needs, and in some

L. Bui-Thanh (✉)
Tra Vinh University, Trà Vinh, Vietnam
e-mail: thlongbui@tvu.edu.vn

L. Morales
Technical University Dublin, Dublin, Ireland
e-mail: lucia.morales@tudublin.ie

B. Andreosso-O'Callaghan
University of Limerick, Limerick, Ireland

Ruhr Universität Bochum, Bochum, Germany
e-mail: Bernadette.Andreosso@ul.ie

B. Andreosso-O'Callaghan et al. (eds.), *Sustainable Development in Asia*,
Contributions to Economics, https://doi.org/10.1007/978-3-030-94679-1_8

cases for their own use. The study identifies the role of women's unions as being crucial to help in bridging loans between microfinance providers and their members while promoting and supporting the development of economic independence and social recognition for Vietnamese women.

Keywords Vietnam · Women's unions · Microfinance · Poor women · Empowerment

1 Introduction

Microfinance is considered a useful financial instrument when targeting poverty reduction, sustainable development, and gender equity in many developing countries. The extant literature in the field has reported strong evidence on how microfinance services have facilitated financial support to poor women. Generally, microfinance tools have been showing benefits for poor and low-income people when providing them access to financial resources (ADB, 2000; Swain 2015). The existing research suggests that microfinance has played a significant role when supporting government strategies that seek to target poverty reduction, to promote sustainable development, and to encourage poor women to become more economically independent; microfinance strategies help narrow the gap between men and women within their households and their communities (Al-Shami et al., 2016). In the past few decades, both governmental and non-governmental organizations have implemented many kinds of policies to support poor women, alongside international organizations who have also been quite active and involved in helping poor women to access financial resources throughout the world (ADB, 2000). The objective of poverty reduction is also identified as a key goal for microfinance institutions (MFI) that also focus on poor women's empowerment and gender equity through the role of women's organizations (D'Espallier et al., 2011). The linkage between MFIs and women's organizations in microfinance programmes is not limited to the provision of financial services; it additionally offers non-financial services including professional and human development, training programmes, and advancing women's awareness about health, legal, and education aspects to their borrowers (Mayoux, 2005). Women borrowers can be trained in financial management thanks to the effectiveness of loans for engaging in small businesses, developing crops, and livestock (Le & Dao, 2013).

Moreover, microfinance programmes target poor women through the roles of women's organizations that present more advantages for empowering women and promoting them economically by targeting poverty and advancing on gender equity, such as in the case of the Grameen Bank in Bangladesh and self-help groups in India (Swain 2015; Pitt et al., 2006; Warnecke, 2015). However, there are unclear results about women's empowerment and how microfinance programmes have contributed to it due to different timeframes, different tools used, differences in socio-economic and political conditions, and differences in terms of the studied environments. In addition, there are significant criticisms with regard to the real value of microfinance and its potential detrimental effects on socially disfavoured classes (Khavul, 2010; Morduch, 1999). Microfinance services that focus on poor women are considered a useful solution to poverty reduction and gender equity issues in developing countries that seek to enhance their economic development goals in a more equitable socially and economically sustainable environment. This chapter examines whether women who access financial resources from microfinance services are impacted in a significant manner in all aspects that relate to economic independence and to their social and family role in the context of Vietnam. The study focuses its attention on the analysis of microfinance resources and how they might have contributed to empowering poor women with the support of the Women Union (WU) in Tra Vinh province that is considered among the poorest provinces within the country. Section 2 discusses some preliminary observations on both microfinance and women's empowerment in Vietnam. Section 3 describes the research sample and the methodology used. Section 4 presents the results and their implications, while Sect. 5 concludes.

2 Background on Microfinance and Women's Empowerment in Vietnam

Over the last two decades, Vietnam has been considered a developing country that has managed to accomplish an impressive reform seeking to support its economic development, whilst still, at the time of writing, being one of the fastest-growing economies in Asia (Fig. 1 below), with a yearly average GDP growth of 6.3 per cent from 2005 to 2018 (WB, 2018).

As a developing country, Vietnam is facing many opportunities but also many challenges linked to its socio-economic development process and to its

Fig. 1 Vietnam annual GDP growth (in percentage). Source: Tradingeconomics.com, General Statistics Office of Vietnam

socio-economic sustainability, such as poverty, gender gaps, employment, welfare, and political participation. Gender inequity in particular is considered a major barrier in terms of the country's sustainable development process, with gender equity issues playing a significant role when designing inclusive strategies and a balanced approach towards stakeholders' engagement (WB, 2012). Poor women are identified as one of the most vulnerable groups in society as they face significant problems in terms of economic and social inclusion; moreover, a sustainable economic development process seeks to address gender inequity issues in society in general and in the Vietnamese society in particular (Lam, 2017; Menon et al., 2017; Tan, 2014). Vietnam is based on a social structure founded by and strongly tied to its patriarchal system that has a significant influence on and repercussions for its culture, with rooted views identifying men as being more important than women in every sphere of society and economic activity. As in many other societies, children have to be named after their father, with the distinction that in Vietnam male children have a stronger role as they are the ones who keep the family lineage and the patrimony from their father, an ideology that is strongly influenced and guided by Confucian teachings[1] (Duong, 2001; Hue, 1999). On the other hand, women are required to be tolerant and to contain themselves both within their family and social environment, and to be submissive to men (Schuler et al., 2006).

Public activities aiming at gender equity and poverty reduction have been implemented by governmental, non-governmental, and international organizations, and social unions bringing financial and non-financial solutions to support and enhance sustainable development goals in Vietnam. Over the years, the government of Vietnam has issued several policies and regulations to support socio-economic development strategies, such as the Land Law in 2003; the Law on Domestic Violence Prevention and Control in 2007; Laws in the Labour Code in 2012; and the Law on Marriage and Family in 2014. These all focus on equal rights between men and women in terms of labour, salary, ownership, inheritance, and marriage in Vietnam. In this context, microfinance tools are considered useful financial solutions in advancing poor women's ability to access financial resources with the aim of improving their livelihood and overcoming disadvantages in developing countries such as Bangladesh, India, Malaysia, and African countries (Hao, 2005; Nghiem et al., 2006, 2007; Vo & Tran, 2013). Vietnam is the country where microfinance performance has been developing significantly in terms of both scale and numbers; microfinance programmes have been implemented by NGOs, banks, MFIs, and

[1] For centuries, Vietnam has been influenced by Confucian culture, which emphasizes patrilineal tendencies (sons carry the family lineage and inheritance), patrilocal traditions (young married couples living with or close to the husband's family), patriarchal traits (male family members represent a great share of the decision-making power), and kinship. These dominant characteristics have guided practices and resource allocation among Vietnamese men and women. However, certain scholars have argued that the Confucian heritage may have had a greater influence on elite populations, and that Vietnamese women in general have shared more power in their day-to-day decision-making process (with their husbands) than their counterparts in China, partly due to the Southeast Asian cultural roots of Vietnam.

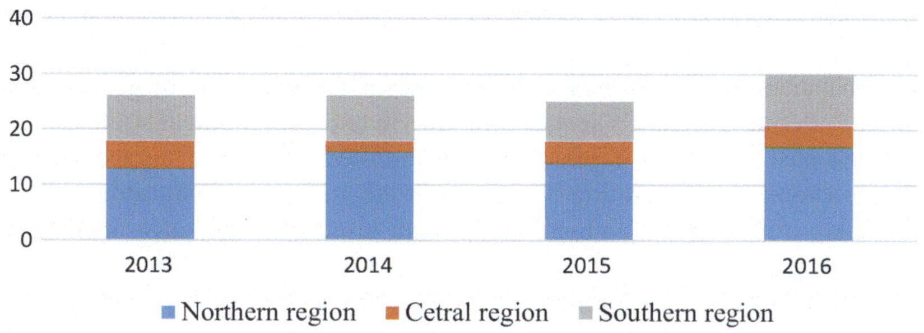

Fig. 2 Establishment of microfinance institutions in Vietnam over the period 2013–2016. Source: Bui-Thanh et al. (2018a) and Nguyen-Kim (2014)

women's organizations with the mobilization of public and private financial resources (Fig. 2).

The government of Vietnam has made significant efforts to develop the microfinance sector with the aim of supporting poverty reduction and socio-economic development, for example by issuing a national strategy on project construction and development of the microfinance system from 2010 to 2020 (Vietnam, 2011). The government of Vietnam established the Vietnam Bank for the Poor (VBP) in 1995 with the help of public financial resources, and it was renamed the Vietnam Bank for Social Policies (VBSP) in 2003 (Swain 2015). The VBSP has been providing credit for poor and quasi-poor Vietnamese people. Microfinance institutions facilitate lending in a more simple and accessible manner to poor women through various microfinance providers (Bui-Thanh et al., 2018b). The Vietnam Women's Union (WU) plays a significant role in terms of collaboration with microfinance actors from banks, international NGOs, and other donors; these actors provide microfinance services that foster gender equity strategies by enabling credit guarantees for their members from both rural and urban areas (Le & Dao, 2013). More specifically, the WU is a social-political organization in Vietnam established in 1930 with the goal of representing Vietnamese women's rights through an extensive system spanning from local areas to the centre, with four levels: commune, district, province, and central (WU, 2019). In 2015, the WU managed up to 90,000 credit and savings groups in 8900 communes to the point that it has become the most effective partner of microfinance provision with very high rates on repayments from women clients (Dineen & Le, 2015). The co-operation between the WUs and microfinance providers focuses on the engagement of poor women with financial and non-financial services through the provision of credits that are integrated as part of training programmes, schemes targeting businesses, and professional and human development programmes, all aimed at empowering women (Huis et al., 2019). The main goal is to advance poor women's competences to gain access to microfinance services with strategic efforts aligning with national goals that seek to support gender equity in terms of women's family planning and health promotion, preventing domestic violence, integrating women in educational and cultural activities, and improving income. In short, these microfinance programmes seek to help poor women clients to solve their financial issues in the short term while helping to alleviate poverty and addressing gender equity imbalances in the long term; all these are critical goals for the government as they seek to define Vietnam's sustainable growth and development strategy.

Over the past few years, researchers have studied the role of microfinance and how it can enable the integration of women in the Vietnamese cultural, social, and economic environment. A summary of the core research in this area is outlined in Table 1.

Table 1 states that most microfinance programmes focus on poor women to target poverty reduction and gender equity so as to foster the socio-economic development processes in Vietnam. The main research findings indicate that there are cases of both success and failure regarding microfinance programmes outreaching poor women borrowers for the purpose of empowering Vietnamese women. A relevant finding indicates that microfinance tools have been identified as useful solutions for gender equity and poverty reduction within an appropriate outreach to women through the combination of non-financial and financial services.

In the context of Tra Vinh province, poor women have access to microfinance programmes from public financial resources in the same national framework, such as the Vietnam Bank for Social Policies (VBSP), the Vietnam Bank for Agriculture and rural Development (Agribank), and the Co-operation Bank of Vietnam (former People's Credit Fund). Furthermore, several microfinance programmes focusing on poor women have been established in recent years. These are, for example, the microcredit programmes as part of the rural development project program for improving market participation of the poor in Ha Tinh and Tra Vinh provinces in 2006; the microcredit programme in a wider project for the adaption to climate change in the Mekong Delta in Ben Tre and Tra Vinh provinces in 2013; the microcredit project of Tra Vinh University in 2011; and the Tra Vinh women's deployment fund in 2014. The outlined programmes show evidence of clear efforts made to advance poor women's access to microfinance services so as to meet the established goals of gender equity and poverty reduction as enshrined in the rural development strategy of Tra Vinh province (Pedersen, 2006; Rath, 2013). However, the existing research has not assessed the impact of microfinance programmes on women's empowerment in Tra Vinh province; since this a very important research gap, it clearly shows the need for a research contribution in this area that helps assess, evaluate, and reflect on the role that microfinance has played in supporting women in a province that is quite diverse and characterized by a significant concentration of ethnic groups where women are in a clearly disadvantaged position.

Table 1 Microfinance and women's empowerment in Vietnam

Authors	Publishers	Findings
Lavoie (2002)	Laval University	• The microcredit approach is opening a new venue for women at the household, community, and society level in the Vietnamese context. However, we must be aware of a destabilization of household dynamics that can emerge from the new phenomenon of women's empowerment in Vietnamese households and society.
Hollister and Nguyen (2012)	Social Development Issues 34 (3) 2012	• Women's perceptions of factors contributing to their success and failure in implementing microenterprises through a microfinance program, including advantages; these factors are weekly payments, loan disbursement in the villages and group solidarity; the reported disadvantages include: high interest rates, low credit limits, and levels of bureaucracy in loan administration.
Le and Dao (2013)	The *International Journal of Interdisciplinary Social and Community Studies* Vol 7, No 1 (2013)	• The study reveals that the perception of empowerment is significantly higher for the borrower group than for the non-borrower group. • The results indicate that the integrated microcredit program significantly enhances women's empowerment, including the ability to express personal views in the community and to offer advice to others. • The study highlights the effectiveness of an approach that integrates the feminist empowerment model with the poverty alleviation and financial self-sustainability models.
Vu et al. (2015)	New Delhi: International Initiative for Impact Evaluation (3ie).	• The study finds that gender and business training programmes improve knowledge, increase the uptake of new business practices, and after some delay cause an increase in profits. • The study provides evidence that female borrowers who receive access to training experience more internal control beliefs and less relational friction, and share more intra-household decision-making power. •The study documents that general business training significantly increases the returns to agricultural practices, even if agriculture was not specifically targeted—an example of household-level spillover effects across economic sectors.

(continued)

Table 1 (continued)

Authors	Publishers	Findings
Dineen and Le (2015)	*The Journal of Developing Areas*, Volume 49 No. 1, Winter 2015	• The findings indicate the importance of the empowerment component in the Peace Trees microcredit program through the role of the Women's Union with the objective of empowering women, which serves as leverage for higher income generation and greater gender equality. • This study supports the importance of the feminist empowerment paradigm in which empowerment is a best practice when a gender equality approach is embedded in program design, rather than an add-on benefit. • The microcredit program has also integrated the poverty alleviation paradigm and the financial self-sustainability paradigm.
Huis et al. (2019)	*World Development*, Volume 120, August 2019, pp. 46–61	• A major contribution of this study is that it focuses on different dimensions of women's empowerment: (1) personal empowerment, measured by control beliefs, and (2) relational empowerment, measured by relational friction and intra-household decision-making power. • The results suggest that it takes some time before the training starts to improve women's empowerment. They reveal no short-term but only mid-term effects from before the training to 12 months after the training.

Source: Compiled by the authors

3 Research Sample and Methodological Framework

3.1 Data Collection Process

The data collection process was focused on Tra Vinh province located in the Mekong Delta area of the southern region of Vietnam. The Tra Vinh population is about 1.1 million people and it consists of three main groups that include: Kinh (Vietnamese), Hoa (Chinese), and Khmer (Cambodian). The Khmer group is considered an ethnic minority group in Vietnam, representing 31 per cent of the provincial population. Tra Vinh province has 9 administrative units with seven districts, one town, and one hub city. Women represent 51.2 per cent of the Tra Vinh population with 30.1 per cent of them being Khmer women (GSO, 2019). Khmer people face many disadvantages such as poor living conditions that are exacerbated by their customs, including, for example, living in remote regions far away from urban areas; their location in shanty towns and home villages; and limits to communication with the external society, limits that have contributed to the creation of limitations regarding access to information, education, and technology. Approximately 75 per cent of the population of Tra Vinh province are living in rural areas and 25 per cent are living in urban areas, of which 10 per cent have been identified as being poor, with roughly 52 per cent of poor households in the province identified as being Khmer (GSO, 2019; WB, 2019). Khmer people are thus clearly one of the ethnic minority groups in Vietnam[2] affected by many disadvantages in the areas of education, information, technology, and daily life needs; this makes them a severely underdeveloped social class in the province and across the country. Women borrowers are considered the focus of this study, specifically women acquiring microfinance loans from programmes enabled by the women's union. The authors obtained a list of women clients from the microfinance providers and from the women's unions and used a random selection process of clients for the data collection exercise. Primary data from a total of 351 women borrowers was collected using a research questionnaire that was filled in through face-to-face interviews during June and September 2018.

Research studies examining women's empowerment and the role played by microfinance offer important insights to this research study, as researchers have developed various indicators to help measure women's level of empowerment that were carefully considered to guide this study. The reviewed literature helped to identify the appropriate research models that have been used to examine how microfinance indicators are helping to explain women's social, economic, and cultural integration and to assess and select the approach that supported the conducted analysis. Table 2 highlights the methodology used by a number of relevant studies and offers a summary of the key research findings.

The research studies presented in Table 2 show key indicators of research frameworks commonly used to analyse the relationship between participation in microfinance programmes and women's empowerment around the world. The logistic regression model is identified as the preferred econometric model to analyse quantitative data collected from interviews and questionnaires from the involved participants. The key independent variables of the logit model seem to be focused on women borrowers' geographies and microfinance accessibility and empowerment measurement. As examples of explanatory variables that help to capture and measure improvements in women's empowerment, researchers use diverse indicators such as income generation, jobs, education, legal awareness, and political rights.

[2]Nearly 85.5 per cent of Vietnam's population belong to the Kinh ethnic group (Vietnamese), and 14.5 per cent of the population belong to 53 other ethnic minority groups, according to official statistics released on April 1, 2019 (Government of Vietnam, 2019).

Table 2 Core methodological research frameworks in microfinance and women's empowerment

Authors, year of publication	Data gathering process	Econometric models	Variables	Services provided	Research outcomes
Hashemi et al. (1996)	Cross-sectional survey	Logistic regression	Independent variables: women's age, education, religion, respondent having sons or daughters, geographic region, economic level of household, respondent's contribution to family support and exposure to credit programmes Dependent variables: respondent's mobility, small purchases, larger purchases, major decisions, freedom from domination, political/legal awareness, protest/campaign, composite empowerment	Credit and savings in group lending model	Increasing women's mobility, their ability to make purchases and major household decisions, their ownership of productive assets, their legal and political awareness and participation in public campaigns and protests
Schuler et al. (1996)	Cross-sectional survey	Logistic regression	Independent variables: women's age, education, religion, whether respondent had any surviving sons or daughters, geographic region, economic level of household, respondent's contribution to family support, and exposure to credit programmes Dependent variable: women's subjection to violence	Credit and savings in group lending model	Decreasing women's vulnerability to family violence Women reporting physical beating by husband in the preceding 12 months
Pitt et al. (2003)	Survey	Probit regression	Dependent variables: women's economic decision making, purchasing capacity, control over loans, control over income and	Credit and savings in group lending model	Increasing women's empowerment in household decision making, having greater access to financial and

(continued)

Table 2 (continued)

Authors, year of publication	Data gathering process	Econometric models	Variables	Services provided	Research outcomes
			savings, mobility, political awareness and activism, networking and friendships, family planning, attitudes, spousal arguments and abuse, and level of household's participating credit programmes Independent variables: male and female credit		economic resources, having greater social networks, having greater bargaining power vis-à-vis their husbands, and having greater freedom of mobility
Garikipati (2008)	Survey	Logistic regression	Independent variables: those relating to the credit program, control variables measuring household characteristics, and those measuring women's personal characteristics The dependent variables in these logit models are vulnerability and empowerment indicators. Vulnerability indicators: drought-related vulnerability, livelihood diversification, entrepreneurial behaviour, investment in and access to social capital, and the composite not-vulnerable indicator Empowerment indicators: ownership of household assets and incomes, control over minor finances, control over major	Credit and savings in self-help group model	While lending to women is likely to strengthen the household's ability to cope with vulnerability across income groups, women themselves, especially the poorest ones, are not likely to see consistent improvements in their household status. In short, although lending to women benefits their households, its benefits for women themselves are not as certain

(continued)

Table 2 (continued)

Authors, year of publication	Data gathering process	Econometric models	Variables	Services provided	Research outcomes
			finances, for example in household decisions, work time allocation, division of domestic chores, and composite empowerment		
Li et al. (2011)	Survey	Logistic regression	Dependent variables: control over own income, control over own cash savings, travel alone to city, ability to visit parental home without asking for consent, independent purchase of utensils, clothes, furniture, jewellery, livestock, and farming machinery, involvement in decisions on house repair/construction, children's education, land lease, what crops to grow, livestock sale/purchase, what farm machinery to buy, what consumer durables to buy, opening bank account, and when to have a child, aware of women rights against domestic abuse, aware of the use of contraception, aware of the incorrectness of arranged marriage, aware of female minimum marriage age, aware of legal	Credit and savings in group lending model	Microcredit has a significant impact on five dimensions of women's empowerment, ranging from economic security to awareness of social/legal issues

(continued)

Table 2 (continued)

Authors, year of publication	Data gathering process	Econometric models	Variables	Services provided	Research outcomes
			method of divorce The independent variables are related to microcredit and the control variables include those reflecting households' socio-economic features, those capturing women's personal characteristics, and a vector of village variables		
Dineen and Le (2015)	Survey	Ordinary least squares regression	The dependent variable addressed 12 questions related to the perceptions of women's empowerment in household decision-making processes, household division of labour, dignity of women, and gender roles in society The independent variables are change in income, training, encouragement, confidence, marriage, and education	Credit and trainings in women's union	The importance of the empowerment components in the microcredit program that serves as leverage for higher income generation and greater gender equality. This is also integrated into the poverty alleviation paradigm and the financial self-sustainability paradigm
Debnath et al. (2019)	Survey	Logistic regression	Dependent variables: control over financial assets/ resources, control over mobility, ability to make purchases independently, and legal awareness Independent variables: age of borrowers, literacy	Credit	Microcredit has a positive and significant impact on enhancing participation in the household decision- making process and in women's legal awareness

(continued)

Table 2 (continued)

Authors, year of publication	Data gathering process	Econometric models	Variables	Services provided	Research outcomes
			level, occupation, family size, average annual household income, and microcredit accessibility		

Source: Compiled by the authors

Table 3 Levels of women's empowerment

Levels	Degree of empowerment	Implication for power
5	Control	Where individuals can make decisions, and these are fully recognized
⇧		
4	Participation & mobilization	Where the equal taking of decisions is enabled
⇧		
3	Conscientization and awareness raising	Where structural and institutional discrimination is addressed
⇧		
2	Access	Where equal access to education, land, and credit is assured
⇧		
1	Welfare	Where basic needs are satisfied. This does not necessarily require structural causes to be addressed and tends to view those involved as passive recipients

Source: Adjusted from Ibrahim and Alkire (2007) and Longwe (2002)

Additionally, the survey method is considered the main approach for data collection in this field.

3.2 Developing Women's Empowerment Indicators

The development of indicators for measuring women's empowerment requires the identification of necessary actions for women to be able to join socio-economic activities across different sectors, activities that can contribute to ensuring that the goals of sustainable development for human equality are transparent and prosperous (Hawk et al., 2011). Longwe (2002) divided the process of women's empowerment into five levels that consider Welfare, Access, Conscientization, Mobilization, and Control, as outlined in Table 3.

First, the level of the first degree of empowerment—Welfare—considers that women have basic needs for their daily life. Second, the level of Access requires that women have access to equal opportunities in socio-economic activities such as education, land, and credit. Third, the level of Conscientization refers to raising awareness through the support of government and legal frameworks for both men and women. Fourth, the level of Participation and Mobilization requires the advance of women's roles of equality in making decisions. Fifth, women have full control for making decisions by themselves within gender equality and without any management or intervention from men or authorities (Longwe, 2002). On the other hand, since empowerment is an internal change relating to power, the process of empowerment follows power over, power to, power with, and power within the community (Ibrahim & Alkire, 2007). Identifying empowerment indicators is considered the most important task for developing variables to measure women's behaviour and socio-economic status in different geographical and physical infrastructures. This study has carefully considered the reviewed literature and different research frameworks used by existing research when identifying both the data and the model needed to support the study of women's empowerment in Tra Vinh province of Vietnam. The study is supported by a questionnaire based on 69 questions drawn from 11 domains to measure the levels of women's empowerment from a microfinance performance for women borrowers (see Appendix for details).

3.3 Empirical Model

The logistic regression model was selected to analyse the impact of microfinance on women's empowerment in Vietnam, as it has been acknowledged as a very suitable technique that helps identify relevant variables when examining the impact of microfinance on women. Moreover, logistic regression has become the analytic technique of choice for multivariate modelling of categorical dependent variables, further justifying its integration as part of this study (Debnath et al., 2019; Garikipati, 2008; Hashemi et al., 1996; Li et al., 2011; Pitt & Khandker, 1998; Pitt et al., 2006). Based on data collection from 351[3] surveys of women borrowers in Tra Vinh province in Vietnam, the empirical model is implemented in a sequential manner to allow examination of the perspectives of microfinance intervention as well as women's empowerment through dependent and independent variables. The impact of microfinance on empowering women in Vietnam is outlined in the equations that follow:

[3]Three questionnaires were incomplete; as a result, valid questionnaires for this study numbered 348.

$$Y_i = \ln \frac{P_i}{1 - P_i} = \alpha_{11} + \beta_{11}X_{11} + \beta_{21}X_{21} + \beta_{31}X_{31} + \beta_{41}X_{41} + \beta_{51}X_{51} + \beta_{61}X_{61} + \varepsilon t_1 \quad (1)$$

$$Y_i = \ln \frac{P_i}{1 - P_i} = \alpha_{21} + \beta_{21}X_{21} + \beta_{22}X_{22} + \beta_{32}X_{32} + \beta_{42}X_{42} + \beta_{52}X_{52} + \beta_{62}D_1X_{62} + \beta_{72}D_2X_{62} + \varepsilon t_1 \quad (2)$$

First, the empowerment indicators were identified through survey questions using a Likert-type five-point scale from low to high (1 to 5) to gather the levels of women's empowerment along three indicators (Table 4). This follows common practice in other studies in this field of research, namely: Xia Li et al. (2011) in the case of China; Supriya Garikipati (2008) for India; Dineen and Le (2015) for Vietnam; Debnath et al. (2019), Rahman et al. (2017), and Hashemi (1996) in the case of Bangladesh; and Coleman (1999) for Thailand. Second, in the above equations, Y_i is identified as the dependent variable capturing empowerment of female borrowers through three different indicators ($I = 1,2,3$), converted in binary form (*id est* the variable is 1 for values ≥ 3; or 0 otherwise, with a scale of five-point scores drawn from the results of the survey questionnaires (Table 4)). P_i is the estimated probability of female borrowers being empowered; consequently, 1–– P_i is the estimated probability of female borrowers not being empowered whereas α is a constant term (Debnath et al., 2019). Three indicators of women's empowerment are considered to help identify women's control over financial assets/resources (Table 4).

Table 4 offers the relevant details regarding the variables that were considered as part of the econometric modelling process, with independent variables defined in two categories including primary variables that relate to microcredit and control variables capturing women's personal information and involvement in the region women's union. In addition, the model is supported by dummy variables that help study potential differences depending on women's ethnicity, an aspect that has not been considered in the reviewed literature.

4 Findings and Discussion

4.1 Descriptive Statistics of Women Borrowers, Women's Union, and Microfinance Performance

The research findings show that 61 per cent of respondents are over 45 year old; in terms of ethnic groups, the Kinh (of Vietnamese ethnicity) represent 72 per cent of the total and the Khmer 27 per cent (Table 5). In terms of education, survey data indicate that 44 per cent of women borrowers have completed primary education,

Table 4 Dependent and independent variables for logistic regression model

X/Y	Indicators	Description	Coding	Referenced studies
Dependent variables Y_i				
Y_1	INCOME	Increase of control over her own income	1 for values ≥3; otherwise 0	Garikipati (2008) and Li et al. (2011)
Y_2	INCOMECP	Her increase in generating income	1 for values ≥3; otherwise 0	Garikipati (2008) and Hashemi et al. (1996)
Y_3	INCOMECBP	Her income contribution for the household	1 for values ≥3; otherwise 0	Hashemi et al. (1996), Li et al. (2011), Pitt and Khandker (1998), and Pitt et al. (2006)
Independent variables X_i				
X_1	AGEP	Age of women borrowers in years	1 = 18–35; 2 = 36–45; 3 = 45–55; 4 >55	Debnath et al. (2019) and Li et al. (2011)
X_2	EDUP	The education of women borrowers	1 = Illiterate; 2 = Primary School; 3 = Secondary School; 4 = Higher Secondary; 5 = Graduation or above higher secondary	Debnath et al. (2019), Garikipati (2008), and Li et al. (2011)
X_3	LOANAM	The loan amount of women borrowers in Vietnamese dong (VND)—(1 euro = 26,000 VND)	1 ≤5,000,000; 2 = between 5,000,000 and 15,000,000; 3 = between 30,000,000 and 15,000,000; 4 ≥30,000,000	Li et al. (2011)
X_4	DURATIONLM	Duration of the last borrowed loans	In years	Rahman et al. (2017)
X_5	DURATIONMW	Duration of a membership of women's union	In years	Garikipati (2008)
Dummy variables				
X_6	ETHINICGP	Ethnic groups	1 = Vietnamese; 2 = Khmer, 3 = Chinese, 4 = Other	Carol (2015) and Imai et al. (2011)
D_1	ETHINICGPVN	Women's ethnic group	1 = Vietnamese, otherwise 0	Dang (2019) and Imai et al. (2011)
D_2	ETHINICGPKM	Women's ethnic group	1 = Khmer, otherwise 0	Imai et al. (2011)

Source: Compiled by the authors

32 per cent secondary education, and 11 per cent have not been engaged in any form of education. Some 57 per cent of participants were identified as self-employed and 16 per cent unemployed. A further 84 per cent of respondents indicated that they were married and as a result have major limitations in terms of access to education,

Table 5 Characteristics of women borrowers

Variables	No.	(%)	Variables	No.	(%)
Age			**Education**		
18–35	42	12	No education	37	11
36–45	93	27	Primary school	155	44
45–55	107	30	Secondary school	112	32
Over 55	110	31	Higher secondary	40	11
Ethnic groups			Graduation or above higher secondary	8	2
Kinh (Vietnamese)	254	72	**Employment status**		
Khmer	95	27	Self-employed	202	57
Hoa (Chinese)	3	1	Wage employed	54	15
Religions			Unemployed	58	16
Buddhism	228	65	Employed in family business	38	11
Catholicism	10	3	**Marital status**		
Protestantism	3	1	Married	295	84
Caodaism	19	5	Unmarried	14	4
Islam	2	1	Divorced	16	5
Atheism	90	26	Separated	5	1
			Widow	22	6

Source: Compiled by the authors

and engaging in remunerated activities as they are responsible for taking care of their children, their families, and the whole household, including looking after their husbands' needs, as is traditionally expected from their role as housewife (Duong, 2001; Le & Dao, 2013). In terms of religion, Buddhism is the main religion in the region, with a representation of 65 per cent of women in Tra Vinh province.

The Vietnam Bank for Social Policies (VBSP) has played a significant role in providing access to financial resources for women borrowers, with a representation of 80 per cent. This shows an effective implementation of government policies in line with Decision No. 2195/QD-TTg dated December 6, 2011, by the Prime Minister who approved the "Project construction and development of the microfinance system in Vietnam 2020", and with Decree No.: 28/2005/ND-CP dated 0/3/2005 by the Prime Minister approaching the Government for Microfinance institutions activity in Vietnam (see Table 6). The VBSP was established by the government of Vietnam through public financial resources, and the work of the institution shows an effective outreach of a formal microfinance provider motivated by the goals of poverty reduction and gender equity (Anh, 2016; Bui-Thanh et al., 2018a). In 77 per cent of cases, the purpose of loans is generating income, with 191 cases for livestock and 22 for crops; this demonstrates the importance of the agricultural sector in this area. In the study by Vu et al. (2015), the agricultural sector is considered the main purpose for microfinance services delivered to improve women's livelihood. The amounts of loans account for 68 per cent of the total,

Table 6 Microfinance providers and loan indicators

Microfinance providers		
Vietnam Bank for Social Policies (VBSP)	283	80%
Vietnam Bank for Agriculture and Rural Development (VBARD)	28	8%
Co-operative Bank of Vietnam (Co-opBank)—Former People's Credit Funds	8	2%
Tra Vinh Women Development Fund (TVWDF)	14	4%
Commercial banks	18	5%
Other resources	1	0%
Purpose of loan		
Generating income (*22 for crops, 191 for livestock, 113 for trades, 6 for manufacturing, and 1 for other*)	271	77%
Non-generating income (*6 for education, 7 for medical, 8 for housing, 9 for ceremonies, and 10 for other*)	37	11%
Both generating income and non-generating income	44	13%
Loan amounts		
Less than 5,000,000 VND	16	5%
5,000,000 VND–15,000,000 VND	239	68%
15,000,000 VND–30,000,000 VND	73	21%
More than 30,000,000 VND	24	7%
Duration of the last borrowed loans in year		
Minimum	Median	Maximum
1	2	15

Source: Compiled by the authors

from 5 million VND[4] to 15 million VND, and the loan duration average is 2 years. Table 6 illustrates that women borrower's businesses are micro-businesses linked to basic purposes such as simply "generating income" (ADB, 2000; Cull et al., 2015; Suesse & Wolf, 2020).

Table 7 shows that 78 per cent of women's union members are interested in benefiting from financial services, while 1 per cent of the members are interested in support unrelated to non-financial activities. Microfinance services play an important role for women's unions in terms of support and outreach to memberships because microfinance can bring financial opportunities for generating income and jobs and overcoming periods of economic difficulty. Approximately 21 per cent of the unions' membership are linked to the purpose of offering support for financial and non-financial services; these are considered critical factors to empower women (Kablan & Boussemart, 2015; Waibel & Glück, 2013).

[4] VND is Vietnamese dong (1 euro = 26.000 VND) (January, 2020).

Table 7 Activities of women's unions

Purpose of joining a women's union		
Financial services (*220 for credits, 227 for savings and insurance, 50 for deposits, 15 for other*)	274	78%
Non-financial services (*2 for training, 41 for health*)	2	1%
Both financial and non-financial services	76	21%
Position in women's union		
Ordinary member	294	84%
Active member	11	3%
Cashier/secretary	2	1%
Leader	43	12%
Other	2	1%
Duration of a membership of women's union in year		
Minimum	Median	Maximum
1	8	30

Source: Compiled by the authors

4.2 *The Impact of Microfinance on Women's Empowerment*

The logistic regression model measures the probability of the relationship between women's empowerment and microfinance accessibility. The women's empowerment variable focuses on three indicators that were used as the dependent variables (Y_i): the increase of women's control over own income (INCOME), women's increase in generating income (INCOMECP), and women's income contribution to the household (INCOMECBP). The impact of microfinance is captured by running the econometric model to consider the case of women borrowers affiliated to women's unions; a distinction is made in terms of the variables that reflect women's empowerment—such as access to loans—and those related to socio-cultural characteristics such as ethnicity in Tra Vinh province. The results of the econometric exercise are presented in Table 8. The outcomes of the logit models led to the analysis of three different scenarios of empowerment as discussed below (see Table 8).

4.2.1 Microfinance and Women's Control Over Own Income (INCOME)

The results show insignificant outcomes for the studied variables, suggesting that microfinance accessibility did not impact on increasing women's control over their own income, as the financial resources appear to be under men's control. Traditionally, Vietnamese women are allowed to keep money for the family besides their responsibilities for expenditures on daily activities but the husband represents the main contribution in terms of income in the household, implying that he keeps a strong control over the family decision-making process and household income (ILO,

Table 8 Logit models outcomes—impact of microfinance on women's empowerment

Y_i/X_i	AGEP	EDUP	LOANAM	DURATIONLM	DURATIONMW	ETHICNICGP	ETHICNICGPVN	ETHICNICGPKM
Scenario 1 (Y_1)								
INCOME	−0.2882 (0.1818)	0.1814 (0.4537)	0.4186 (0.2416)	0.3229(0.1027)	−0.0043(0.9110)	−2.6978 (0.0000)*		
INCOME	−2.2830 (0.1873)	0.1646 (0.4935)	0.3533 (0.3149)	0.2391(0.2247)	−0.0006(0.9878)		3.7406(0.0067)*	0.3439(0.6017)
INCOME	−0.2790 (0.1928)	0.1647 (0.4918)	0.3356 (0.3342)	0.2194(0.2503)	0.0014(0.9714)		3.0712(0.0000)*	
INCOME	−0.2615 (0.2189)	0.1768 (0.4549)	0.3033 (0.3735)	0.2003(0.2862)	0.0064(0.8691)			−1.4310(0.0000)*
Scenario 2 (Y_2)								
INCOMECP	−0.0948 (0.4494)	−0.1312 (0.2953)	−0.1576 (0.3257)	0.0829(0.2614)	0.0354(0.0917)	−0.8067 (0.0031)*		
INCOMECP	−0.0932 (0.4567)	−0.1298 (0.3005)	−0.1607 (0.3167)	0.0818(0.2675)	0.0359(0.0864)		0.7996(0.0042)*	
INCOMECP	−0.0884 (0.4791)	−0.1246 (0.3193)	−0.1643 (0.3068)	0.0823(0.2645)	0.0369(0.0776)			−0.3689(0.0085)*
Scenario 3 (Y_3)								
INCOMECBP	−0.0975 (0.6811)	0.1804 (0.4431)	0.4441 (0.1948)	−0.1452 (0.1837)	−0.0661 (0.0600)**	0.3469 (0.5071)		
INCOMECBP	−0.0989 (0.6782)	0.1795 (0.4455)	0.4459 (0.1932)	−0.1456 (0.1831)	−0.0664 (0.0587)**		−0.3310(0.5358)	
INCOMECBP	−0.1004 (0.6721)	0.1776 (0.4504)	0.4481 (0.1915)	−0.1467 (0.1803)	−0.00668 (0.0568)**			0.1480(0.5803)

Total observations: 351. This table presents the coefficients and the probabilities for results of logistic regression models. The probabilities of logit models tend to be insignificant in most cases

Source: Derived from the authors' findings

* 1% significance level

** 10% significance level. The logit models have been checked by the log-likelihood test and deviance residuals with a goodness of model fit. Independent variables which were correlated did not show any multicollinearity.

2008; Kabeer, 2005; Li et al., 2011; Schuler et al., 2006). There are no differences between Vietnamese and Khmer women in terms of exercising control over income; this clearly shows that income remains under the control of men, with minor improvements being made in this respect (Hue, 1999; Tan, 2014; Vu et al., 2014).

4.2.2 Microfinance and Women's Income Generation (INCOMECP)

With regard to the second dependent variable, the results show evidence of microfinance effectively helping to increase women's ability to generate income. Women spend more time taking care of children, their family, and the household, with, as a result, the concentration of income generation being placed on husbands because men spend more time in their jobs or businesses with a significant lack of involvement in caring duties and household chores. This result is not surprising as Vietnamese culture considers that wives are responsible for household chores, and husbands take control of all resources in the family for generating income (Duong, 2001; FAO, 2017; Lam, 2017; Nguyen & Hollister, 2012). In this regard, women have managed to gain access to microfinance services but men still lead the family and their dominant role prevents women's ability to increase income or to become more economically independent (Berge et al., 2016; Mazumder & Lu, 2015).

4.2.3 Microfinance and Women's Income Contribution (INCOMECBP)

The research findings for the third dependent variable suggest the existence of a positive impact between women's membership in women's unions and women's ability to make an income contribution to their families. The women's unions in the province have a mission to promote gender equity through the provision of both financial and non-financial services for their members. This implies that the longer a women remains a member of the union, the more likely it is that she is able to benefit from different training and coaching programmes that enable her to start making more significant contributions to her household (Aggarwal et al., 2015; Swain 2015).

Overall, the research findings suggest that microfinance services do not have an impact on women's empowerment in Tra Vinh province. Microfinance providers focus on offering only microcredits, with 68 per cent of the loans amounting to 5,000,000 VND–15,000,000 VND (Table 6), which is revealed as the highest amount of available loans for women.

Moreover, Vietnam's traditional culture builds on social norms that have strict limitations for women's roles and responsibilities within their families, and communities represent the biggest challenges to empowering women in Vietnam. Vietnamese women can access microfinance services, but financial resources are still under men's control within the household, with limited changes regarding women's role in the context of rigid patriarchal cultures such as in the case under study here. However, women borrowers do benefit from membership in the Vietnam women's unions as they are able to access additional services that are not only financially related but also offer valuable support to contributing to their social role. As members of women's unions, women not only can access financial services from the co-operation between women's unions and microfinance institutions, but can also enjoy non-financial services such as training in the areas of business, health, legal awareness, and political rights, all empowering women in terms of their knowledge and ability to generate income for their household.

5 Conclusion

The present study evaluates the impact of microfinance on women's empowerment in Tra Vinh province in Vietnam. The research findings indicate that microfinance programmes in the province did not have a direct impact on empowering women borrowers by themselves. Microfinance institutions provide financial services for women borrowers who are not able to make significant changes with regard to women's gender inequities in the family and social contexts. However, the research outcomes suggest that the co-operation between microfinance providers and the women's unions plays an important role in delivering a combination of financial and non-financial services. The present findings suggest several courses of action for policymakers, financial providers, and social unions in Vietnam in terms of advancing the effectiveness of microfinance services in empowering women out of poverty and inequity.

- The government of Vietnam should redesign microfinance policies with the goals of gender and ethnic equity to close large gaps between ethnic groups. Microfinance tools should enable mechanisms that target poor women in ethnic minorities that are at clear disadvantage in the economic development process taking place in Vietnam. This would enhance sustainable forms of economic development. Policymakers should look at financial inclusion in terms of safety for microfinance providers, women clients, and stakeholders through ceilings on interest rates and taxation levels.
- The Vietnam women's unions should engage in co-operation agreements with microfinance providers with the aim of reaching ethnic minorities by offering specific access to financial and non-financial services.

In conclusion, the government of Vietnam should play a central role regarding the efforts in terms of gender and ethnic equity through the development of sustainable polices that can be supported by the use of microfinance tools. The government should become an active player that encourages and supports the role of the women's unions by enabling women's access to financial and non-financial services that help to reduce gaps between women minorities and with regard to women's roles in the development of the country's economic and social model for the years to come.

Appendix

Indicators of women's empowerment

	Indicators	Description
1	**FASSETE**	**Do you think since using microfinance services and joining a women's union you have control over your financial assets? Could you please mention some improvements?**
2	**INCOME**	Do you have increased control over your own income?
3	**SAVINGE**	Do you have increased control over your own savings?
4	**MONEYE**	Do you have increased control over access to money for your own use?
5	**MOFREE**	**Do you feel you have more mobility and freedom since using microfinance services and joining a women's union? Could you please mention some activities?**
6	OTUSITE	Do you have to ask your husband or a senior family member for permission to go outside the local ward/commune?
7	VPHE	Do you visit your parental home without asking for permission?
8	GLOCALE	Do you have to ask your husband/a senior family member for permission to go to a community centre, park, or plaza in the local ward/commune?
9	VFRIENDE	Do you have to ask your husband/a senior family member for permission to visit friends/relatives?
10	GSOE	Do you have to ask your husband/a senior family member for permission to go to a social union/NGO/MFI office?
11	GHEALTHE	Do you have to ask your husband/a senior family member for permission to go to the health centre?
12	**MAKEPE**	**Do you have the ability to make a purchase since using microfinance services and joining a women's union? Could you please respond to the following questions?**
13	FURNITURE	Do you buy household furniture independently?
14	CLOTHE	Do you buy clothing for yourself independently?
15	UTENSILE	Do you buy utensils for the household independently?
16	JEWELLERYE	Do you purchase jewellery independently?
17	CCLOTHE	Do you purchase clothes for your children independently?
18	CFOODE	Do you buy daily consumable food items independently?
19	CBYE	Do you buy ice creams, candies, or cookies for your children independently?
20	**EDME**	**Are you involved in economic decision making since using microfinance services and joining a women's union? Could you please respond to the following questions?**
21	HOUSE	Do you participate in decisions on house repair/construction?
22	CEDUE	Do you participate in decisions on children's education?
23	DURABLE	Do you participate in decisions on what consumer durable to buy?
24	BANKAE	Do you participate in deciding to open a bank account?
25	PSHOUSE	Do you participate in the purchase/sale of the house?
26	USEME	Do you participate in decisions on the use of borrowed money?

(continued)

	Indicators	Description
27	BUYFRRE	If you wanted to buy yourself a dress/sari, would you feel free to do it without consulting your husband (or a senior member of your family)?
28	BUYSIE	If you wanted to buy yourself a small item of jewellery, such as bangles or beads, would you feel free to do it without consulting your husband (or a senior member of your family)?
29	**LEGALE**	**Do you have legal awareness since using microfinance services and joining a women's union? Could you please respond to the following questions?**
30	ADOMESTICE	Are you aware of women rights against domestic abuse?
31	BSALARYE	Do you know about basic salary per month?
32	MMAGE	Are you aware of women's minimum marriage age?
33	LMDIVORCE	Are you aware of the legal method of divorce?
34	LWHOUSE	Do you know about the maximum legal working hours per day or week?
35	**COERCIVE**	**Do you have control over interpersonal coercive tactics since using microfinance services and joining a women's union? Could you please respond to the following questions?**
36	COERCIVE	Are you afraid to disagree with your husband for fear he may become angry with you?
37	BEATE	Does your husband hit or beat you?
38	CDVIOLENCE	Do you have a better check on domestic violence/alcoholism from your husband?
39	**DFMILYSIZE**	**Can you make decisions on family size since using microfinance services and joining a women's union? Could you please respond to the following questions?**
40	WCHILDE	Do you participate in deciding when to have a child?
41	NCHILDE	Do you participate in deciding how many children to have?
42	FDCHILDE	Do you make the final decision to have children?
43	**HEALTHSE**	**Do you receive better health services since using microfinance services and joining a women's union? Could you please respond to the following questions?**
44	BTREATE	When you are ill do you receive better treatment?
45	RPHEALTHE	Do you have a regular plan to seek health services?
46	EHEALTHSE	Do you have easy access to medical facilities through local health services?
47	CHEALTHYE	Can you complain directly to health workers when you are not satisfied?
48	CONTRACE	Do you know about the use of contraception?
49	TCREPROHE	When you born the child do you get the take care of health from your husband?
50	**POLITICALE**	**Do you have political empowerment services since using microfinance services and joining a women's union? Could you please respond to the following questions?**
51	LOCALME	Do you participate in the meetings of the local (ward/commune) people's committee?
52	PARTYME	Do you participate in the meetings of the local level of the Communist party?
53	VOTE	Do you participate in the elections of the people's council as a voter?

(continued)

	Indicators	Description
54	CANDIDATE	Do you participate as a candidate in local body elections?
55	SELECTE	Have you ever been selected as a member of local government?
56	**GIRLVOICE**	**Do you have a voice for your girl children since using microfinance services and joining a women's union? Could you please respond to the following questions?**
57	SCHOOLGE	Can you make a decision about choosing a school for your girl child?
58	BCLOTHEGE	Can you make a decision about buying clothes for your girl child?
59	CAREERGE	Do you participate in decision making in career choices for your girl child?
61	WOMENDAYE	Do you celebrate International Women's Day with your girl child?
62	HSGIRLE	Do you take the advice of health services for your girl child?
63	**PROBLEMCE**	**Do you have any problems and challenges since using microfinance services and joining a women's union? Could you please respond to the following questions?**
64	STREESE	Do you have additional stress about saving and repayment of loan?
65	WORKEFFE	Is your routine/daily work affected?
66	CHILDNE	Do you have neglected children?
67	NONCOPE	Has non-co-operation from your family/husband increased?
68	SOLVEPINDE	Do you think you will be able to solve the problems independently?
69	NCONFIDENCE	Do you have confidence to work?

Source: Compiled by the authors

References

ADB. (2000). *Finance for the poor: Microfinance development strategy*. Asian Development Bank.

Aggarwal, R., Goodell, J. W., & Selleck, L. J. (2015). Lending to women in microfinance: Role of social trust. *International Business Review, 24*(1), 55–65. https://doi.org/10.1016/j.ibusrev.2014.05.008

Al-Shami, S. S. A., Razali, M. M., Majid, I., Rozelan, A., & Rashid, N. (2016). The effect of microfinance on women's empowerment: Evidence from Malaysia. *Asian Journal of Women's Studies, 22*(3). https://doi.org/10.1080/12259276.2016.1205378

Anh, N. K. (2016). Microfinance in Vietnam: Lessons learnt from transformation. *Vietnam Microfinance Working Group, 2016*.

Berge, L. I. O., Juniwaty, K. S., & Sekei, L. H. (2016). Gender composition and group dynamics: Evidence from a laboratory experiment with microfinance clients. *Journal of Economic Behavior & Organization, 131*(Part A), 1–20. https://doi.org/10.1016/j.jebo.2016.07.015

Bui-Thanh, L., Morales, L., & Andreosso-O'Callaghan, B. (2018a). Microfinance in South-East-Asia: The case of Vietnam over the period 2005–2015. In M. B. Zolin, J. Jaussaud, & B. A.-O. Callagha (Eds.), *Asian nations and multinationals: overcoming the limits to growth*. Palgrave Macmillan.

Bui-Thanh, L., Morales, L., & Andreosso-O'Callaghan, B. (2018b). Microfinance notes in the context of Vietnam. *Advances in Natural and Applied Sciences (ANAS), 12*(3), 21–30. https://doi.org/10.22587/anas.2018.12.3.2

Carol, N. (2015). Gender inequality and the empowerment of women in rural Viet Nam. *WIDER Working Paper Series* (066). http://hdl.handle.net/10419/126324

Coleman, B. E. (1999). The impact of group lending in Northeast Thailand. *Journal of Development Economics, 60*(1), 105–141. https://doi.org/10.1016/S0304-3878(99)00038-3

Cull, R., Navajas, S., Nishida, I., & Zeiler, R. (2015). A new index of the business environment for microfinance. *World Development, 70*, 357–388. https://doi.org/10.1016/j.worlddev.2014.11.023

Dang, T. T. H. (2019). Does horizontal inequality matter in Vietnam? *Social Indicators Research, 145*(3), 943–956. https://doi.org/10.1007/s11205-018-1896-1

Debnath, D., Rahman, M. S., Acharjee, D. C., Latif, W. U., & Wang, L. (2019). Empowering women through microcredit in Bangladesh: An empirical study. *International Journal of Financial Studies, 7*(3), 37. https://doi.org/10.3390/ijfs7030037

D'Espallier, B., Guérin, I., & Mersland, R. (2011). Women and repayment in microfinance: A global analysis. *World Development, 39*(5), 758–772. https://ideas.repec.org/a/eee/wdevel/v39y2011i5p758-772.html

Dineen, K., & Le, Q. V. (2015). The impact of an integrated microcredit program on the empowerment of women and gender equality in rural Vietnam. *Journal of Developing Areas, 49*(1), 23–38.

Duong, W. N. (2001). Gender equality and women's issues in Vietnam: The Vietnamese woman-warrior and poet. *Pacific Rim Law & Policy Journal, 10*(2), 136.

FAO. (2017). Land tenure and related Institutions | Gender and Land Rights Database | Food and Agriculture Organization of the United Nations. http://www.fao.org/gender-landrights-database/country-profiles/countries-list/land-tenure-and-related-institutions/en/?country_iso3=VNM

Garikipati, S. (2008). The impact of lending to women on household vulnerability and women's empowerment: Evidence from India. *World Development, 36*(12), 2620–2642. https://doi.org/10.1016/j.worlddev.2007.11.008

GSO. (2019). Information publication. http://www.gso.gov.vn/Default_en.aspx?tabid=491

Hao, Q. M. (2005). *Access to finance and poverty reduction: An application to rural Vietnam*. PhD thesis. The University of Birmingham.

Hashemi, S. M., Schuler, S. R., & Riley, A. P. (1996). Rural credit programs and women's empowerment in Bangladesh. *World Development, 24*(4), 635–653. https://doi.org/10.1016/0305-750X(95)00159-A

Hawk, J. L., Wynhoven, U., Mills, L., & Gula, L. (2011). Women's Empowerment Principles: Equality Means Business. *UN Women Headquarters*, 16.

Hollister, D. C., & Nguyen, H. T. (2012). Microfinance in Vietnam: Advantages and disadvantages from the perspectives of women participants. *Social Development Issues, 34*, 81–93.

Hue, G. T. T. (1999). Gender and gender issues in Vietnam. *Ha Noi, 1999*.

Huis, M., Lensink, R., Vu, N., & Hansen, N. (2019). Impacts of the gender and entrepreneurship together ahead (GET ahead) training on empowerment of female microfinance borrowers in Northern Vietnam. *World Development, 120*, 46–61. https://doi.org/10.1016/j.worlddev.2019.04.001

Ibrahim, S., & Alkire, S. (2007). Agency and empowerment: A proposal for internationally comparable indicators. *Oxford Development Studies, 35*(4), 379–403. https://doi.org/10.1080/13600810701701897

ILO. (2008). *Small change, big changes: Women and microfinance*. Paper presented at the International Women's Day 2008: Investing in Decent Work for Women: Not Just Right, but Smart, Geneva, Switzerland. https://www.ilo.org/gender/Events/WCMS_091581/lang%2D%2Den/index.htm

Imai, K. S., Gaiha, R., & Kang, W. (2011). Poverty, inequality and ethnic minorities in Vietnam. *International Review of Applied Economics, 25*(3), 249–282. https://doi.org/10.1080/02692171.2010.483471

Kabeer, N. (2005). Is microfinance a 'magic bullet' for women's empowerment? Analysis of findings from South Asia on JSTOR. *Economic and Political Weekly, 40*(44/45), 4709–4718. http://www.jstor.org/stable/4417357

Kablan, S. A., & Boussemart, J. P. (2015). Bootstrapping efficiency scores of microfinance institutions in West African economic and monetary union. *Economics Bulletin, 35*(4), 2220–2232.

Khavul, S. (2010). Microfinance: Creating opportunities for the poor? *Academy of Management Perspectives, 24*(3), 58–72.

Lam, N. T. (2017). Even it up: How to tackle inequality in Vietnam. *Oxfam Digital Repository*. http://hdl.handle.net/10546/620171

Lavoie, M. (2002). Women and microcredit in Vietnam. Localized poverty reduction in Vietnam. *Field report 1999–2000*. Anthropology Department, Laval University.

Le, Q. V., & Dao, H. T. (2013). Microcredit and women's empowerment in rural Vietnam. *The International Journal of Interdisciplinary Social and Community Studies, 7*(1), 61–76. http://www.i-scholar.in/index.php/IJISCSCG/article/view/61954

Li, X., Gan, C., & Hu, B. (2011). The impact of microcredit on women's empowerment: Evidence from China. *Journal of Chinese Economic and Business Studies, 9*(3), 239–261. https://doi.org/10.1080/14765284.2011.592352

Longwe, S. H. (2002). *Addressing rural gender issues: A framework for leadership and mobilisation*. Paper presented at the III World Congress for Rural Women, Madrid. https://sarpn.org/documents/d0000055/

Mayoux, L. (2005). *Women's empowerment through sustainable micro-finance: Rethinking 'best practice'*. Enterprise Development Impact Assessment Information Service.

Mazumder, M. S. U., & Lu, W. C. (2015). What impact does microfinance have on rural livelihood? A comparison of governmental and non-governmental microfinance programs in Bangladesh. *World Development, 68*, 336–354. https://doi.org/10.1016/j.worlddev.2014.12.002

Menon, N., Rodgers, Y., & Kennedy, A. R. (2017). Land reform and welfare in Vietnam: Why gender of the land-rights holder matters. *Journal of International Development, 29*(4), 454–472.

Morduch, J. (1999). The microfinance promise. *Journal of Economic Literature, XXXVII*, 1569–1614.

Nghiem, H. S., Coelli, T., & Rao, P. (2006). The efficiency of microfinance in Vietnam: Evidence from NGO schemes in the north and the central regions. *International Journal of Environmental, Cultural, Economic and Social Sustainability, 2*(5), 8.

Nghiem, H. S., Coelli, T., & Rao, P. (2007). *The welfare effects of microfinance in Vietnam: Empirical results from a quasi-experiment survey*. Paper presented at the Annual Conference of the Australian Agriculture and Resources Economics Society, Queenstown, New Zealand.

Nguyen, H., & Hollister, C. D. (2012). Microfinance in Vietnam: Advantages and disadvantages from the perspectives of women participants. *Social Development Issues, 3*, 81–93.

Nguyen-Kim, A. (2014). *Microfinance in Vietnam: Reaility and policy recommendations*. Hanoi.

Pedersen, H. V. (2006). Programme for improving market participation of the poor in Ha Tinh and Tra Vinh Provinces. *Duration 2006–2012*. https://www.ifad.org/en/web/operations/project/id/1100001374

Pitt, M. M., & Khandker, S. R. (1998). The impact of group-based credit programs on poor households in Bangladesh: Does the gender of participants matter. *Journal of Political Economy, 105*(5), 958–996.

Pitt, M. M., Khandker, S. R., & Cartwright, J. (2003). Does micro-credit empower women: Evidence from Bangladesh. *Policy research working paper; No. 2998, 1*. http://hdl.handle.net/10986/19162

Pitt, M. M., Khandker, S. R., & Cartwright, J. (2006). Empowering women with micro finance: Evidence from Bangladesh. *Economic Development and Cultural Change, 54*(4), 791–831. https://doi.org/10.1086/503580

Rahman, M. M., Khanam, R., & Nghiem, S. H. (2017). The effects of microfinance on women's empowerment: New evidence from Bangladesh. *International Journal of Social Economics, 44*(12), 1745–1757. https://doi.org/10.1108/IJSE-02-2016-0070

Rath, T. (2013). Project for adaption to climate change in the mekong delta in Ben Tre and Tra Vinh Provinces, Viet Nam. *Duration 2013–2020.* https://www.ifad.org/en/web/operations/project/id/1100001664/country/viet_nam

Schuler, S. R., Anh, H. T., Ha, V. S., Minh, T. H., Mai, B. T. T., & Thien, P. V. (2006). Constructions of gender in Vietnam: In pursuit of the 'three criteria'. *Culture, Health & Sexuality, 8*(5), 383–394. https://doi.org/10.1080/13691050600858924

Schuler, S. R., Hashemi, S. M., Riley, A. P., & Akhter, S. (1996). Credit programs, patriarchy and men's violence against women in rural Bangladesh. *Social Science & Medicine, 43*(12), 1729–1742. https://doi.org/10.1016/S0277-9536(96)00068-8

Suesse, M., & Wolf, N. (2020). Rural transformation, inequality, and the origins of microfinance. *Journal of Development Economics, 143*, 102429. https://doi.org/10.1016/j.jdeveco.2019.102429

Swain, RB. (2015). Can microfinance empower women?: Self-help groups in India. *Luxembourg: Appui au Développement Autonome (ADA), 37*(May), 61–82. http://urn.kb.se/resolve?urn=urn:nbn:se:sh:diva-27238

Tan, T. M. (2014). *Gender equity and development.* Training Center for Elected Representatives. http://tailieu.ttbd.gov.vn:8080/index.php/tai-lieu/tai-lieu-bien-tap/item/93-binh-dang-gioi-trong-phat-trien

Vietnam. (2011). *Decision No. 2195/QD-TTg dated 06/12/2011 the Prime Minister approved the "Project construction and development of the microfinance system in Vietnam 2020".*

Vo, K. T., & Tran, V. H. (2013). The microfinance in countries around the world and the experienced lessions for poverty reduction in Vitenam (Vietnamese). [Tài chính vi mô tại một số nước trên thế giới và bài học kinh nghiệm nhằm hạn chế đói nghèo tại Việt Nam]. *Development and Intergration, 9*(19), 16–21.

Vu, H. S., Schuler, S., Hoang, T. A., & Quach, T. (2014). Divorce in the context of domestic violence against women in Vietnam. *Culture, Health & Sexuality, 16*(6), 634–647. https://doi.org/10.1080/13691058.2014.896948

Vu, N. T. H., Velzen, R. V., Lensink, R., & Bulte, E. (2015). *The impact of gender and business training for female microfinance clients in Vietnam.* International Initiative for Impact Evaluation, 3ie. https://doi.org/10.23846/ow31132

Waibel, G., & Glück, S. (2013). More than 13 million: Mass mobilisation and gender politics in the Vietnam Women's Union. *Journal Gender & Development, 21*(2). https://doi.org/10.1080/13552074.2013.80

Warnecke, T. (2015). "Greening" gender equity: Microfinance and the sustainable development agenda. *Journal of Economic Issues, 49*(2), 553–562. https://doi.org/10.1080/00213624.2015.1042803

WB. (2012). Gender equality and development. *World Development Report 2012.* http://hdl.handle.net/10986/4391

WB. (2018). Vietnam: GDP growth (annual %) | Data. https://data.worldbank.org/indicator/NY.GDP.MKTP.KD.ZG?locations=VN

WB. (2019). MapVietnam. http://www5.worldbank.org/mapvietnam/

WU. (2019). Introduction of Vietnam Women's Union. http://hoilhpn.org.vn/?Lang=EN

Environmental Management Accounting in European Countries and Japan: A Literature Survey

Bruno Amann , Jacques Jaussaud , Shuji Mizoguchi, and Hiroyuki Nakamura

Abstract A lot of research has been carried out in Japan as in Western countries on Environmental Management and on the question of corporate environmental data collection and reporting through effective Information Systems. However, most research by Japanese scholars has been published only in Japanese, and thus is not available to most Western researchers. The aim of this research paper is to carry out a survey of the Japanese literature on this topic, including references in Japanese, so as to make them more widely available.

The process of developing environmental and social reporting on the one hand, and environmental management accounting on the other hand, under the aegis of international organizations, including the United Nations, and replicated by the European Union and by the authorities in Japan, will be underlined. The differentiation will then be made clearer between the close and related concepts of environmental accounting, environmental management accounting, environmental and social reporting, and integrated reporting etc. Specific indicators that have been developed to assess the impact of firms' activity on the environment, such as the eco-efficiency approach, will be presented and discussed. Finally, different cases in Europe and in Japan of innovative firms in the field of environmental management accounting and integrated reporting will also be presented.

B. Amann
University of Toulouse 3 Paul Sabatier, Toulouse, France

Tianjin Foreign Studies University, Tianjin, China
e-mail: courriel@bruno-amann.fr

J. Jaussaud (✉)
E2S-UPPA, TREE UMR CNRS 6031, University of Pau, Pau, France
e-mail: jacques.jaussaud@univ-pau.fr

S. Mizoguchi · H. Nakamura
Yokohama National University, Yokohama, Japan
e-mail: shujim@ynu.ac.jp; nakamura-hiroyuki-tf@ynu.ac.jp

B. Andreosso-O'Callaghan et al. (eds.), *Sustainable Development in Asia*, Contributions to Economics, https://doi.org/10.1007/978-3-030-94679-1_9

Keywords Corporate governance · Corporate Social Responsibility (CSR) · Eco-efficiency approach · Environmental management · Environmental accounting · Environmental management accounting · Environmental and social reporting · Integrated reporting · Japan

1 Introduction

Accounting has a very long history and has traditionally served as an essential information system for companies. Accounting systems provide useful information to various company stakeholders who are interested in the real situation of their companies. Stockholders want mainly to know the operating performance and financial condition of the company. They need this information to be checked by entities from outside the firm through audits. On the other hand, managers have to evaluate staff members' performance and to carry out decision making within the company. Based on these information needs, accounting is classified as financial accounting on the one hand, and management accounting on the other hand.

Management accounting is designed as an accounting information system for internal users in the company. It provides broad information and doesn't have to comply with standardized accounting rules. Consequently, management accounting includes not only financial but also non-financial information. Recently, management accounting has started providing information about environmental matters also.

In this chapter, we will carry out a literature survey on the topic of Environmental Management Accounting in European countries and Japan. In particular we take into account references in the Japanese language, in order to make them more available to researchers outside Japan.

The chapter is structured as follows. Section 2 underlines the global trend supported by international organizations, particularly the United Nations, and replicated by the European Union and by authorities in Japan, leading to the development of environmental and social reporting on the one hand, and environmental management accounting on the other hand, and eventually to integrated reporting. Section 3 will make clearer the distinction between the close and related concepts of environmental accounting, environmental management accounting, environmental and social reporting and integrated reporting etc. Finally, Sect. 4 will present different cases in Europe and in Japan of innovative firms in the field of environmental management accounting and integrated reporting.

2 The Emergence of Environmental Management Accounting (EMA)

Environmental management has been developed globally, under the aegis of the United Nations. In 1987, the United Nations (UN) World Commission on Environment and Development published a report entitled "Our Common Future," also known as "the Brundtland Report." This report innovatively deployed the expression "sustainable development", which has been more widely deployed since then. Sustainable development was defined in the Brundtland report as "development that meets the needs of present generations without compromising the ability of future generations to do the same." Future generations are thus regarded as major stakeholders in current economic activity and decision making. Firms were urged in the report to reduce pollution, invest in environmental protection equipment, and to provide compensation for residual pollution etc.

Thus, measuring polluting emissions, and evaluating environment protection investments and costs became crucial issues, which is the aim of environmental accounting, and of environmental management accounting which was designed to support managers' decision making. In 1992, the United Nations Conference in Rio de Janeiro on the environment, the so-called Earth Summit, recognized environmental accounting as a major instrument for developing a consistent policy of sustainability (Baldarelli et al., 2017). At the same summit, the Convention on Biological Diversity was ratified. Biological diversity and climate change became major (related) concerns, which led to the Kyoto Protocol in 1997, aimed at curbing CO_2 and other greenhouse gases emissions contributing to ongoing global warming. The strong involvement of the United Nations in promoting sustainable development has been replicated by the government in Japan and the authorities in the European Union, the two areas we focus upon in this chapter, leading to the gradual development of environmental management and environmental accounting.

In Japan, the following highlights in respect of environment related accounting are noteworthy:

- in 1999 the Ministry of International Trade and Industry (MITI) entrusted the responsibility of carrying out environmental management accounting research to The Japan Environmental Management Association for Industry (JEMAI);
- in 2000 the Environment agency published *Environmental Accounting Guidelines* for the first time;
- in 2002 the Ministry of Economy, Trade and Industry (METI) published the *Environmental Management Accounting Techniques Workbook*;
- in 2018 the Ministry of the environment of Japan (MOEJ) updated *Environmental Accounting Guidelines* as *Environmental Reporting Guidelines*.

Clearly, public institutions are actively promoting the introduction of environmental-related accounting in Japan and METI and MOEJ have played important roles in this. METI's *Environmental Management Accounting Techniques Workbook* contains five important environmental management accounting techniques. These techniques are Environment-conscious capital investment management, Environment-conscious cost management systems, Material Flow Cost Accounting (MFCA), Life Cycle Costing and Environment-conscious performance evaluation systems. The *Environmental Management Accounting Techniques Workbook* was prepared for internal use by each company for planning and control. On the other hand, the *Environmental Accounting Guidelines* was prepared for external use by the various stakeholders, as a part of a disclosure process.

The same trend occurred in Europe. The European Commission launched in 1994 its strategy for "green accounting". Since then, it has supported Eurostat and Member States in developing environmental accounting methods, in close liaison with the United Nations and the Organisation for Economic Co-operation and Development (OECD), regarding physical flow accounts of emissions, particularly but not only of greenhouse gases, and material consumption on the one hand, and on the other hand monetary accounts of costs and expenses relating to the environment (Baldarelli et al., 2017). In 2003, the European Union launched the CSR Europe campaign, which strongly promoted Corporate Social Responsibility throughout the continent, and supported Social and Environmental Accounting Research.

Environmental accounting and environmental management accounting are strongly related and Ogawa (2013) in his study highlighted the strength of this relationship. In his view, the development of environmental accounting is an explanatory variable and the emergence of environmental management accounting is the explained variable. Several phenomena (environmental problems, climate change) and environmental-related events (the 1992 Earth Summit, the issuance of ISO 14001 and the publication of environmental accounting guidelines) have influenced the development of environmental accounting, the explanatory variable. In addition, there are some moderators (restriction by accounting techniques, positive research by the METI and the International standard of the MFCA) which promote or restrict the emergence and development of environmental management accounting.

As Figure 1 suggests, environmental accounting as a part of environmental management evolved into environmental management accounting. As a consequence, there are currently mainly two types of accounting in respect of the environment, i.e., environmental accounting and environmental management accounting.

3 Environmental Accounting, Environmental Management Accounting (EMA) and Integrated Reporting

Environmental accounting and Environmental management accounting aim to measure the environmental damage resulting from the working of businesses with a view to it being reduced as much as possible, and to measure the investment and other costs directed at reducing the damage on the one hand, and on the other hand

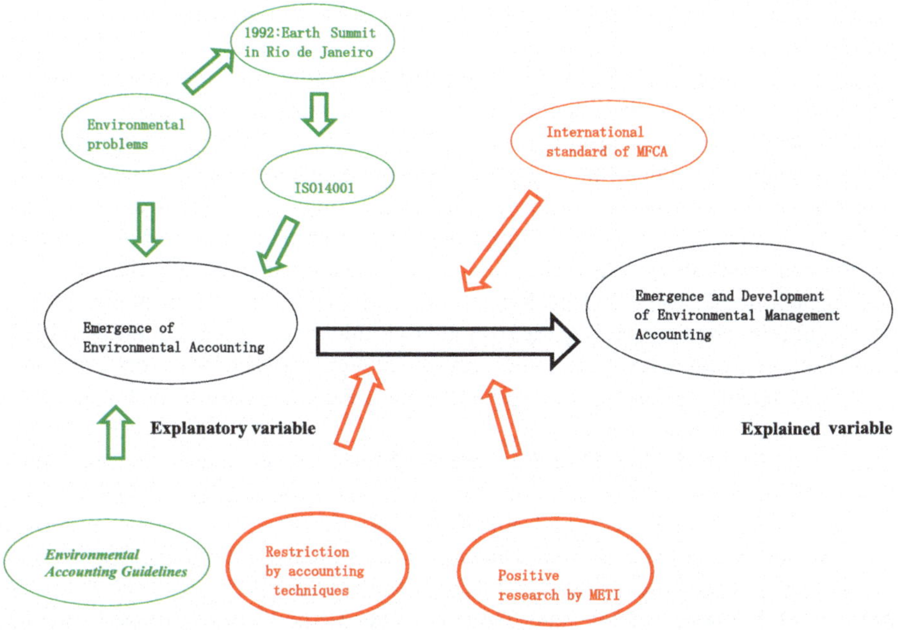

Fig. 1 Analytical model of Environmental Management Accounting evolution. (Source: Ogawa, 2013—小川 哲彦, 2013)

measuring the benefits and potential returns derived from such investments and other related expenditure. A number of non-financial quantitative measurement indicators have been suggested for deployment by the different guidelines mentioned above, that are widely accepted, such as cubic metres for the release of several polluting materials and tons for CO_2 and other emissions etc. Such indicators are for instance provided by Toyo Keizai in its CSR Directory of firms published every year in Japanese (Keizai, 2015 in the reference list). A number of other synthetic indicators, financial and non-financial ones, have been provided also, which, although also widely accepted, require some care when referred to in order to avoid any misunderstanding. Let us consider for instance the question of eco-efficiency measurement, a short word for ecological efficiency measurement.

Eco-efficiency measurement has been adopted by a growing number of companies, in Japan (Burritt & Saka, 2006) and elsewhere (Baldarelli et al., 2017). In general terms, efficiency measures the ratio between the output obtained from a process and the inputs that this process require. Output and inputs may be measured in physical or in monetary terms. Thus, ecological efficiency is measured as the ratio between an output and the assessment of its environmental impact: eco-efficiency = output/estimated environmental impact. As emphasized by Burritt and Saka (2006), two kinds of eco-efficiency are often calculated by firms: the first one focusing on production (the output is thus a production amount); the second one focusing on function i.e., considering the full life cycle of a product (for instance, calculating the ecological function efficiency of a car in transporting a person over a specific distance).

Such calculations are useful in accurately assessing the improvement in the reduction of the environmental impact of a firm's production process (eco-efficiency focused on production) or of a firm's products design and production (eco-efficiency focused on function). They are however subject to continual review, as a firm may improve eco-efficiency over time, while it increases its overall ecological impact, by increasing for instance its production and sales. In the current environment, with the world facing dramatic climate change and biodiversity collapse, which most people and institutions are aware of, firms should improve their ecological efficiency and reduce the overall environmental impact of their activities. Thus, both eco-efficiency type indicators and overall impact indicators are commonly calculated, and are also promoted by the guidelines (Burritt & Saka, 2006; Baldarelli et al., 2017).

In Japan, Material Flow Cost Accounting (MFCA) is nowadays the most well-known EMA tool. MFCA is a method that helps organizations identify the environmental consequences and financial costs derived from under-optimized flows of materials and energy used. Developed in Germany in the 1980s, the method has been enthusiastically adopted in Japan, with the strong support of the Japanese Ministry of Economy, Trade and Industry. The method has developed into an international standard, ISO 14051, released in 2011, which aims at improving material and energy efficiency. Material Flow Cost Accounting is a powerful cost reduction tool through material loss reduction.

As already pointed out, management accounting is an internal accounting information system. It provides information to help managers in their performance evaluation and decision making. Companies, however, have been encouraged to increase their reporting on environmental issues and environmental management since the beginning of the present century. This relates to the issue of *accountability*. For instance, the EU Commission's recommendation of 30 May 2001/453/EC emphasized the need for companies to provide environmental information and reports in addition to financial statements. In line with the Brundtland report of 1987 however, the need for a more integrated approach to reporting has been promoted, which would combine economic, financial, social, and environmental information in a so-called sustainability report. This led for instance to the formation of the Global Reporting Initiative (GRI), in 1997, a private international standards organization involving environmental Non-Governmental Organizations (NGO) and large firms, with the support of the United Nations Environment Programme—UNEP.

Another initiative for global integrated reporting was launched in 2010 by the Prince of Wales, with the support of a number of investors, NGOs, large businesses from a number of countries, the International Federation of Accountants (IFAC), the Global Reporting Initiative organization and the United Nations, in order to set up the International Integrated Reporting Committee (IIRC). Renamed as the International Integrated Reporting Council (IIRC) in November 2011, it aimed at providing a globally accepted Integrated Reporting framework that would help understand the creation of value process of the reporting firm through an integrated, standardized and comparable reporting format. Reporting within such a framework would provide financial and non-financial information in terms of strategy, operations, financial and human capital management practices, and on environmental, social and governance performance.

In 2018, 414 Japanese companies published integrated reports. The number of companies publishing integrated reports is increasing continuously, in Japan as in Europe and elsewhere. Integrated Reporting is mainly guided by International Integrated Reporting Council (IIRC). Several Japanese professors carry out research in respect of integrated reporting. Uchiyama (2016) emphasized how value creation was related to human capital in the integrated reporting framework. Four company cases were analyzed by him from this perspective, which will be outlined in following section. In addition, Y. Ito (2014, 2016) discussed the contribution of integrated reporting to management accounting. He suggested that the Balanced Scorecard (BSC) can be used as the basis of integrated reporting preparation by companies. In the BSC, both the vision and mission are necessarily made clear and this is the same in integrated reporting. The BSC and integrated reporting have the same starting point for their preparation. They share the same point of view and they both consist of financial and non-financial information. This is a very beneficial revelation. It shows that the contribution area of management accounting is expanding further and the BSC can become the model for integrated reporting.

4 Environmental Management Accounting (EMA) Cases in Europe and Japan

There are two main EMA research areas. One is integrated reporting and the other one is Material Flow Cost Accounting, MFCA.

In respect of Europe, Baldarelli et al. (2017) developed a case study of two Italian firms (not to mention the case of Casio computers from Japan). The first Italian case is the giant firm ENI, a well-known listed and globalized company in the field of energy, which since 2011 has started to prepare integrated reports. ENI was one of the companies participating in the pilot program of the International Integrated Reporting Council (IIRC). The second one is the SGR group, an unlisted holding company based in Rimini (Italy), with all its affiliated firms being family owned, and which is in the energy sector also. The SGR group case study focuses on the preparation of their sustainability reports. As details of the cases are provided by Baldarelli et al. (2017), in their book (in English), we do not develop the cases here and strongly advise interested readers to refer to the book itself. Because of limited space, we prefer to focus on Japanese sources, not easily available to most of Western researchers.

In respect of Japan, Uchiyama (2016) analyzed 4 cases of Japanese companies from the perspective of the three essential criteria based on the value creation process as listed by the IIRC (International Integrated Reporting Council): (1) mission, vision, strategy; (2) input and output of human capital; (3) results, performance and outcome. These four companies, Asahi Group Holdings, Itochu Corporation, MS&AD Insurance Group Holdings Inc. and Omron Corporation, received an award from The World Intellectual Capital/Assets Initiative of Japan because of their endeavors.

Asahi Group Holdings Inc. manages 244 companies, which operate mainly in the beverages-related industry. Asahi Breweries Ltd., a well-known Japanese brewer, is one of these subsidiaries. According to the 2015 integrated report of Asahi Group Holdings, they provided details on the above three criteria and showed the relationships between them in the exhibit of their value creation process. The top management of the company highlighted their invisible assets and acknowledged the importance of the management of intangibles in relation to strategy and operating performance.

Itochu Corporation is one of the famous *Sôgô Shôsha* (総合商社), or General Trading Companies of Japan (Jaussaud, 1999). According to its Home Page, it is involved in domestic trading, import/export, overseas trading of various products such as textiles, machinery, metals, minerals, energy, chemicals, food, general products, information and communications technology, finance, as well as business investment in Japan and overseas. According to its 2015 integrated report, Itochu emphasizes the development and involvement of human capital and recognizes the importance of having a stable corporate mission and human capital.

As stated in its Home Page, MS&AD Insurance Group Holdings, Inc. is the insurance holding company of the new Group formed in April 2010 through the merger of Aioi Insurance Co., Ltd., Nissay Dowa General Insurance Co., Ltd., and Mitsui Sumitomo Insurance Group. The integrated report of MS&AD includes all relevant information about the above-mentioned three important criteria. Linkage of these items is shown as an exhibit of MS&AD's value creation story. MS&AD measures human capital in relation to strategy and operational performance and promotes diversity through this value creation story in its integrated reporting.

Omron Corporation markets various innovative products all over the world. As a global leader in the field of automation, Omron's businesses cover a broad spectrum, ranging from industrial automation and electronic components to social systems including automated ticket gates, solar power conditioners, and healthcare equipment and devices. Currently, Omron markets products and services in around 120 countries and regions. In its integrated 2015 report, Omron declared its mission as being to improve people's lives and to contribute to a better society. Omron recognizes that women managers are not significantly represented in Japanese companies and it has computed and displayed the ratio of women in managerial roles in Japan in the non-financial highlights of its integrated report. In addition, various indices and key performance indicators (KPI) were shown based on Omron's business systems. For example, Omron's Down-Top ROIC tree approach is a unique management system, which is highly praised in Japan.

In addition to integrated reporting cases, a growing number of MFCA cases have been studied in Japan. Many companies have some dedicated information systems in this field. As is well known, cost accounting requires an information system which provides financial and non-financial quantitative information. Both cost accounting and MFCA are material loss reduction oriented. Prof. Kokubu and Prof. Nakajima are distinguished Japanese researchers in MFCA. In Kokubu (2004), four MFCA cases were studied: Nitto Denko, Tanabe Seiyaku, C.I. Takiron and Canon.

According to its Home Page, Nitto group has created various products based on 4 core technologies. It has expanded into diversified business domains by applying advanced technologies. These core technologies are adhesion technology, polymer function control technology, polymer analysis and evaluation technology, and coating technology. Nitto first introduced a typical MFCA system in Japan in 2000. MFCA, according to the case study, provides many benefits to Nitto, such as:

- as a result of loss reduction activities, material losses were reduced by 7% in the cutting center;
- MFCA reports help top management in decision making in the acquisition of new equipment;
- not only is specific process improvement made possible, but also the improvement of the manufacturing process as a whole.

Tanabe Seiyaku Co., Ltd. (Mitsubishi Tanabe Pharma Corporation from 2007) is a pharmaceutical manufacturer. It introduced MFCA in conjunction with an Enterprise Resource Planning (ERP) system in 2002. The ERP system was SAP R/3. This is a rare case because most Japanese companies tended to utilize in-house-designed MFCA information systems. Generally, MFCA data collection and processing are carried out by stand-alone PCs in Japan. By the adoption of MFCA, Tanabe Seiyaku realized that the waste disposal costs in one factory's synthetic process operations amounted to about one million Euro. In order to reduce this cost, equipment investment was decided upon. As a result, Tanabe Seiyaku achieved both environmental load reduction and increased profitability.

According to its Home Page, C.I. Takiron pursues business in four major fields: Construction Materials, Environmental Materials, High Functional Materials, and Specialty Films. Its mission is to "Create a people- and earth-friendly future through plastics technology". C.I. Takiron tries to analyze the financial implications of recycling materials based on an MFCA model. MFCA was introduced in 2001 in the manufacturing process of synthetic resin sheet. In the midst of this process, defective material is recycled and mixed again with zero emissions. For information gathering, a cross functional team was organized involving both headquarter staff and factory staff. This team collected and recorded quantifiable data manually because this data was kept in many separate departments of the factory. As a result, Takiron could consider the economic implications of undertaking a recycling process.

The well-known Japanese Canon Group promotes environmental activities as "Action for Green", as stated in its homepage. Canon consists of four business units (BUs). They are the Office BU, the Imaging System BU, the Medical System BU and the Industry and Others Businesses BU. In 2000, a project MFCA team in a lens manufacturing line was assembled involving many related departments. Most members came from the environmental management department. Project team members consisted not only of environmental department staff but also manufacturing, production engineering and production management staff etc. Data were inputted daily to Excel sheets from each process. The Excel sheets recorded lens manufacturing transactions, such as processing time, processing costs, spoilage, volume of shavings etc. Glass grinding was the most significant aspect of the camera lens manufacturing from the view point of MFCA. About 70 percent of material loss costs occurred in this glass grinding process. As a result, it was clear that the shape of the glass had to be reviewed with the supplier to achieve lower shavings. It was a new idea arising from the use of MFCA in the supply chain.

5 Conclusion

Accounting has traditionally provided important information in respect of businesses both internally and externally. It is an essential business information system for the various stakeholders, whatever its country location. Nowadays, accounting has expanded its scope to environment protection. In relation to this, management accounting also has enlarged its scope to environment protection. A lot of meaningful research has been carried out in Japan, as in Western countries, on this process. With this research contribution, we aim to make references in the Japanese language regarding this field more available to Western researchers.

As explained in this chapter, Japanese environment accounting has evolved to environmental management accounting in tandem with governmental support, as it did in Europe, North America, and elsewhere (South-Africa particularly, for instance). The strong encouragement and support by the United Nations, and related initiatives supported by the United Nations, should be underlined once more, including the GRI and IRRC mentioned earlier, for establishing a global Integrated Reporting format.

References

Baldarelli, M.-G., Del Baldo, M., & Nesheva-Kiosseva, N. (2017). *Environmental accounting and reporting, theory and practice*. Springer.

Burritt, R. L., & Saka, C. (2006). Environmental management accounting applications and eco-efficiency: Case studies from Japan. *Journal of Cleaner Production, 14*.

Ito, K. (2014). *The strategy formulation and execution using the balanced scorecard*. Dobunkan Shuppan (in Japanese). [伊藤和憲『BSCによる戦略の実行と策定-事例で見るインタンジブルズのマネジメントと統合報告への管理会計の貢献-』同文舘出版]

Ito, Y. (2016). The effects of integrated reporting on the research and practice of management accounting. *The Waseda Commercial Review*, (446), pp. 329–351 (in Japanese). [伊藤嘉博 (2016),「統合報告が管理会計研究・実践に及ぼす影響」『早稲田商学』第446号]

Jaussaud, J. (1999). Group relationships and business strategy of Japanese trading companies in the Chinese market. In S. Sam Dzever & J. Jaussaud (Eds.), *China & India, economic performance and business strategies of firms in the mid 90s*. Macmillan.

Keizai, T. (2015). *CSR Kigyô Sôkan* (for "CSR Directory of firms", in Japanese). Tôyô Keizai.

Kokubu, K. (2004). *Introduction to environmental management accounting, Japan environmental management association for industry* (in Japanese). [國部 克彦編著(2004)『環境管理会計入門:理論と実践』産業環境管理協会]

Ministry of Economy, Trade and Industry. (2002). *Environmental management accounting workbook*. Ministry of Economy, Trade and Industry (in Japanese). [経済産業省(2002)『環境管理会計手法ワークブック』経済産業省]

Ogawa, T. (2013). Expansion of information needs and revolution of management accounting in Environmental Accounting Area. In H. Nakamura & M. Takahashi (Eds.), *The revolution of management accounting: The advancement of theory and practice through information needs expansion*. Chuo- Keizai- Sha (in Japanese). [小川 哲彦(2013)「環境会計分野における管理会計の変容」(中村博之・高橋 賢『管理会計の変革』中央経済社、pp 99–112)].

Uchiyama, T. (2016). Measurement on human assets and value creation: The case of integrated reporting. *Economic Journal of Chiba University, 31*, pp. 51–75 (in Japanese). [内山哲彦(2016)「人的資産にかかわる測定と価値創造—統合報告を例に—」『千葉大学経済研究』第31巻第1号]

Funding and Management Control of Hospitals: A France–Japan Comparison

Emmanuelle Cargnello-Charles, Isabelle Franchisteguy-Couloume, Jacques Jaussaud, Julien Martine, and Hiroyuki Nakamura

Abstract The objective of this chapter is to compare the hospital funding and management control systems in two countries with ageing populations, France and Japan. Due to significant financial constraints in the context of strong growth in health needs, powerful mechanisms for disseminating funding and hospital management practices between countries are being put in place, which neo-institutional theory helps to analyse.

In this chapter, we present the funding systems of hospitals in the two countries, both of which are being forced to constrain their health expenditure, each within its own institutional framework. We then analyse, on the basis of in-depth interviews in both countries, the impact of the characteristics of their hospital funding systems on the development of hospital management control. The consequences of the current Covid-19 health crisis are also considered.

Keywords Management control · Hospital management · Activity-based funding · France · Japan

---

E. Cargnello-Charles · I. Franchisteguy-Couloume
Department of Management Sciences, E2S UPPA, Laboratoire de Recherche en Gestion (LiREM), Université de Pau et des Pays de l'Adour (UPPA), Pau, France
e-mail: emmanuelle.cargnello@univ-pau.fr; isabelle.franchisteguy@iutbayonne.univ-pau.fr

J. Jaussaud (✉)
Department of Management Sciences, E2S UPPA, Transitions Energétiques et Environnementales (TREE, UMR CNRS 6031), Université de Pau et des Pays de l'Adour (UPPA), Pau, France
e-mail: jacques.jaussaud@univ-pau.fr

J. Martine
Department of Japanese Language and Civilization, Centre de Recherche sur les Civilisations Orientales (CRCAO), University of Paris, Paris, France
e-mail: julien.martine@univ-paris-diderot.fr

H. Nakamura
Department of Management Accounting, Yokohama National University, Yokohama, Japan
e-mail: nakamura-hiroyuki-tf@ynu.ac.jp

B. Andreosso-O'Callaghan et al. (eds.), *Sustainable Development in Asia*, Contributions to Economics, https://doi.org/10.1007/978-3-030-94679-1_10

1 Introduction

Developed countries with ageing populations face serious problems in financing healthcare expenditure. The same underlying factors in France and Japan produce the same effects, beyond the specificities of each country and each healthcare system. The size of governmental budgetary deficits and the potential consequences in terms of the sustainability of healthcare financing systems have led to the development of powerful mimetic mechanisms between countries. Exchanges of experience and innovative solutions are being sought, as shown, for example, by the spread of hospital activity-based funding, basing hospital revenues on the volume of their actual medical activities. Developed in the United States, this method has been adopted by a growing number of countries, including France and Japan, which will be of particular interest to us in this chapter. The role and intensity of these mimetic mechanisms lead us to refer to the framework of neo-institutional theory (Di Maggio & Powell, 1991; North, 1994).

Differences from one country to another remain strong, however, in terms of population health, healthcare financing and hospital management. These are frequently highlighted in comparisons between European countries, France and the United Kingdom in particular, but also more widely between different OECD countries (OECD, 2018). In this chapter, we wish to highlight both the impact of mimetic mechanisms in terms of hospital funding and management and, conversely, the weight of the national institutional context. To this end, we have chosen France and Japan, both of which are confronted with health financing problems due to population age maturity, but which are characterized by contrasting institutional contexts. Our research question can be formulated as follows: To what extent do hospital (including clinic) financing methods in France and Japan affect their management control practices?

The chapter is structured as follows. The first part specifies the mechanisms of convergence or hybridization in the efforts to disseminate more efficient hospital management methods at the international level. We then compare the respective methods of hospital funding in Japan and France, both inspired by the American system, but each retaining strong national specificities. The second part, based on in-depth interviews in both countries, investigates and compares the approaches and management control methods that hospitals in France and Japan are implementing as a result.

2 Hospital Funding, Between Convergence and National Specificities

Neo-institutional theory has been particularly interested in the phenomenon of mimetism, according to which, faced with the same pressures in a given environment, organizations adopt the same types of solutions (Di Maggio & Powell, 1991).

As we have seen, such mechanisms are at work in the healthcare sector, with the same types of solutions being adopted from one country to another in the face of the same financial constraints and the same growth in needs. We will first recall (1.1) how institutional theory analyses the phenomenon of mimetism, then underline (1.2) how the French and Japanese healthcare systems are both under severe financial constraints, and finally, analyse (1.3) the methods of funding hospital structures in the two countries.

2.1 *Economic Constraints, Institutional Pressures and Healthcare Systems*

Institutional theory (Di Maggio & Powell, 1991) identifies two types of isomorphisms that leads organizations to adopt similar solutions in terms of strategy, organization, managerial practices and even management tools. These are competitive isomorphism and institutional isomorphism.

Competitive isomorphism leads firms to choose and implement solutions when they prove to be more efficient than any others, as with the massive adoption of just-in-time production principles by most industrial firms in developed countries in the 1980s and 1990s (Jaussaud & Kageyama, 1991). Institutional isomorphism results from the pressure by institutions on organizations, the concept of institutions being defined by North (1994, p. 360) as the constraints established by human beings that structure their interactions. Some of these constraints are formal, for instance legal or contractual, while others are informal, such as conventions, in particular.

Institutional isomorphism results from powerful mechanisms that Di Maggio and Powell (1991) identify and characterize as follows:

- coercive isomorphism, resulting from the constraint imposed by a powerful economic agent or authority, a State for example, or in our case in France a Regional Health Agency concerned with regulating healthcare supply at regional level
- normative isomorphism, resulting from the dissemination of professional standards, as in the case in healthcare, both for medical personnel and for managers of healthcare systems
- mimetism, leading organizations, in adverse and uncertain contexts, to imitate the decisions and solutions adopted by their counterparts when they appear to work

In the healthcare sector, for ageing population countries, the rapid growth in demand for healthcare in a context of slow economic growth is putting strong pressure on funding systems, whether they are primarily public, as in France or Japan, or more broadly private, as in the United States. Resource constraints undoubtedly fuel both competitive isomorphism and, in the case of public health systems faced with major collective challenges, institutional isomorphism. Governments are critically involved in the management and restructuring of healthcare systems. The solutions adopted in one country, when they appear to be efficient, are taken up by others, such as the activity-based funding system that we mentioned in the introduction. This is also the case, for example, when setting up long-term healthcare systems for the care of dependent or chronically ill elderly people, with Japan followed by South Korea drawing heavily on the German experience (Campbell et al., 2009). As a result, we can expect a strong convergence of practices in the organization and management of healthcare systems, across borders.

The neo-institutional theory, however, envisages that an organization may be subject to pressure from institutions at different levels, pressures that may be partially contradictory, which it will have to find ways to reconcile. This is the case, for example, with subsidiaries of multinationals that, in a given country, are subject to the pressure of the local institutional environment, on the one hand (the country's laws and regulations, business practices, etc.), and those imposed by the framework that the multinational has set up to manage its affairs, on the other (Kostova & Roth, 2002).

Such institutional dualism will undoubtedly be at work in the management of healthcare systems, particularly hospital management systems. On the one hand, there are the strong constraints imposed by the similarities resulting from ageing populations and the international dissemination of efficient solutions, favoured by national governments and the various healthcare funding organizations. On the other hand, however, the weight of national institutions remains strong, particularly in fields such as healthcare. It can therefore be expected that the solutions transferred will be frequently adapted to take into account the specificities of the local context. In other words, a phenomenon of hybridization will be at work, echoing that identified in the case of the transfer of practices within multinational firms (Kostova & Roth, 2002). This phenomenon of adaptation to the local environment is particularly strong in public management (Politt & Bouckaert, 2006).

In the case of hospital management, we wish to ascertain how these partially contradictory forces, some of which lead to similarities and others to diversity, are reflected in the choices relating to the organization and financing of healthcare services. We intend to do this by comparing the condition and practices of hospital management in two countries with significantly different institutional contexts, France and Japan. We then aim to see how these forces translate into hospital management practices, particularly in terms of cost control.

The funding of hospital structures is strongly determined by the constraints that weigh heavily on the healthcare systems of the countries under consideration. First, let us highlight the strong convergence of health spending between France and Japan, and the main characteristics of their respective healthcare systems. These contextual elements are largely the result of the high degree of economic, demographic and social maturity of the two countries.

2.2 France and Japan: Healthcare Systems Under Severe Financial Constraints

Countries' healthcare expenditures are frequently assessed as a percentage of GDP and in per capita terms. For a long time expenditure was thought to be lower in Japan than in France, but the expenditure associated with Japan did not take into account the new healthcare criteria adopted by the OECD, namely long-term care (OECD, 2018). Taking these new criteria into account in 2016 has moved Japan from eighth place (10.2 per cent of GDP in 2014) to sixth place (10.9 2 per cent of GDP in 2016) in the ranking of OECD countries by level of healthcare expenditure, just after France, in fifth place (11 per cent of GDP in 2016). The two countries' expenditures are thus very similar, both in terms of their weight in GDP and per capita annual spending (around 4500 euros).

Spending on hospital care accounts for a significant share of healthcare spending in all OECD countries. This is particularly the case in France, where it accounts for around 37.2 per cent, which is higher than the OECD average of 28.2 per cent. In Japan, hospital spending equals the OECD average (OECD, 2017).

However, growth rates in healthcare spending have declined in recent years, from 3.62 per cent per year over the period 2003–2009 to 1.42 per cent over the period 2009–2016 (average of OECD countries, OECD, 2017). The year 2009–2010 marks a break in this progression, as a result of the 2008 financial crisis. Numerous measures have been taken in the two countries under consideration, in terms of workforce reductions, lower salaries for healthcare professionals and lower compensation for healthcare providers. The change was particularly noticeable in Japan and France: in Japan, the growth rate in healthcare spending was 2.9 per cent over the 2003–2009 period, then 1.8 per cent over the 2009–2016 period; in France the rates were 1.6 per cent and 0.9 per cent respectively (OECD, 2017).

In Japan, as can be seen, growth in healthcare spending remains relatively high, even after the severe global subprime financial crisis in 2007–2008. This is due in particular to the declining birth rate, the accelerated ageing of the population and the development of lifestyle-related diseases. Japan is striving to implement a systematic preventive healthcare policy. Costs associated with advances in medical technology and new treatments must also be taken into account (Henke et al., 2009).

However, since the early 1980s, the government of Japan has been pursuing a policy of controlling healthcare spending, trying to ensure that the rate of increase in national healthcare expenditure does not exceed the rate of increase in national income. As early as the 1970s, the existing copayment system was refined to limit the growth of expenditure. The copayment system, currently capped at 130,000 yen, means there is a 30 per cent copayment requirement in respect of healthcare fees for patients between 6 and 69 years of age, reducing to 20 per cent for those between 70 and 74, and to 10 per cent for those 75 years and older. However, for people over 70 years of age in the high-income category, their contribution remains at 30 per cent. At the same time, efforts are being made to reduce the length of hospital stays.

Table 1 Share of health expenditure by type of financing (2015)

	Japan		France		OECD average	
Public administration	10%	Public share 85%	4%	Public share 79%	36%	Public share 72%
Health insurance	75%		75%		36%	
Households	13%	Private share 15%	7%	Private share 21%	20%	Private share 26%
Private insuran-ce companies	2%		14%		6%	

Source: Health at a Glance (OECD, 2017)

This measure is particularly necessary in Japan where there is a tradition of "social hospitalization" for the elderly (Imai, 2002).

France, for its part, has taken significant measures to reduce the growth in healthcare spending in recent years. It has tightened control over the reimbursement of medicines and adopted a policy of developing generics. The search for improved performance is also spreading to all levels of healthcare. In France the National Agency for Supporting the Performance of Medical and Medico-social Healthcare Institutions (French acronym ANAP) was created in 2009 to support healthcare institutions in improving their performance.

In overall terms, there are two sources of funding for health expenditure: public sources and private sources. The public sources are provided by government general tax revenues, and by social insurance funds, which often bear the largest share of the funding. The private sources are made up of direct payments by households, as well as the many private health insurances that supplement the publicly funded coverage. In most OECD countries, the public sector is the main source of financing; this is particularly the case in Japan and France (Table 1).

The majority of funding for both countries is public (around 80 per cent), divided between social security and general taxation.

Beyond certain differences in terms of organization in particular, the similarities between the healthcare systems in Japan and France are considerable, particularly in terms of objectives and population coverage.

As outlined by Shimazaki (2011) and Ikegami et al. (2011), in Japan the system is characterized by: universal coverage for all inhabitants since 1961; collective financing through public health insurance funds; essentially private healthcare services providers (82 per cent of facilities with more than 20 beds are private, i.e. in 2014, 6876 private facilities of various types of status and 57 facilities run by health insurance companies, managing 1,064,624 and 16,824 beds respectively) (Ministry of Health, Labor and Welfare, 2016); a uniform fee schedule for all healthcare facilities and all insurance companies; a third-party payment system, with beneficiaries paying only the copayment segment; and the right of everyone to select the healthcare facility of their choice.

In addition, in order to rationalize healthcare services, the search for synergies between public and private hospitals is, as in France, increasingly systematic. In Japan, a real division of labour has been established between the different types of hospitals. The governor of each prefecture is empowered to restructure the supply of healthcare, particularly between the public and private sectors. For example, the country has three times more beds per head of population than the OECD average, i.e. eight beds per thousand population in 2011 compared to 3.4 in France (Keizai Koho Center, 2014). This does not, however, eliminate the serious waiting time problems in hospitals in large cities, which have difficulties in meeting healthcare demands. Moreover, there are still too many small facilities in Japan. Structures that are too small generate significant costs and cannot offer specialized services (Henke et al., 2009). The existence of so many small facilities can be explained by the historic right of doctors for many years to set up their own clinics wherever they wanted to in the country.

Japan also has a great deal of work to do in rationalizing its healthcare spending. For example, it spends three to four times more on magnetic resonance imaging (MRI) and scanners per capita than the average of developed countries. Similarly, the number of visits to doctors is 14 per year on average per individual, compared to three for all developed countries. This apparent medical over-consumption can be explained in particular by very systematic follow-up visits in schools and at work, and in municipal settings for non-salaried workers. The elderly also consult doctors more often, and are encouraged to do so.

In France, beginning in 1996, an annual National Health Insurance Expenditure Target (French acronym ONDAM)[1] is set to control healthcare expenditure growth. Each year, parliament debates healthcare budgets and agrees on the healthcare expenditure target, which then forms the basis for allocating resources among the various healthcare providers, particularly hospitals.

More recently, the Hospital Patient Health Region Act (French acronym HPST[2]) of 2009 plays an important role in the spatial organization of care. It has led to the creation of Regional Health Agencies (French acronym ARS[3]), one per region, which are responsible for organizing the provision of healthcare in their region. Their responsibilities include seeking synergies between healthcare structures, in particular between public hospitals and private clinics. The aim is to avoid duplication in the supply of healthcare services as much as the emergence of supply gaps. The Regional Health Agencies encourage/impose collaboration between the various healthcare actors to improve the supply of healthcare in the regions, at lower cost. In the Aquitaine region, for example, the recent restructuring of several private clinics into a new grouping was only authorized by the Regional Health Agency on condition that the cardiology activity was transferred to a nearby public hospital. The aim is to avoid waste resulting from an excess of service providers, while improving the quality of healthcare through economies of scale (use of more sophisticated equipment, and the creation of larger specialized teams).

In 2004, France also introduced the concept of the Preferred Doctor scheme. This is used as a gatekeeping process aimed at regulating access to outpatient specialist

[1]ONDAM: *Objectif National d'Evolution des Dépenses d'Assurance Maladie* in French.

[2]*Loi Hôpital Patient Santé Territoire (loi HPST)* in French.

[3]*Agence Régionale de Santé (ARS)* in French.

care. Patients must initially consult their preferred doctor (usually the family doctor) or other general practitioner in order to be eligible to receive the higher reimbursement rates in respect of healthcare fees from the French national health insurance schemes. More recently, "care pathways" in respect of certain pathologies have been developed throughout the country, with the aim of improving patient care, but also with a view to putting the financing of the services on a more harmonized and equitable basis. At the same time, the State is determined to develop ambulatory care (healthcare received on an outpatient basis without staying more than one day in hospital), with the aim of saving money, but also to reduce the burden of patient care. The development of telemedicine and e-health, which consists of using digital technology in the relationship between caregivers and patients, particularly in the case of care pathways, complements this search for greater efficiency. The "My health 2022[4]" strategy, announced in September 2018 by the French president, reaffirms the dual objective of better patient care and economic efficiency (Report from the Ministry of Solidarity and Health, 2019).

It is in this context of financial constraints, at a time when the demand for healthcare is growing rapidly under the dual effect of an ageing population and the desire for better coverage, in Japan as in France, that the organization and evolution of the funding of hospital structures in these two countries needs to be analysed.

2.3 Financing of Hospital Structures in Japan and France

Both Japan and France have adopted a system of activity-based hospital funding, which was initially developed in the United States. But the two countries have adopted this innovation in significantly different ways. Let us first consider the case of Japan, and then France.

The Japanese hospital sector is characterized by the strong heterogeneous nature of its service providers. Public hospitals may be state hospitals or hospitals attached to national universities, prefectures or cities; private hospitals may be affiliated to a mutual or associative organization (e.g. a mutual insurance company), attached to a private university, or owned by private investors, doctors or others (Kato et al., 2014). Hospitals run by for-profit investment funds are prohibited in Japan (Ikegami & Campbell, 1995, p. 1296).

Hospitals and clinics in Japan are mostly private. Public sector establishments account for only 31 per cent of the beds managed by establishments with more than 20 beds (Ministry of Health, Labor and Welfare, 2016). While in France the term hospital is reserved for public healthcare establishments, and the term clinic for private establishments, it is not the same in Japan, where people speak of public hospitals and private hospitals if the establishment in question has more than

[4] *Ma santé 2022* in French.

Table 2 Healthcare facilities in Japan, as of October 2014; all medical activities excluding dental clinics

	Public sector		Private sector	
	State, national level	Prefectures, cities and others	health insurance companies, private institutions	Private investors, individuals and others
Hospitals (more than 20 beds)	329	1231	57	6876
Clinics (up to 20 beds)	532	3593	513	95,823
Total	861	4824	570	102,699

Source: Ministry of Health, Labor and Welfare (2016)

20 beds, and of clinics if it has fewer than 20 beds. Table 2 breaks down the different types of hospitals and clinics in Japan.

Since 2003, as outlined by Uetsuka (2012), the Japanese government has introduced a method of reimbursing hospitals, whether public or private, based on payment in respect of the number of patients treated, known as "Diagnosis Procedure Combination" (DPC) financing. This method of financing, initiated in the United States in the 1980s under the name Diagnosis Related Groups (DRG) financing, was subsequently widely adopted by a large number of OECD countries. It consists of classifying patients into categories based on their diagnoses and reimbursing hospitals based on the number of patients treated in these different diagnostic categories. Using this method, hospitals receive the funding they need for their healthcare activity, no more, no less, and have no incentive to increase the number of procedures undertaken in respect of the same patient. According to Ikegami and Campbell (2004), this method of financing is based on three dimensions: standardization (diagnoses are coded and grouped homogeneously), transparency (information must be revealed, without ambiguity) and accountability (hospitals are made responsible for the expenses generated).

There are two peculiarities in the Japanese system. The first is that reimbursement is not only based on DPC, but also on a fee-for-service (FFS) basis. Thus, both systems are simultaneously utilized in determining hospital reimbursements. DPC ensures that hospitalized patients are funded for their entire stay in hospital. The DPC-based coverage only applies to certain basic expenses related to hospitalization, i.e. hospital admission, initial examination, drugs, laboratory, radiology and other care fees costing less than 10,000 yen each; the FFS coverage, on the other hand, applies to surgical, anesthetic, radiotherapy and any other healthcare expenses costing more than 10,000 yen each (Matsuda et al., 2008; Annear et al., 2018). Thus, the hospital reimbursement system in Japan, although partially based on DPC, is very different from that in other developed countries.

The second peculiarity is that refunding in Japan is made on the basis of degressive DPC payments (which became per diem payments) according to the length of hospital stay. Three separate rates apply depending on hospital stay duration: for short stays (shorter than that required for uncomplicated treatments), the reimbursed cost is on the basis of DPC costs plus 15 per cent; for average length stays, the reimbursed cost is on the basis of DPC costs; for long stays (longer than that provided for uncomplicated treatments), the reimbursed cost is on the basis of DPC costs less 15 per cent for the part of the stay exceeding the average stay length (Matsuda, 2007). For exceptionally long stays, funding reverts to the FFS basis (Annear et al., 2018).

The primary outcome of this pricing system has been a reduction in the length of patient hospital stays, although it remains the longest among OECD countries. When 82 hospitals in Japan adopted DPC, beginning in 2002, the length of hospital stays in Japan fell from 20.4 days to 18.8 days between 2002 and 2003 (Randall, 2009). By 2017, hospital stays averaged 16.3 days in Japan (the longest among OECD countries), compared with 5.7 days in France (OECD, 2017).

With the introduction of the DPC, healthcare acts have been standardized, and it is now possible to make comparisons between different hospitals using data-based care standards as well as pricing information. Most importantly, the government can now have a real impact on healthcare spending by setting reimbursement payments for DPCs, which it reviews every two years.

The political will to improve healthcare services by putting the service providers in competition with each other has not always had the desired effect. Control of private establishments had to be strengthened by legislation, by amending healthcare insurance legislation in May 2008, in order to combat, in particular, the practice of billing for the over-coding of medical services (Naïto 2009, p. 73). For their part, Kato et al. (2014) studied the impact of the public and private status of the different hospital establishments on the average length of hospital stays. They point out that private establishments deliberately choose better paid care, i.e. specialized care with limited hospital stays with the reimbursement of additional healthcare costs, and specialized long-term healthcare, particularly of the elderly. Conversely, public institutions are more inclined to provide limited hospital stay care in accordance with public policies, without being able to target more profitable specific healthcare markets.

In France, the majority of establishments are public (62 per cent of beds), and private clinics account for the rest, with 24 per cent of beds belonging to profit-making establishments and 14 per cent to non-profit-making establishments (DREES, 2017). Until 2008, public establishments received a global operating allowance (French acronym DGF),[5] renewed yearly, by being simply adjusted for the rate of growth in spending under the ONDAM. This quasi-fixed envelope budgeting did not reflect the actual activities of each healthcare institution. Each public hospital was certain, year after year, of receiving an allocation close to that of the previous year. The private establishments, for their part, invoiced the Health Insurance Companies the per diem fees (associated with the structure's operational expenses) and for the medical procedures undertaken. These fees varied

[5] DGF for *Dotation Globale de Fonctionnement*, in French.

geographically but were negotiated with the regulatory authorities (Halgand, 1995; Mougeot & Naegelen, 2011; Holcman, 2018; Moisdon, 2010).

There was thus a difference in funding between public and private hospitals, making it difficult to control spending. In addition, no accurate calculations of the costs of medical procedures for all establishments (public and private) were made at the time.

All of these elements have led to a major reform in terms of the funding of healthcare institutions by the adoption of activity-based funding (French acronym T2A). Here again, the system is largely inspired by the funding methods of American hospitals through diagnosis-related group-based payments. The main objective of this funding reform, which was road tested from 1999 onwards and incorporated nationally from 2005 to 2008, was to harmonize reimbursement methods between the public and private sectors, but also to make health structures more accountable in order to better control spending (Angelé-Halgand & Garrot, 2014). In this way, the framework for the reimbursement of public and private establishments is standardized and resources are allocated depending on the nature and volume of care activities. This is in line with the spirit of the Organic Law on Finance Laws (French acronym LOLF) of 2012,[6] set up to monitor the performance of public services as closely as possible.

It should be emphasized that in the spirit of T2A, each healthcare institution is responsible for its own budget, and cannot ask the State to make up any deficits. In the event of budget overruns, which are currently becoming increasingly common (the deficit tripled to a record €1.5 billion in 2017), the Regional Health Agencies are setting up Contracts for the Return to Financial Sustainability (French acronym CREF[7]) with hospitals, which determine areas of savings and improvement for institutions. In France, therefore, unlike in Japan, the government does not automatically cover budget deficits. It is up to the institutions themselves to do so within the framework of the CREF, through improvements in efficiency. This situation is clearly different from the case of Japanese public hospitals, where deficits are more readily financed by the State, even if this is not done without conditions or sanctions, as we shall see later.

Since March 2008 in France, T2A funding has been available for activities in the fields of Medicine, Surgery, Obstetrics and Dentistry (French acronym MCOO).[8] Psychiatry as aftercare and rehabilitation activities are not covered by T2A and continue to be financed by a global endowment. For MCOO activities, payments are set for the Health Insurance Companies by Homogeneous Hospital Stay Group (French acronym GHS) fees, which can be compared to the American DRG fees, and are derived from the calculations of the costs of the Diagnosis Related Groups (French acronym GHM) from hospital cost databases. It should be noted that the GHSs are identical whether in the public or private sector, but that reimbursement

[6] *Loi Organique relatives aux Lois de Finance (LOLF)* in French.

[7] *Contrats de Retour à l'Equilibre Financier (CREF)* in French.

[8] *Médecine, Chirurgie, Obstétrique et Odontologie* in French.

rates are different depending on the sector (O'Reilly et al., 2012): reimbursement in the public sector includes the remuneration of physicians who are salaried in this sector, whereas they are not in the private one, fees being paid separately; furthermore certain procedures are reimbursed separately in the private sector (e.g. radiology), which explains the higher reimbursement rates for the public sector.

Convergence between the two systems, initially planned for 2013 and subsequently postponed to 2018, no longer seems to be a priority. Reimbursement of hospitals via T2A represents approximately 80 per cent of their funding. The remaining funding concerning specific public sector activities, such as emergencies and research, is done separately through flat-rate FFS payments.

The literature on hospital financing, both academic and professional, remains relatively limited, often fragmented, particularly with regard to Asian countries (Annear et al., 2018). To our knowledge, the literature on hospital management control is even more limited (Halgand, 1995; Lartigau, 2009). Studying the link between financing methods and hospital management control in France and Japan requires substantial exploratory fieldwork.

3 Fieldwork: Financing of Hospital Structures and Management Control

In an attempt to answer our research question on the links between hospital funding and management control in France and Japan, in addition to reviewing the academic, institutional and professional literature presented in the first part of the chapter, we conducted in-depth interviews with hospital directors and their direct collaborators, both in France and Japan, between 2015 and 2019. We conducted nine in-depth interviews in Japan, with seven respondents (two of them, very cooperative, were met twice), from five public hospitals and one private hospital in and around Tokyo, one public hospital in Iwate Prefecture, in the northeast of the country, and one private hospital in Hokkaidô, the large northern island. In France, we conducted nine interviews with nine respondents from five hospital structures in the southwest and the Regional Health Agency of New Aquitaine (Table 3).

The semi-directive interviews lasted from one to four and a half hours in Japan, and from one and a half to four hours in France. The same questions were asked in respect of the different institutions, to understand how they were adjusting to the constraints imposed by changes in the way healthcare is financed and other pressures to rationalize supply, both in Japan and France. In particular, we wished to obtain an understanding of the tools developed by those responsible for management control and how the institutions, under pressure to be more efficient, used these tools. In Japan, the interviews were conducted using both English and Japanese, according to the respective language levels of the different interlocutors, and in such a way as to avoid any risk of misunderstanding.

Table 3 Profile of interviewees and their work institutions

Japan		France	
Interviewed	Institution	Interviewed	Institution
General Manager	Public Hospital J1, Tokyo	General Manager	Public Hospital F1, Pau
General Manager	Public Hospital J2, Tokyo	Management Accounting Chief Executive	Public Hospital F1, Pau
General Manager	Public Hospital J3, Iwate	Vice General Manager	Public Hospital F1, Pau
Administrative Chief	Public Hospital J3, Iwate	Financial Chief Executive	Public Hospital F2, Bayonne
Vice General Manager	Private Hospital J4, Tokyo	Management Accounting Chief Executive	Public Hospital F2, Bayonne
General Manager	Public Hospital J5, Yokohama	Financial Chief Executive	Public Hospital F3, Tarbes
General Manager	Private Hospital J6, Yokohama	General Manager	Public Hospital F4, Oloron
		Financial Chief Executive	Public Hospital F5, Bordeaux
		Financial Chief Executive	ARS, F6, New Aquitaine

Letter J for Japanese hospitals, letter F for French hospitals

The results are presented in two parts. We first consider (2.1) the use of activity-based funding (DPC in Japan, T2A in France) and its failures in each of the two countries; second (2.2), we consider the consequences of this funding method for the development of management control practices.

3.1 Areas of Failure in Activity-Based Funding

The implementation of activity-based funding has not been without difficulties requiring further modifications, both in Japan and in France.

In Japan, it emerged from our interviews that the introduction of activity-based funding has led to an increase in the number of repeat hospital admissions by the same patients. Thus, the reduction in the length of stays may lead to the need for readmission to hospital because the patient has not been comprehensively treated. This may even correspond to a desire on the part of physicians to have the patients return to hospitals. With a per diem DPC system in operation, it is financially advantageous to bill for several short-term stays, rather than a single long-term stay. In addition, as our interlocutors confirmed, there have been cases of "over-coding" of certain procedures: by classifying patients in diagnostic categories that require more intensive and therefore more expensive treatment, the hospital obtains higher reimbursements. In France, as in Japan, a trend towards over-coding was also observed, according to our respondents, in order to get higher reimbursements.

Between 2006 and 2009, measures were taken by French supervisory bodies to combat this overbilling through a large number of hospital audits, which resulted in financial penalties where fraud was discovered.

In Japan, as in France, our interlocutors underline a second drift linked to activity-based funding. It may be financially advantageous to ask patients to have certain procedures performed in hospital outpatient departments (such as blood tests and imaging), rather than during the mere hospitalization, for which, as we have seen, the payment is a flat-rate fee. In the case of Japan, the former are billed on a "Fees For Service" basis, which is more advantageous for the hospital, while the latter are billed on a DPC basis, which is less advantageous (Randall, 2009). In France, our interlocutors speak of "border acts", like in Japan, where the reimbursement system is manipulated with the focus on increased financial reimbursement rather than on patient care.

Another major criticism concerns the risk of selecting patients according to their pathologies. This is particularly true in the case of private for-profit institutions, which specialize in well-reimbursed healthcare that generates significant financial returns. This was seen in the case of Japan, as outlined in the previously cited study by Kato et al. (2014), and our interlocutors addressed this point. This is also the case in France, where emergency care and care for the elderly, often costly and under-reimbursed, are generally left to public hospitals, which are obliged to provide these services.

In the search for increased profitability, it is possible to observe drifts associated with the premature discharge of patients from hospitals. Hospitals no longer have incentives to retain patients because they are reimbursed only according to the number and type of cases treated.

Given the financial constraints generated by activity-based funding, it is common in Japan to hire low-skilled staff in order to reduce the payroll or to report fictitious care services hours to the financing authorities. As our interlocutor at Iwate Hospital told us, between 2000 and 2006, 478 healthcare organizations, the vast majority of them private, had their licences revoked for such practices. In order to strengthen control over private institutions, as we have seen, legislation on healthcare insurance reimbursements was amended in May 2008 (Naïto, 2009, p. 73).

As far as the adequacy of hospital funding is concerned, there is also a need to look at how health services are coping with the most recent developments. The Covid-19 health crisis in France has revealed the extent to which decades of cost reductions have weakened the whole hospital sector. However, despite the enfeebled nature of the hospital sector, hospital staff have been widely praised and supported by the public and by the authorities for their tremendous work dealing with the pandemic. In 2020 this led the government to organize a 50-day consultation process between 25 May and 10 July with 90 stakeholders and trade unions, the so called Ségur de la Santé. This consultation process covered various subjects such as the upgrading of career structures, the organization of care in the regions, healthcare investment, digital health, governance and the inclusion of carers in decision-making, the fight against health inequalities, psychiatry and research, but also the health of the elderly and the disabled. It gave rise to 33 major recommendations aimed at continuing the modernization of the French health system. The main measures include:

- 19 billion euros of investment in the healthcare system to improve patient care and the daily lives of caregivers
- 8.2 billion euros per year to upgrade the healthcare establishments and homes for the elderly, and to recognize the commitment of carers to the health of the French people
- 15,000 new jobs in public hospitals
- effective exit from the "all T2A" activity-based funding in developing the fee-for-service system and giving priority to the quality of care
- opening or reopening of 4000 beds where needed

Most of these measures are currently under way. However, it remains to be seen how the exit from the "all T2A" activity-based funding through the development of a fee-for-service system will be designed and implemented.

In Japan, the consequences of the pandemic crisis have been totally different. Unlike France, the health system registered a huge drop in activity, largely explained by a comparatively limited circulation of the Covid-19 virus and by a massive reduction in the number of consultations linked to the population's reluctance to expose itself to the risk of contamination. As a result, according to a study by the Japan Hospital Association (Nihon Byôin Kai 日本病院協会), the All Japan Hospital Association (Zennihon Byôin Kyôkai 全日本病院協会) and the Association of Japanese Healthcare Corporations (Nihon Iryô Hôjin Kyôkai 日本医療法人協会), nearly 70 per cent of the 1459 hospital facilities surveyed were in deficit over the period April to June 2020 (Nihon Byôin Kai et al., 2020a). A second study conducted by these three entities shows that the decline in revenue, compared to the previous year, was 13.9 per cent for April and 17.4 per cent for May 2020 (Nihon Byôin Kai et al., 2020b).

Some institutions, already financially weak before the health crisis, could not bear the financial losses and filed for bankruptcy. This was the case of the orthopaedic clinic "Kishimoto Seikei Gekaiin" (Okayama prefecture), regarded as the first case of "Corona bankruptcy" in the hospital sector. In order to compensate healthcare institutions for losses and reduce the real risk of increasing bankruptcies, the government introduced a number of aids. For example, a mortgage-free, interest-free loan scheme has been set up and has benefited 1475 healthcare institutions to a total amount of 372.8 billion yen as of 31 August 2020 (Okada, 2020). In addition, the fee-for-service index for the resuscitation of patients with Covid-19 has been increased fivefold (Okada, 2020).

3.2 Consequences of Activity Financing for Management Control

As all of our interviewees in Japan explained to us, there is a major difference between public and private hospital structures in respect of reimbursements. Both are reimbursed on the basis of the DPC system, but public hospitals benefit from subsidies to cover their chronic deficits, whereas private structures have not benefited from such supports since the early 1980s. The amount of subsidy, which is renewed yearly, is subject to periodic renegotiation between the management of the public hospital in question and its supervisory authorities.

For our interlocutors, this difference in the treatment of public and private hospitals is justified by the fact that the former are often located in sparsely populated and low-income rural areas. In any case, this exemplifies that public and private hospitals in Japan have very different approaches to management control. The management control systems of public hospitals in Japan are essentially oriented towards "budget monitoring". The overriding aim is to avoid any slippage in spending that would lead to having to ask for larger allocations than budgeted for at the beginning of the year. We know that budgetary overruns translate into increased pressure from the supervisory authorities, and if such problems persist, into the implementation of restructuring operations, or imposed mergers with other, better managed hospitals. According to one of our respondents, the Prefecture of Iwate lost seven public hospitals in about 10 years, following such closures or mergers.

Budgets are therefore well monitored in public hospitals, but according to our respondents, there are no accurate cost calculations undertaken, for example by type of patient or type of hospital stay. Private clinics and hospitals, conversely, not only accurately track their budgets, but also perform such cost calculations in order to improve their profitability, developing their most lucrative activities, and reconfiguring those that are less lucrative, either by offering them differently or by ceasing to offer them.

Conversely, importance given to the calculation of costs is found in all the hospital structures encountered in France, both public and private. As our interviewees in France pointed out, cost monitoring has become essential in the context of the funding based on the GHS. This explains the significant development of cost accounting and management control services in French hospitals. New tools are being developed in order to better monitor costs and results, both internally and externally, to facilitate comparisons with other hospital establishments. To this end, the National Costs Studies (French acronym ENC)[9] play an important role through annual surveys of hospital establishments, conducted by the Technical Agency for Information on Hospitalization[10] (French acronym ATIH), which serve as a

[9] *Echelle Nationale des Coûts (ENC)* in French.

[10] *Agence Technique de l'Information sur l'Hospitalisation (ATIH)* in French.

reference for comparisons of the costs of medical, surgical and obstetric (French acronym MCO) care, follow-up and rehabilitation care (French acronym SSR) and home hospitalization (French acronym HAD) care. Similarly, the so-called Angers database, which focuses on logistics and medico-technical activities, serves as a reference point for comparing the administrative costs of hospital establishments. Standardized cost calculation tools have been developed and distributed at the initiative of the regulatory authorities, particularly the Regional Health Agencies.

These tools thus make it possible to determine the funding associated with each care activity, based on average costs between all hospital structures. They also make it possible to analyse the results of the various institutions, and to understand why they differ so much from one institution to another. This leads to the identification of the most efficient hospitals or clinics, exemplary in terms of controlling costs. Finally, at the level of each institution, they are of course essential management tools.

However, this system is not free of criticism. The first, and most problematic according to the hospital managers we met in France, is that the determination of fees in respect of the GHSs is not based on consistent cost logic. If consistent cost logic were applied, the fees for the different GHSs would be based on their costs, determined using the National Costs Scale (ENC), which calculates, each year, the average cost of each GHS treatment of the hospitals deemed most representative. However, the GHS fees are also reviewed each year according to the budget envelope allocated to the hospital sector within the framework of the ONDAM National Health Insurance Expenditure Target outlined above. Thus, a hospital, although it may have increased its volume of activity, may see its resources decrease. This situation may partially explain the increase in the financial imbalances of some hospitals.

3.3 Discussion of Results

Basing the funding of hospital structures on their actual activity, in France and in Japan, requires a particularly accurate monitoring of the registration of medical activities. All those involved in hospital structures are therefore made aware of the need to monitor as closely as possible the measurement of the various activities carried out, because the amount of funding depends directly on this monitoring. The aim is to give the hospital establishment the funding it needs for its activities, no more and no less. Moreover, this method of funding implies, for the bodies that provide funding for the hospital structures (social security or other), the implementation of rigorous control mechanisms to reduce information asymmetry and limit excesses linked to opportunistic behaviour by certain actors, public or private, as suggested by agency cost theory.

As the developments in neo-institutional theory outlined in Sect. 2 suggest, Japan and France demonstrate remarkable elements of convergence in terms of healthcare objectives, and the organization of health systems. In particular, the hospital funding systems in Japan and France were both inspired by Anglo-Saxon activity-based systems. It was the need to control hospital spending that led legislators in these two countries to introduce this method of hospital funding. The idea was to avoid inflating the number and the costs of services provided to patients, by standardizing the expected services and utilizing activity-based funding systems.

The coercive isomorphism of Di Maggio and Powell (1991) is clearly seen at work here. At a different level, it can also be seen at work in France in the state pressure for the harmonization of cost calculation systems within the public hospital sector and private clinics. Such harmonization also contributes to better controlling of expenditure, both through the comparisons it allows and through better knowledge of the actual costs borne by the different structures and the potential for improvement.

Beyond the identified elements of convergence, there are differences between Japan and France. These differences can largely be explained by the economic, institutional and demographic contexts of the two countries. For example, the longer length of hospital stays in Japan, given the more marked ageing of the population than in France, and in a context where cramped housing conditions and the geographical mobility of the younger generations in recent decades makes it difficult to keep sick people, particularly the elderly, at home. The mechanisms of institutional dualism highlighted by Kostova and Roth (2002), presented in the first part of this chapter, are clearly at work.

We also tried to understand how the different funding models in the two countries have an impact on the management of hospital structures, and what consequences can be observed at the level of the management control tools deployed. In terms of healthcare financing, France and Japan have comparable systems, based mainly on contributions to the public social security system. The systems in the two countries seek to provide universal healthcare coverage for all. Hospital funding in both countries is based on the measurement of medical diagnostic activities, with a particularity associated with the Japanese system, as we have seen, which does not finance all hospitalization benefits through DPC, and which modulates reimbursements according to the length of hospital stay. This latter measure is explained by a strong desire to reduce the length of hospital stays, which, as we have seen, are much longer than in other OECD countries.

We also identify significant differences in the control tools developed in hospitals. In Japan, public hospitals essentially undertake simple budgetary follow-ups of their expenses, with cost calculations not fully developed for the moment, whereas private hospitals perform detailed, often sophisticated, but not harmonized cost calculations. In France, conversely, all hospitals, both public and private, are developing, under the aegis of the Regional Health Agencies, detailed and harmonized cost calculation systems to complement their budget monitoring tools.

4 Conclusion

Hospital funding can differ considerably from one country to another, including between countries at the same level of development. Some countries opt for financing by global financial envelopes allocated to each hospital, while others, such as France and Japan, are inspired by Anglo-Saxon models: they base allocations on the volume of activity carried out by the hospitals (activity-based funding). Hospitals are then funded on the basis of the level of care provided, which avoids the wastage of public funds observed in the case of financing by global envelope, particularly when expenditure exceeds what is strictly necessary.

The adoption of such an approach by countries that are in some respects as different as France and Japan is the result of the fact that they are both facing the same types of difficulties, with severe financial constraints while at the same time wanting to offer broad healthcare coverage to their populations, and facing a sharp increase in health needs (ageing populations, development of chronic diseases). Consequently, the healthcare management practices deemed most effective are spreading across borders, in accordance with the powerful mechanisms identified by neo-institutional theory, sometimes with hybridization, as shown by the Japanese version of the financing of activity-based hospitals. It remains to be seen how the activity-based funding system will be changed in France, following the Covid-19 health crisis, and the resulting Ségur de la Santé round of negotiations in 2020.

Therefore, the differences that remain in terms of how hospital structures are funded are translated into differences in terms of hospital management control. Whereas in France the rigorous financial constraints linked to the radical application of activity-based funding leads to the diffusion of standardized and sophisticated cost calculation tools under the watchful eyes of Regional Health Agencies, both in public hospitals and private clinics, the situation is different in Japan. In Japan, activity-based funding only applies to a portion of hospitalization costs, and public hospitals, unlike private hospitals, have room for negotiation to cover their budgetary deficits with their supervisory authorities. As a result, while the latter, which have been financially constrained for a long time, have developed sophisticated cost calculation systems that are not yet fully harmonized, public hospitals have management controls that are essentially oriented towards accurate budget monitoring.

Future research will be needed to consider the extent to which harmonized management control systems in France meet the needs of both public and private hospitals. It is easy to understand the reasoning behind the setting up of the Regional Health Agencies, which are concerned about standardized controls. Are these agencies appropriate for the specific problems facing each type of healthcare structure? Similarly, should the management control systems developed by private hospitals in Japan also be adapted to the country's public hospitals? Such questions will be addressed in new in-depth interviews that we plan to conduct in France and Japan in the near future.

References

Angelé-Halgand, N., & Garrot, T. (2014). Les biens communs à l'hôpital: De la 'T2A' à la tarification au cycle de soins. *Comptabilité—Contrôle—Audit, tome, 20*(3), 15–41.

Annear, P. L., Kwon, S., Lorenzoni, L., Duckett, S., Huntington, D., Langenbrunner, J. C., Murakami, Y., Shon, C., & Xu, K. (2018). Pathways to DRG-based hospital payment systems in Japan. *Korea and Thailand, Health Policy, 122*, 707–713.

Campbell, J. C., Ikegami, N., & Kwon, S. (2009). Les enseignements politiques tirés de l'expérience d'autrui et des échanges internationaux en matière d'assurance sociale des soins de santé de longue durée: Allemagne, Japon et République de Corée. *Revue internationale de sécurité sociale, 62*(4), 73–94.

Di Maggio, P. J., & Powell, W. W. (1991). The iron cage revisited: Institutional isomorphism and collective rationality in organizational fields. In W. W. Powell & P. J. Di Maggio (Eds.), *The new institutionalism in organizational analysis* (pp. 63–82). The University of Chicago Press.

DREES. (2017). *Panorama des établissements de santé*, édition 2017.

Halgand, N. (1995). Problèmes de pertinence des coûts pour le contrôle: le cas hospitalier. Comptabilité—Contrôle—Audit, 1995/2 (Tome1).

Henke, N., Kadonaga, S., & Kanzler, L. (2009). Improving Japan's health care system. *McKinsey Quarterly*, March, publication en ligne sur http://www.mckinsey.com/industries/healthcare-systems-and-services/our-insights/improving-japans-health-care-system

Holcman, R. (2018). *Management hospitalier.* Manuel de gouvernance et de droit hospitalier, Dunod.

Ikegami, N., & Campbell, J. C. (1995). Medical care in Japan. *The New England Journal of Medecin, 333*(19), 1295–1299.

Ikegami, N., & Campbell, J. C. (2004). Japan's health care reform system: Containing costs and attempting reform. *Health Affairs, 23*, 26–36.

Ikegami, N., Byung-Kwang, Y., Hashimoto, H., Matsumoto, M., Ogata, H., Babazono, A., Watanabe, R., Shibuya, K., Yang, B.-M., Reich, M., & Kobayashi, Y. (2011). Japanese universal health coverage: Evolution, achievements, and challenges. *The Lancet, 378*, 1106–1115.

Imai, Y. (2002). *Health care reform in Japan.* OECD Economics Department Working Papers, No. 321, Publication de l'OCDE, Paris, Février, 21 p.

Jaussaud, J., & Kageyama, T. (1991, September–October). Juste à temps ou la gestion de la production en flux tendus. Revue Française de Gestion, n°85.

Kato, N., Kondo, M., Okubo, I., & Hasegawa, T. (2014). Length of hospital stay in Japan 1971–2008: Hospital ownership and cost-containment policies. *Health Policy*, n°115, 180–188.

Keizai Koho Center. (2014). *Japan 2014, An International Comparison.* Keizai Koho Center (Japan Institute for Social and Economic Affairs).

Kostova, T., & Roth, K. (2002). Adoption of an organizational practice by subsidiaries of multinational corporations: Institutional and relation effects. *Academy of Management Journal, 45*(1), 215–233.

Lartigau, J. (2009). L'évolution de la fonction contrôle de gestion à l'hôpital. *Journal d'économie médicale, 27*(7), 371–391.

Matsuda, S., 松田 晋哉 (2007). Kisokara yomitoku DPC—Tadashiirikaito jisen no tameni 基礎から読み解くDPC—正しい理解と実践のために (understanding the basics of DPC—For a good understanding and application.), Tokyo, igakushoin医学書院.

Matsuda, S., Ishikawa, K., Kuwabara, K., Fujimori, K., Fushimi, K., & Hashimoto, H. (2008). Development and use of the Japanese case-mix system. *Eurohealth, 14*, 25–30.

Ministry of Health, Labor and Welfare. (2016). *Handbook of health and welfare statistics 2015.* Japan Health, Labor and Welfare Association.

Moisdon, J.-C. (2010). L'évaluation du Changement Organizationnel par l'approche de la Recherche Intervention. *L'exemple des Impacts de la T2A, Revue française des affaires sociales*, n°1, 213–226.

Mougeot, M., & Naegelen, F. (2011). *Régulation et Tarification des Hôpitaux*, Economica.

Naïto, K. (2009). Assurance de soins de santé au Japon: au-delà de la vision binaire entre Etat et famille. *Revue internationale de sécurité sociale, 62*(3), 55–84.

Nihon Byôin Kai (日本病院会), Zennihon byôin kyôkai (全日本病院協会), Nihon Iryô Hôjin Kyôkai (日本医療法人協会). (2020a). *Shinkorona uirusu kansen kakudai ni yoru byôin keiei jôkyô no chôsa* (新型コロナウイルス感染拡大による病院経営状況の調査), 1st Quarter, https://www.ajha.or.jp/topics/4byou/pdf/200805_6.pdf

Nihon Byôin Kai (日本病院会), Zennihon byôin kyôkai (全日本病院協会), Nihon Iryô Hôjin Kyôkai (日本医療法人協会). (2020b). Shinkorona uirusu kansen kakudai niyoru 2020 nen 7gatsu bun byôin keiei jôkyô chôsa (新型コロナウイルス感染拡大による 2020年7月分病院経営状況調査), 10/09/2020, http://www.hospital.or.jp/pdf/06_20200910_01.pdf

North, D. N. (1994). Economic performance through time. *The American Economic Review, 84*(3), 359–368.

O'Reilly, J., Busse, R., Hakkinen, U., Or, Z., Sreet, A., & Wiley, M. (2012). Paying for hospital care: The experience with implementing activity-based funding in five European countries. *Health Economics, Policy and Law, 7*, 73–101.

OECD. (2017). Organization for Economic Co-operation and Development, 'Panorama de la santé 2017: les indicateurs de l'OCDE'. http://www.oecd-ilibrary.org

OECD. (2018). https://www.oecd.org/fr/sante/

Okada, H., 岡田 広行. (2020). Korona de iryôkai no kukyô ga 15 nen maedaoshi ni natta (コロナで医療界の苦境が15年前倒しになった), Tôyô keizai Kaisetsubu Koramunisuto (東洋経済解説部コラムニスト), 2020/10/06. https://toyokeizai.net/articles/-/379745

Politt, C., & Bouckaert, G. (2006). *Public management reform: A comparative analysis*. Oxford University Press.

Randall, J. (2009). *Health-care reform in Japan: Controlling costs, improving quality and ensuring equity*. Economic Department Working Paper, N°739.

Rapport Ministère des Solidarités et de la Santé. (2019). Réformes des modes de financement et de régulation: vers un modèle de paiement combiné. https://solidarites-sante.gouv.fr/IMG/pdf/dicom_rapport_final_vdef_2901.pdf

Shimazaki, K., 島崎謙治. (2011). *Nihonno iryôseido to seisaku*日本医療-制度と政策*Politique et système de soin au Japon*. Tōkyōdaigaku shuppankai 東京大学出版会.

Uetsuka, Y. (2012). Characteristics of Japan's healthcare systems and the problems. *Japan Society for Healthcare Administration, 55*(4), 330–333.

Trade Cooperation Between China and Vietnam from the Perspective of Intra-Industry Trade

Yan Tan and Yang Yang

Abstract Exchange rate pass-through (ERPT) indicates the impacts of an effective exchange rate change on the trading prices of a country's commodities. After more than two decades of Doi Moi, Vietnam has highly been involved in international economies. Upon its internationalization, RMB (Chinese Renminbi) has been empirically proven to be an invoicing currency of Vietnam when Vietnam imports goods from abroad. Based on our preliminary research, two main findings are noteworthy. Firstly, the degree of intra-industry between the trade of Vietnam and China has been increasing. In particular, the vertical intra-industry trade accounts for the biggest proportion of the Vietnam–China intra-industry trade. Secondly, most of Vietnam's trading goods are of low quality in relation to China. Nevertheless, Vietnam's quality of goods has witnessed an improvement from 2001 to 2016. The main objective of this part is to research the heterogeneous ERPT into Vietnam's import prices from China using highly disaggregated 6-digit HS data from 2001 to 2016.

Keywords China–Vietnam trade · ERPT · Intra-industry trade · Kernel density non-parameter estimations · Panel data

1 Introduction

Exchange rate pass-through (ERPT) indicates the impacts of an effective exchange rate change on the trading prices of a country's commodities. After more than two decades of Doi Moi, Vietnam has highly been involved in international economies. The trade performance is expected to be dramatically promoted since Vietnam has signed up bilateral and multilateral FTAs (Free Trade Agreements) with many trade partners. Although this trend is believed to offer Vietnam several opportunities, it will face many challenges in its economy and enterprises. Because of the economic

Y. Tan (✉)
School of Business, Yulin Normal University, Yulin, China

Y. Yang
College of ASEAN Studies, Guangxi University for Nationalities, Nanning, Guangxi, China

B. Andreosso-O'Callaghan et al. (eds.), *Sustainable Development in Asia*,
Contributions to Economics, https://doi.org/10.1007/978-3-030-94679-1_11

integration, huge changes will be brought into the relationship between the Vietnamese Dong (VND) and the currencies of her main trading partners. The external risk that poses challenges in the local economy is expected to increase significantly.

China is one of the most significant trade markets of Vietnam. This country is also the biggest source of Vietnam's trade deficit. Upon its internationalization, RMB (Chinses Renminbi) has been empirically proven to be an invoicing currency of Vietnam when Vietnam imports goods from abroad (Nguyen et al., 2019). However, the research on the exchange rate pass-through into Vietnam's import prices from China is quite limited. The empirical studies on the Vietnam–China trading prices do not draw enough attention.

As discussed in the second part of this chapter, most studies on the ERPT focus on the developed countries, for example, the United States or Europe. In Asia, most studies attempt to research the cases of Japan, Korea, and China. Meanwhile, there has rarely been any empirical works in the case of Vietnam. To the best of our knowledge, while only one paper approaches the case between Vietnam and China (Nguyen et al., 2019), it only studies the manufacturing industries.

Therefore, the main objective of this part is to research the heterogeneous ERPT into Vietnam's import prices from China using highly disaggregated 6-digit HS data from 2001 to 2016.

Based on our preliminary research, two main findings are noteworthy. Firstly, the degree of intra-industry between the trade of Vietnam and China has been increasing. In particular, the vertical intra-industry trade accounts for the biggest proportion of the Vietnam–China intra-industry trade. Secondly, most of Vietnam's trading goods are of low quality in relation to China. Nevertheless, Vietnam's quality of goods has witnessed an improvement from 2001 to 2016.

The results of the most recent papers on the issues of ERPT documented that the intra-industry trade and the quality of goods were the main factors that led to the heterogeneity of ERPT. Meanwhile, we further research the roles of vertically differentiated production and quality of goods in the ERPT into Vietnam's import prices from China.

The rest of this chapter is arranged as follows. Section 2 presents the literature review; Sect. 3 discusses the theoretical framework of the exchange rate pass-through; Sect. 4 defines the empirical models and illustrates the data; Sects. 5 and 6 discuss the results and the conclusions, respectively.

2 Literature Review

2.1 Literature Review on the Exchange Rate Pass-Through

Modeling and examining the connections between the exchange rates and trading prices have received considerable attention during the last three decades (Hong & Zhang, 2016; Goldhammer et al., 2013; Kim, 2007; Wickremasinghe & Silvapulle, 2004; Pollard & Coughlin, 2004; Knetter, 1989; Marston, 1990). However, the policy outcomes taken by some developing countries—which leaned toward weakening home currencies—disappointingly failed to achieve desirable economic goals. This result subsequently refutes the theoretical expectations that the depreciation of a currency would promote exports and reduce imports, leading to an equilibrium in a country's trade. Although the Vietnamese Dong (VND) was depreciating, Vietnam had a significant trade deficit against China for a long time, indicating that the fluctuation in the exchange rates was not completely transferred into import prices. Pioneering studies on the exchange rate pass-through relationship stemmed from exploring the import/export demand and supply elasticities (Branson, 1972).

According to new trade theory, the incomplete pass-through mainly owes to the market structure and product differentiation (Menon, 1996). Under the assumption of a market with perfect competition, imported and domestic goods can substitute each other perfectly. As a result, the evaluation pass-through is like that of the elasticities approach. In the real world, an imperfectly competitive market usually exists. Mark-ups can be added up to a firm's cost to gain extra profits, which can be changed according to the degree of substitutions between domestic and imported goods. The degree of substitutions is determined by the product differentiation and the level of market integration and separation.

Many empirical papers have researched the ERPT by adopting different methodologies and data across various economies in the past three decades. They are classified into two groups based on the results.

In the first group, the ERPT to import prices was found to be incomplete. Aron et al. (2014) explored the exchange rate pass-through to the monthly import price index in South Africa from 1980 to 2009. The results show that the average pass-through was about 50 percent within a year and 30 percent in six months, which indicated that the exchange rate pass-through to import prices to South Africa was incomplete.

Similarly, Campa et al. (2006) estimated the exchange rate pass-through to import prices utilizing the industry-level data from European Union countries. The results from the error correction model confirmed that ERPT was incomplete. Furthermore, the pricing behavior of manufacturing industries was different from the homogenous products produced in the primary industries.

Menon (1996) explored the ERPT to import prices of automobiles adopting Engle-Granger's cointegration tests and error correction models. The paper concluded that ERPT to import prices of automobiles was incomplete in the long run. Two possible explanations are given in the paper for the incomplete pass-through: the existing quantitative limitations and the pricing behaviors on intra-firm sales by multinational companies.

Twelve European countries were examined in the work of Lutz and Reilly (1997). They found that the exchange rate pass-through was smaller than 50 percent for all 20 selected countries. It was also revealed that the low level of pass-through was not connected to the market share of domestic companies or nontariff barriers. However, in the work of Adolfson (2001), he argued that the pricing to market behavior in most industries was the reason for incomplete pass-through.

In the second group, the ERPT to import prices was found to be complete. For example, in the work of Dwyer and Lam (1994), the exchange pass-through to both export and import prices of the docks was complete for Australian manufactured industries. Another work of Dwyer and Lam (1994) also had a similar conclusion.

2.2 *Literature Review on the Heterogeneous Exchange Rate Pass-Through*

Recently, research started to examine ERPT to trading prices from the perspective of commodity heterogeneity. They believed that the product-specific characteristic significantly contributed to the exchange rate pass-through (Auer et al., 2018; Chen & Juvenal, 2016; Bernini & Tomasi, 2015; Antoniades & Zaniboni, 2016; Han & Shen, 2016; Bacchetta & Van, 2005; Athukorala & Menon, 1994; Dornbush, 1987).

The above-mentioned papers support the assumption that the production differentiation led to the heterogeneous ERPT to trading prices. In the work of Auer et al. (2018), they explored the pricing-to-market behaviors of firms in vertically differentiated industries. They incorporated the quality of goods and consumers' income in the empirical models, through which their conclusions shed light that the pricing-to-market decisions could be attributed to the interaction of consumer income and product quality.

Chen and Juvenal (2016) scrutinized the impacts of real exchange rate changes on the pricing behaviors of firms exporting various commodities with heterogeneous quality. The result suggested that the prices of lower quality products were more exposed to the real exchange rate variation while the prices of higher quality products responded less sensitively to the real exchange rate.

Using the HS data at a 6-digit level from 1991 to 2001, estimated the ERPT to product import prices with different quality levels in the USA. They found out that the import prices of low-quality products were more sensitive to the variation of real exchange rate than the high-quality ones.

Athukorala and Menon (1994) argued that the reaction of the intermediate goods in response to the exchange rate determined the exchange rate pass-through to different industries. Further, the degree of dependence on the intermediate goods affected the degree of exchange rate pass-through. The industries with high degrees of intra-industry had lower ERPTs, for instance, electronics and mechanical industries. On the contrary, industries like the chemical industry had higher ERPTs because of the low degree of intra-industry trade.

2.3 Literature Review on the Case of Vietnam

Most literature on the ERPT to the trading prices apparently focuses on developed countries. Meanwhile, studies in the case of Vietnam are scarce. On the other hand, as Vietnam's biggest trade partner, studies on the trading prices of China and Vietnam do not receive enough attention either. To the best of our knowledge, only one paper can be found that studied Vietnam's import prices from China (Nguyen et al., 2019), which adopted the fixed effect model using the monthly data from December 2007 to December 2015. They concluded that Chinese RMB was an invoicing currency for Vietnam. The price-to-market decisions were detected across the manufacturing industries in Vietnam's imports from China.

The following limitations are notable in the papers on the exchange rate pass-through to Vietnam's import prices from China. Firstly, the empirical evidence supporting the exchange rate pass-through to Vietnam's import prices from China is scarce. Secondly, the heterogeneities of the exchange rate pass-through to Vietnam's import prices from China are never studied from the perspective of product differentiation.

Therefore, our work attempts to contribute and fill the gaps in the existing literature.

Firstly, we experiment with the perspective of intra-industry. International trade can be divided into two types: the inter-industry and the intra-industry trade. The difference in factor endowment between the two countries leads to inter-industry trade, while the economies of scale and product differentiation result in intra-industry trade. The product differentiation is implemented to measure the degree of intra-industry trade in many empirical works (Azhar & Elliott, 2008; Ghosh & Rajan, 2007; Aturupane et al., 1999; Krugman, 1991) and to estimate the role of product differentiation on exchange rate pass-through (Auer et al., 2018; Athukorala & Menon, 1994).

Based on our preliminary studies in Sect. 4.4, the degree of intra-industry trade between Vietnam and China is increasing significantly over time. Therefore, it is necessary to reinvestigate the ERPT in this context using the G-L (Grubel-Lloyd index) index to measure the degree of intra-industry trade. As far as our knowledge is concerned, this factor is included for the time in analyzing the ERPT in the case of Vietnam.

Secondly, we apply the quality of goods as a factor into our empirical model to test the heterogeneous ERPT across products with different qualities. Based on our preliminary results in Sect. 4.4, the quality of Vietnam's goods is generally lower than that of China's. However, the gap in the quality of goods between these two countries is shrinking. According to Auer et al. (2018), Chen and Juvenal (2016), and Han and Shen (2016), the quality is both theoretically and empirically proved to affect ERPT, thereby stimulating our interest to investigate the ERPT to Vietnam's import prices from China by including the quality of goods—the first work conducted in the case of the Vietnam–China trade.

3 Theoretical Framework

The exchange rate pass-through effects to trading prices originate from the *Law of One Price*. Based on the assumptions of the inexistence of trade barriers in international trade, the domestic price of a product in a country is equal to the price in the international markets. Under the premise of profit maximization, the basic production function of a producer can be written as:

$$MAX\Pi_{\mathrm{i}} = P_i^x Q_i - C_i(Q_{\mathrm{i}}, Inp_i), \tag{1}$$

where Π_i represents the maximized profit of industry i, P_i^x denotes the trading price in the home currency in foreign country x, and C_i represents the cost of production, which is a function of quantity (Q_i) and intermediate input price INP_i. When we connect the production function in international trade, the trading price should be exchanged into the currency of the foreign market, as follows:

$$MAX\Pi_{\mathrm{i}} = \mathrm{e}P_i^x Q_i - C_i(Q_{\mathrm{i}}, Inp_i) \tag{2}$$

In Eq. (2), everything can be interpreted in the same way. However, the export price is now expressed as $\mathrm{e}P_i^x Q_i$, where e represents the bilateral exchange rate. In other words, the export price is now represented in the foreign currency. To get the optimal price that can maximize export producers' profit, we make the first-order derivative of Eq. (2) against price and get Eq. (3):

$$P_i^x = \frac{MC_i}{e} \times \frac{\varphi_i}{\varphi_i - 1} = \frac{MC_i}{e} \times \theta_i, \tag{3}$$

where P_i^x is the export price of the exporting producers with maximized profit, pricing on the currency of the foreign market—in our case, in Chinese *Renminbi*. When a domestic trading firm prices an export commodity, it is assumed that a markup θ_i, which is an equation of the price elasticity of demand (φ_i) in the foreign market, will be added to the marginal cost (MC_i) of production. e is the exchange rate, defined as units of home currency per unit of foreign currency. When e increases (decrease), it means the depreciation (appreciation) of the domestic currency. As a result, when we take the natural logarithm of both sides of Eq. (3), the basic exchange rate pass-through effects to export price can be written as Eq. (4):

$$\log(EXP_i) = \beta_1 + \beta_2 \log(MC_i) + \beta_3 \log(ER_i) + \varepsilon_t, \tag{4}$$

where ε_t is the error term, and β_1 is the constant; β_2 is the parameter for export producers' marginal cost, which indicates how much the marginal cost of producers will change the export price; and β_3 is the elasticity of the exchange rate pass-through to export price. There are five possible occasions of β_3.

Firstly, if β_3 equals to -1, it reflects the complete exchange rate pass-through. Specifically, if there is 1 percent depreciation (1 percent increase in the exchange rate) in a domestic currency, the export price (priced by the foreign currency) will decrease by 1 percent; the exchange rate fluctuation effect is wholly transmitted to export price. On the contrary, if there is a 1 percent appreciation of the domestic currency (1 percent decrease in the exchange rate), the export price quoted by the foreign currency will increase for the same level (which is also 1 percent), the appreciation of the domestic currency is thoroughly passed through to the export price.

Secondly, if $-1 < \beta_3 < 1$, in this case, the fluctuation of the exchange rate is not 100 percent passed through to the export price. In other words, the exchange rate variation is only partially delivered to the export price in the export market. When the domestic currency depreciates (appreciates) by 1 percent, the export price in the foreign currency will decrease (increase) by less than 1 percent. The closer β_3 is to -1, the larger is the exchange pass-through effect. Meanwhile, the closer β_3 is to 0, the smaller is the exchange pass-through effect.

Thirdly, if β_3 equal to 0, the export price is not affected by the exchange rate fluctuation. Fourthly, $\beta_3 < -1$ denotes excessive exchange rate transfer. A 1 percent depreciation or appreciation will cause more than 1 percent fluctuation in the export price. Fifthly, if $\beta_3 > 0$, it indicates that the exchange rate is reversely passed through to the export price. For example, a 1 percent depreciation in the domestic currency will lead to an increase in the export price.

When the Law of One Price is upheld, the exchange rate pass-through should be complete and symmetric and $\beta_3 = -1$. A 1 percent depreciation in the home currency will decrease the export price in the foreign currency by 1 percent. On the other hand, a 1 percent appreciation in the home currency will lead to the same magnitude of change in the export price but the opposite side of the depreciation. However, in the reality of international trade, the Law of One Price is difficult to realize. Krugman (1986), the pioneer of the Pricing-to-Market theory, argues that most industries face imperfect competition in the real-world economy. Thus, to keep the market share, some industry producers will adjust their marginal profits or cost makeups to absorb the fluctuations of the exchange rate. Consequently, the export prices for the same products to different destinations vary, and the ERPT is usually incomplete, under the assumption of profit maximization.

4 Methodology and Data

4.1 Intra- and Inter-Industry Trade

Following the considerable literature on the evaluation of the degree of intra-industry trade originating from the work of Balassa (1986) and Grubel and Lloyd (1971), we adopt the weighted G-L index to measure the level of intra-industry trade between Vietnam and China from 2001 to 2016.

$$\mathrm{GL}_{it} = 1 - \frac{|X_{it} - M_{it}|}{X_{it} + M_{it}}, \tag{5}$$

where X_{it} indicates the export of commodity i from Vietnam to China, at time *t*; and M_{it} denotes the import of industry *I* from Vietnam to China, at time *t*. The index will range from 0 to 1. The closer it is to 1, the deeper the intra-industry trade level of industry *i* between Vietnam and China. Further, WTO (World Trade Organization) suggested that it is more accurate to calculate the G-L index from the SITC-3-digit level. Therefore, we compute the weighted G-L index based on the HS 6-digit level.

Furthermore, we adopt Abd-el-Rahman's (1991) index to distinguish the inter- and intra-industry trade, as follows:

$$\mathrm{AER}_{it} = \frac{\min\ (X_{it}, M_{it})}{\max\ (X_{it}, M_{it})} > \alpha, \tag{6}$$

where $\alpha = 0.1$ or $\alpha = 0.2$. Following the previous literature, we adopt $\alpha = 0.1$. As a result, we can get the standard to distinguish the inter- and intra-industry trade, as follows:

$$\mathrm{AER}_{it} > 0.1, IIT = 1;\ \ \text{Otherwise}\ \ IIT = 0, \tag{7}$$

where $IIT = 1$ indicates the existence of intra-industry trade; otherwise, inter-industry trade.

4.2 Vertical and Horizontal Intra-Industry Trade

A quality-based methodology was proposed to capacitate the researcher to scrutinize the dynamic import and export patterns of quality-varied goods. The inter-industry trade can be divided into vertical IIT (VIIT) and horizontal IIT (HIIT), based on the quality of goods (Azhar & Elliott, 2008; Greenaway et al., 1995, 1994; Abd-el-Rahman, 1991). The researchers argued that the differentiated quality of goods distinguishes the VIIT from the HIIT. Quality differentiation leads to VIIT, while the variety of customers' tastes results in HIIT.

Following the above-mentioned papers, we adopt the unit price ratio to measure the quality of goods, as follows:

$$\frac{UVX_{it}}{UVM_{it}}, \tag{8}$$

where UVX_{it} is the unit price of Vietnam's export to China of commodity *i* at time *t*; and UVM_{it} is the unit price of Vietnam's import price of the same commodity *i* at time *t*. If the $(UVX_{it})/(UVM_{it}) > 1$, it reveals that Vietnam's commodity *i* has better quality than the same commodity *i* of China.

If the price ratio lies between the interval of $(1/(1+\alpha), 1+\alpha)$, it is recognized as HIIT. The equation is as follows:

$$\frac{1}{1+\alpha} \leq \frac{UVX_{it}}{UVM_{it}} \leq 1+\alpha \tag{9}$$

Similarly, the high-quality vertical intra-industry trade (HVIIT) is defined by the following equation:

$$\frac{UVX_{it}}{UVM_{it}} > 1+\alpha \tag{10}$$

The low-quality vertical intra-industry trade VIIT (LVIIT) is defined by the following equation:

$$\frac{UVX_{it}}{UVM_{it}} < \frac{1}{1+\alpha} \tag{11}$$

The $\alpha = 0.15$ or $\alpha = 0.25$. Meanwhile, we adopt $\alpha = 0.15$ in our work.

4.3 Empirical Model Specification

Based on the discussions of the theoretical framework, the basic empirical model to test the ERPT to Vietnam's import price from China can be written as follows:

$$\mathrm{UVM}_{it} = \alpha_{it} + \beta RER_{it} + \gamma MC_{it} + \delta CP_{it} + \varepsilon_{it}, \tag{12}$$

where UVM_{it} is the import price from China to Vietnam, in VND; and *RER* is the real bilateral exchange between Vietnam and China, which can be calculated as$RER_t = (NER \times CPI_{VNM})/(CPI_{CHN})$. The nominal bilateral exchange rate is written as *NER*. The increase (decrease) of *NER*, which indicates the depreciation (appreciation) of VND/RMB, will result in import prices going down (going up). CPI_{VNM} and CPI_{CHN} are consumer price indexes for Vietnam and China at time t, respectively. MC_{it} is the marginal cost of exporter China, which is proxied by its PPI (Producer Price Index).

We let the lower case represent the nature logarithmic forms of the variables. Equation (12) can be rewritten as follows:

$$\mathrm{uvm}_{it} = \alpha_{it} + \beta_1 rer_{it} + \beta_2 mc_{it} + \beta_3 cp_{it} + \varepsilon_{it} \tag{13}$$

To test the role of the quality of goods on the heterogenous ERPT to Vietnam's import prices from China, an interaction term $rer_{it} \times \mathrm{Quality}_{it}$ is added to Eq. (13), as Eq. (14), where Quality is proxied by the price ratio $(UVX_{it})/(UVM_{it})$.

$$\text{uvm}_{it} = \alpha_{it} + \gamma_1 rer_{it} + \gamma_2 mc_{it} + \gamma_3 cp_{it} + \gamma_4 rer_{it} \times \text{Quality}_{it} + \varepsilon_{it} \quad (14)$$

To test the degree of intra-industry trade on the ERPT into Vietnam's import prices from China, an interaction term $rer_{it} \times GL_{it}$ is added to Eq. (13), as Eq. (15), where GL_{it} denotes the GL index of commodity i at time t.

$$\text{uvm}_{it} = \alpha_{it} + \gamma_1 rer_{it} + \gamma_2 mc_{it} + \gamma_3 cp_{it} + \gamma_4 rer_{it} \times GL_{it} + \varepsilon_{it} \quad (15)$$

To test the HIIT on the ERPT to Vietnam's import prices from China, an interaction term $rer_{it} \times HIIT$ is added to the Eq. (13), as Eq. (16), where $HIIT$ is a dummy variable, which equals to 1 if industry i is recognized at $HIIT$ at time t; otherwise, 0.

$$\text{uvm}_{it} = \alpha + \delta_1 rer_{it} + \delta_2 mc_{it} + \delta_3 cp_{it} + \delta_4 rer_{it} \times HIIT + \varepsilon_{it} \quad (16)$$

To test the LVIIT on the ERPT to Vietnam's import prices from China, an interaction term $rer_{it} \times LVIIT$ is added to Eq. (13), as Eq. (16), where $LVIIT$ is a dummy variable, which equals to 1 if industry i is recognized at $LVIIT$ at time t; otherwise, 0.

$$\text{uvm}_{it} = \alpha + \theta_1 rer_{it} + \theta_2 mc_{it} + \theta_3 cp_{it} + \theta_4 rer_{it} \times LVIIT + \varepsilon_{it} \quad (17)$$

To test the HVIIT on the ERPT to Vietnam's import prices from China, an interaction term $rer_{it} \times HVIIT$ is added to Eq. (13), as Eq. (16), where $HVIIT$ is a dummy variable, which equals to 1 if industry i is recognized at $HVIIT$ at time t; otherwise, 0.

$$\text{uvm}_{it} = \alpha + \varphi_1 rer_{it} + \varphi_2 mc_{it} + \varphi_3 cp_{it} + \varphi_4 rer_{it} \times HVIIT + \varepsilon_{it} \quad (18)$$

4.4 Variable and Data

Variables and data are defined in this part. Table 1 outlines the names and definitions of variables. Table 2 gives the sources of data of variables. uvm_{it} is the unit price of import price from China to Vietnam. rer_{it} is the bilateral real effective exchange rate. mc_{it} denotes the marginal cost of exporters, which is proxied by China's PPI. cp_{it} represent the competitors' price in Vietnam, proxied by Vietnam's PPI. Quality_{it} is the price ratio, which is used to measure Vietnam's quality of goods. GL_{it} is the GL index measuring the degree of intra-industry trade between Vietnam and China. *HIIT*, *HVIIT*, and *LVIIT* are dummy variables.

Table 1 Variable and data

Variable	Description
uvm_{it}	Unit Value of import, which is calculated by dividing the trade value by the quantity
rer_{it}	Real bilateral exchange rate between Vietnam and China
mc_{it}	The marginal cost is proxied by the PPI (Producer Price Index) of China
cp_{it}	The domestic competitor's price is proxied by the PPI of Vietnam
$\mathrm{Quality}_{it}$	The price ratio is calculated by Vietnam's export unit price over import unit price
$\mathrm{GL}_{\mathrm{it}}$	GL index of commodity i at time t
HIIT	Dummy variable of HIIT
HVIIT	Dummy variable of HVIIT
LVIIT	Dummy variable of LVIIT

Table 2 Data

Variable	Period	Source
uvm_{it}	2001~2016	China's General Administration of Customs
rer_{it}	2001~2016	IMF, World Bank
PPI_CHN	2001~2016	Statistical Bureau of China
PPI_VNM	2001~2016	General Statistics Office of Vietnam
$\mathrm{Quality}_{it}$	2001~2016	Authors' own calculation based on the data from China's General Administration of Customs
$\mathrm{GL}_{\mathrm{it}}$	2001~2016	
HIIT	2001~2016	
HVIIT	2001~2016	
LVIIT	2001~2016	

The span of the data is from 2001 to 2016. Trade data is at a 6-digit HS level, allowing us to have a sample of around 40,000 observations. All data is abstracted from recognized databases.

5 Estimation Results

This section reports the qualitative and quantitative results based on the above methodologies, with corresponding discussions.

5.1 GL index of Vietnam Vis-à-vis China

Figure 1 The Weighted GL Index of Vietnam Vis-à-vis China, 2001~2016 portrays the GL index of Vietnam vis-à-vis China from 2001 to 2016. WTO suggested that it is more accurate to measure the degree of intra-industry trade from the 3-digit SITC level, at least. If the data is aggregated, the degree of intra-industry trade will be overestimated. Therefore, we compute the GL index based on the HS 6-digit level

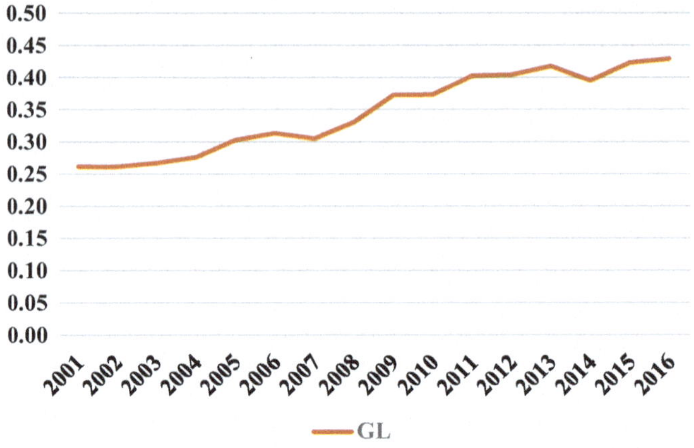

Fig. 1 The Weighted GL Index of Vietnam Vis-à-vis China, 2001~2016 (Note: Author's calculation based on the HS 6-digit level data from China's General Administration of Customs)

data and aggregate it to the country level by the weight of the trade volume of each commodity.

It is clear in Fig. 1. The Weighted GL Index of Vietnam Vis-à-vis China, 2001~2016 that the GL index of Vietnam vis-à-vis China witnessed an increasing trend from 2001 to 2016, which reveals that the degree of intra-industry between these two economies is deepening.

5.2 Vietnam's Goods Quality

To shed light on the dynamic patterns of Vietnam's quality of goods, we conduct the Kernel density non-parameter estimations on Vietnam's total commodities and 12 industries. For comparison, we plot the density curves of 2001~2003 and 2013~2016, respectively. Kernel density estimation is a non-parametric statistical methodology to estimate the probability density function of a variable.

For convenience, we take the nature logarithm of the price ratio as follows. If the price ratio is bigger than 0, it indicates that the price of Vietnam's commodity i is bigger than the import price from China of the same commodity. As a result, Vietnam's commodity i is of higher quality than China, and vice versa.

$$\ln\left(\frac{UVX_{it}}{UVM_{it}}\right) > 0 \quad \text{or} \quad \ln\left(\frac{UVX_{it}}{UVM_{it}}\right) < 0 \tag{19}$$

As shown in Fig. 2, the Kernel density curves of two subsamples are distributed on the left-hand side of 0. It reveals that most of Vietnam's trading commodities have lower quality than China. By comparing the two subsamples, the curve of

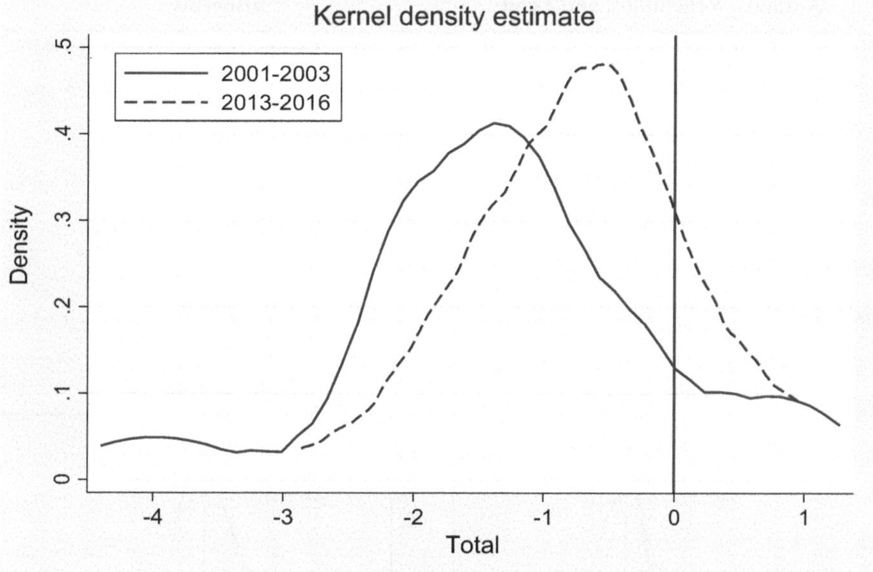

Fig. 2 The density estimation for all commodities (Note: Author's estimation based on the HS 6-digit level data from WITS)

2013~2016 moves closer than 0 than 2001~2013. This finding denotes that the quality of Vietnam's trading commodity is improving in relation to China.

Figure 3 shows the results of the kernel density estimations of the 12 main industries of Vietnam. The curves of 8 industries are distributed on the left-hand side of 0. These industries are hides and skins, textiles and clothing, footwear, stones and glass, metals, machinery and electronics, and transportation. This finding indicates that for these industries, Vietnam's export prices to China are smaller than the same commodities that China exports to Vietnam. The quality of goods of these industries of Vietnam is relatively lower than China's.

On the contrary, the quality of goods of Vietnam's export to China in animals, vegetables and food, minerals, chemicals, plastic or rubber, and wood is relatively higher than China's export to Vietnam (Fig. 4).

5.3 *The Composition of Vietnam's Intra-Industry Trade Vis-À-Vis China*

Table 3 reports the composition of Vietnam's intra-industry trade vis-à-vis China from 2001 to 2016. The percentage of the intra-industry trade over Vietnam's total trade with China is more than 50 percent, except for 2006~2010. This finding reveals that intra-industry trade, which is mainly vertically distributed, plays a significant

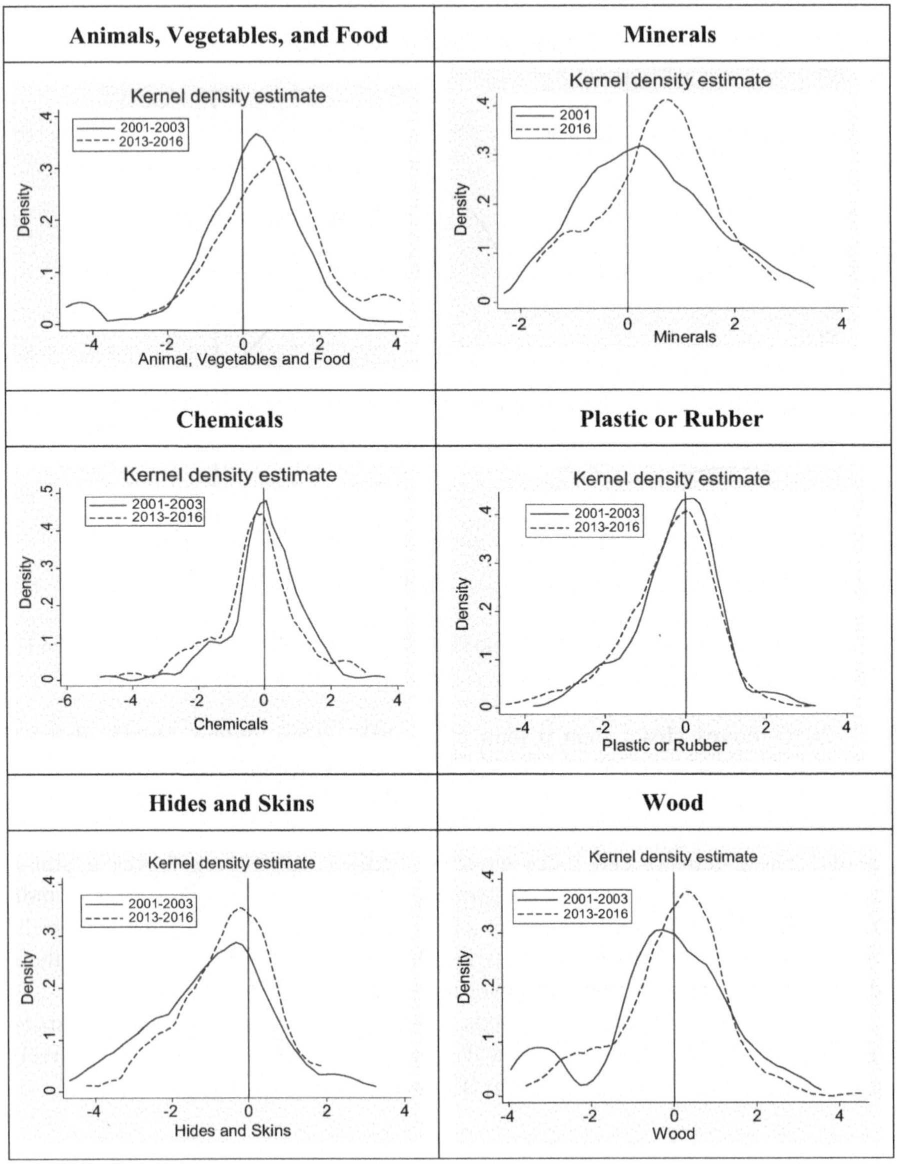

Fig. 3 The density estimation, at an industry level (Note: Author's estimation based on HS 6-digit level data from WITS)

role in the Vietnam–China trade. The vertical intra-industry trade accounts for more than 70 percent of the intra-industry trade from 2001 to 2016. However, the percentage of the high-quality vertical intra-industry trade is relatively low, ranging from 2 percent to 20 percent of the VIIT from 2001 to 2016.

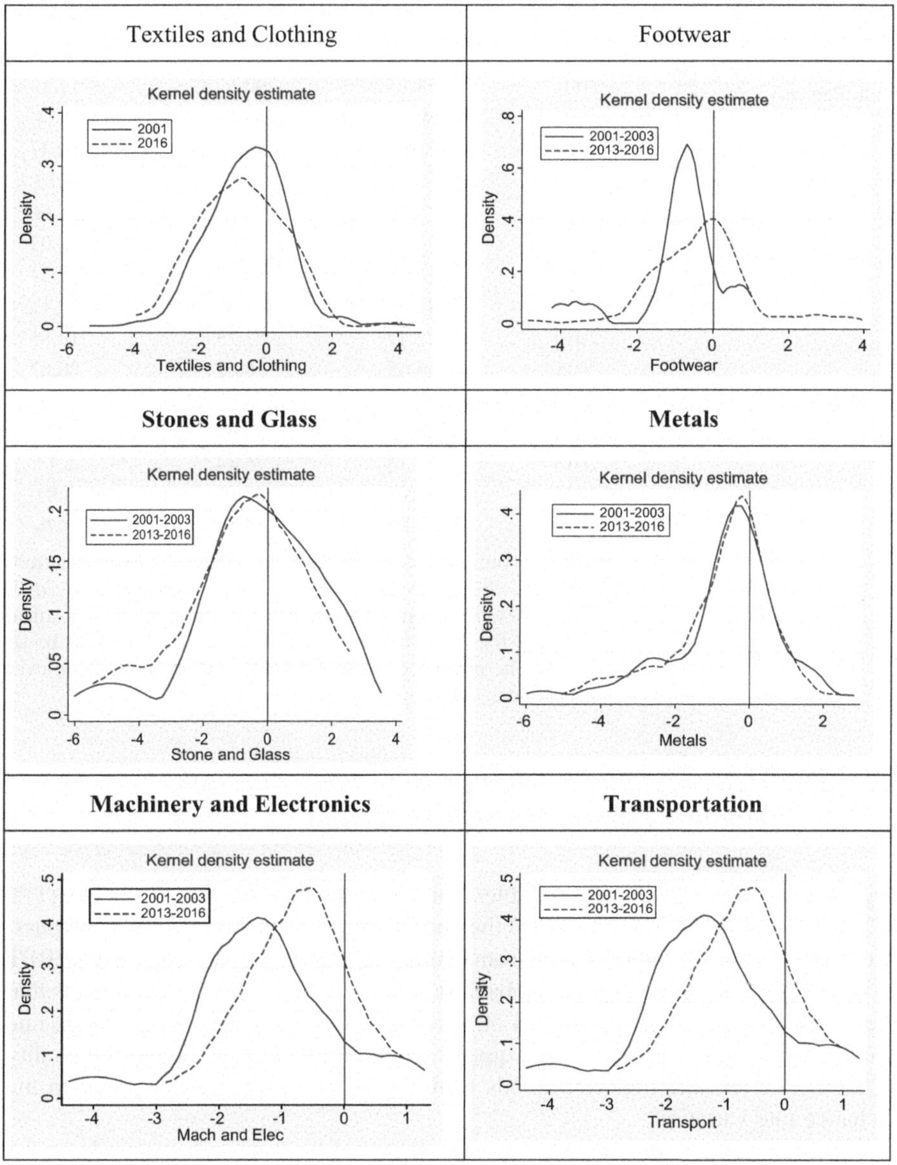

Fig. 4 The density estimation, at an industry level (Note: Author's estimation based on HS 6-digit level data from WITS)

In summary, even the intra-industry trade has become a major form between the trade relations of Vietnam and China. A big proportion of Vietnam's export to China is relatively lower in quality than China's export to Vietnam. However, the gap in the quality between the goods of Vietnam and China has shrunk from 2001 to 2016.

Table 3 The composition of Vietnam's intra-industry trade vis-à-vis China, 2001~2016 (Unit: Percent)

Year	IIT%	VIIT%	HVIIT%
2001	57.59	90.16	5.67
2002	58.14	90.69	11.13
2003	69.06	81.73	3.34
2004	71.77	79.41	10.47
2005	59.83	75.86	8.13
2006	37.06	63.69	21.66
2007	37.58	77.48	18.07
2008	42.85	87.07	12.37
2009	21.53	84.64	12.11
2010	42.49	83.73	18.85
2011	56.65	76.87	20.67
2012	56.72	95.77	7.39
2013	60.09	72.04	6.28
2014	51.74	76.44	5.17
2015	58.42	73.57	4.91
2016	59.84	74.10	9.76

Notes: 1. Authors' calculation based on HS 6-digit level data from WITS; 2. IIT: The percentage of intra-industry trade over Vietnam's total export to China; VIIT: The percentage of vertical intra-industry trade over Vietnam's total intra-industry trade; HVIIT: The percentage of high-quality intra-industry trade over vertical intra-industry trade

5.4 The Heterogenous Exchange Rate Pass-Through to Vietnam's Import Prices from China

Regression results are reported in Tables 4 and 5, based on Eqs. (14), (15), (16), (17), and (18). Equation (14) is used to test the quality of goods on the exchange rate pass-through to Vietnam's import prices from China. Generally, we can see that the ERPT is incomplete but relatively high in absolute value (−0.55). This finding reveals that Vietnam's importers take more than 50 percent of the risk when the exchange rate fluctuates. The positive value of the quality index reveals that the higher the quality of goods, the less the imported goods from China to Vietnam are exposed to the exchange rate variation.

Equation (15) is implemented to test the degree of the intra-industry trade on the ERPT to Vietnam's import prices from China. The positive coefficient (0.15) is statistically significant at a 5 percent level. This finding reveals that the tendency of the intra-industry trade between Vietnam and China decreases the ERPT to Vietnam's import prices from China. It is consistent with the previous literature that the production fragmentation and the existence of intra-industry trade affect the degree of ERPT to a country's trading prices. As Athukorala and Menon (1994) discussed, the industries with a higher degree intra-industry level in Japan had a lower degree of ERPT because the correlative independence of industries decreases

Table 4 The heterogenous exchange rate pass-through to Vietnam's import prices from China, 2001~2016

Equation	Eq. (14) uvm_{it}	Eq. (15) uvm_{it}	Eq. (16) uvm_{it}
rer_{it}	-0.55^{**}	-0.56^{*}	-0.47^{***}
	(3.24)	(−2.43)	(−5.14)
cp_{it}	3.24	8.25^{*}	7.98
	(1.69)	(1.74)	(1.69)
mc_{it}	0.821^{*}	1.33^{***}	1.23^{**}
	(2.12)	(3.41)	(3.17)
$rer_{it} \times \text{Quality}_{it}$	0.03^{***}		
	(15.48)		
$rer_{it} \times \text{GL}_{it}$		0.15^{**}	
		(2.62)	
$rer_{it} \times HIIT$			−3.87
			(−0.97)
$rer_{it} \times HVIIT$			
$rer_{it} \times LVIIT$			
_cons	−8.15	-1.66^{**}	-3.30^{***}
	(−0.73)	(−2.70)	(−3.53)
Model	Fixed	Fixed	Fixed
R^2-Adj	0.10	0.08	0.11
F-stats	15.01	14.99	13.29
N	42557	42557	42557

Notes: 1. t statistics are in the parentheses, $^{*}p < 0.05$, $^{**}p < 0.01$, $^{***}p < 0.001$; 2. Authors' own estimations

the variation of trading prices in response to the exchange rate. The same can be explained in the case of Vietnam.

Equation (16) reveals that the horizontal intra-industry does not significantly affect the ERPT to Vietnam's import prices. The underlying reason can be that the proportion of the horizontal intra-industry trade between Vietnam and China is small.

The results of Eq. (17) and (18) proved that the ERPT is heterogeneous across the vertically differentiated goods imported from China to Vietnam. It further supports that the quality of goods plays a significant role in the ERPT to Vietnam's import prices from China. The negative coefficient (−0.91) of the dummy variable of LVIIT reveals that the LVIIT significantly increases the ERPT of Vietnam's imports from China. On the contrary, the HVIIT (0.14) significantly decreases the ERPT of Vietnam's imports from China. In other words, the import prices of LVIIT of Vietnam from China are at greater risks of exchange rate fluctuations, while the import prices of HVIIT of Vietnam from China are more stable in response to the exchange rate.

In summary, the level of intra-industry trade is a significant factor that can affect the ERPT to Vietnam's import prices from China. The increase of the degree of intra-industry trade reduces the level of ERPT to Vietnam's import prices from China, in general.

Table 5 The heterogenous exchange rate pass-through to Vietnam's import prices from China, 2001~2016

Equation	Eq. (17)	Eq. (18)
	uvm_{it}	uvm_{it}
rer_{it}	−0.36***	−0.67***
	(−5.00)	(−4.98)
cp_{it}	7.75	7.84
	(1.64)	(1.66)
mc_{it}	1.31***	1.32***
	(3.35)	(3.37)
$rer_{it} \times Quality_{it}$		
$rer_{it} \times GL_{it}$		
$rer_{it} \times HIIT$		
$rer_{it} \times HVIIT$		0.14**
		(−2.61)
$rer_{it} \times LVIIT$	−0.91**	
	(−2.64)	
_cons	−4.78***	−4.66***
	(−3.77)	(−3.69)
Model	Fixed	Fixed
R^2 Adjusted	0.09	0.10
F-stats	16.64	15.79
N	42557	42557

Notes: 1. t statistics are in the parentheses, $^{*}p < 0.05$, $^{**}p < 0.01$, $^{***}p < 0.001$; 2. Authors' own estimations

Furthermore, the ERPT effects are heterogeneous across commodities based on quality in the vertically differentiated industries. The degree of ERPT of commodities in which Vietnam has a lower position in quality than China is bigger. The underlying explanation is as follows. If Vietnam has a lower quality position when importing a commodity from China, the corresponding commodity imported from China is of higher quality and has a smaller price elasticity of demand in Vietnam. Chinese exporters can pass most proportions of risk to Vietnam and maintain their profit markup. Therefore, the level of ERPT to the import prices of this commodity from China to Vietnam is larger when Vietnam's commodity is in the lower quality position in relation to China. Lastly, no impact of the HIIT on the ERPT into Vietnam's import prices from China is detected.

The F-statistics reveals that all models are valid, at a 5 percent significant level. Based on the Hausman test, fixed effect models are selected for all estimations. The adjusted R square and the number of observations are also provided to support the effectiveness of the models.

6 Conclusion

Utilizing the HS 6-digit level data from 2001 to 2016, we calculate the GL index between Vietnam and China. Moreover, we distinguish the trade between Vietnam and China into intra- and inter-industry trades. Lastly, we decompose the intra-industry trade based on quality into horizontal intra-industry trade, high-quality vertical intra-industry trade, and low-quality vertical intra-industry trade. For the first time in the case of Vietnam, we incorporate all these factors into our empirical models to estimate the heterogeneous exchange rate pass-through to Vietnam's import prices from China.

The main findings are as follows. Based on the results of the weighted GL index, the degree of intra-industry trade between Vietnam and China has been increasing from 2001 to 2016. The vertical intra-industry trade accounts for more than 80 percent of the intra-industry trade between Vietnam and China. However, the percentage of high-quality vertical intra-industry trade is still quite low in the Vietnam–China trade. According to the Kernel density estimations, the quality of goods of Vietnam's export to China is generally lower than China's export to Vietnam.

According to the results of the estimated equations, we found out that the deepening of intra-industry trade between Vietnam and China weakens the impact of the exchange rate on Vietnam's import prices from China. Secondly, the quality of goods plays a significant role in the ERPT to Vietnam's import prices from China. Specifically, the lower quality commodities of Vietnam in relation to China have higher ERPT effects on the import prices than the higher quality commodities. Thirdly, we have not detected any impact of the horizontal intra-industry trade on the ERPT.

Based on our findings, the policy implications are proposed as follows. At the macro level, the exchange rate policy is still a crucial tool to adjust Vietnam's import prices from China. However, deepening the intra-industry trade between the two countries might make the exchange rate policy less effective. The heterogeneous ERPT based on quality also suggests that implementing the exchange rate policy alone might lead to the deterioration of the trade imbalance of some industries.

Therefore, more specific policies should be considered. For example, improving the quality of goods can be one practical tool, especially considering that we found that Vietnam's commodities are of lower quality in the industries of hides and skins, textiles and clothing, footwear, stones and glass, metals, machinery and electronics, and transportation equipment, compared to China. Therefore, Vietnam should strive to accelerate product upgrades and improve the product quality of these industries to promote the positions of enterprises in international trade and strengthen the pricing power in the Chinese market.

Lastly, from the perspective of import enterprises of Vietnam, our work is vital in showing them their positions in the Vietnam–China trade, in regard to the product quality, as well as how much degree of the exchange rate will affect their trading prices. This information can instruct Vietnamese trading enterprises to make appropriate pricing strategies when trading with Chinese companies.

References

Abd-el-Rahman, K. (1991). Firms' competitive and national comparative advantages as joint determinants of trade composition. *Review of World Economics, 127*(1), 83–97.

Adolfson, M. (2001). Export Price responses to exogenous exchange rate movements. *Economics Letters, 71*(1), 91–96.

Antoniades, A., & Zaniboni, N. (2016). Exchange rate pass-through into retail prices. *International Economic Review, 5*(74), 1425–1447.

Aron, J., Farrell, G., Muellbauer, J., & Sinclair, P. (2014). Exchange rate pass-through to import prices, and monetary policy in South Africa. *Journal of Development Studies, 50*(1), 144–164.

Athukorala, P., & Menon, J. (1994). Pricing to market behavior and exchange rate pass-through in Japanese exports. *The Economic Journal, 104*(423), 271–281.

Aturupane, C., Djankov, S., & Hoekman, B. (1999). Horizontal and vertical intra-industry trade between Eastern Europe and the European Union. *Weltwirtschaftliches Archiv, 135*(1), 62–81.

Auer, R. A., Chaney, T., & Sauré, P. (2018). Quality pricing-to-market. *Journal of International Economics, 110*, 87–102.

Azhar, A. K., & Elliott, R. J. (2008). On the measurement of changes in product quality in marginal intra-industry trade. *Review of World Economics, 144*(2), 225–247.

Bacchetta, P., & Van, W. E. (2005). A theory of the currency denomination of international trade. *Journal of International Economics, 67*(2), 295–319.

Balassa, B. (1986). The determinants of intra-industry specialization in United States trade. *Oxford Economic Papers, 38*(2), 220–233.

Bernini, M., & Tomasi, C. (2015). Exchange rate pass-through and product heterogeneity: Does quality matter on the import side? *European Economic Review, 77*, 117–138.

Branson, W. H. (1972). The trade effects of the 1971 currency realignments. *Brookings Papers on Economic Activity, 1972*(1), 15–69.

Campa Fernández, J. M., González Mínguez, J. M., & Sebastia-Barriel, M. (2006). *Non-linear adjustment of import prices in the European Union*. Documentos de trabajo/Banco de España, 0635.

Chen, N., & Juvenal, L. (2016). Quality, trade, and exchange rate passthrough. *Journal of International Economics, 100*, 61–80.

Dornbush, R. (1987). Exchange rate and prices. *The American Economic Review, 77*, 93–106.

Dwyer, J., & Lam, R. (1994). *Explaining import price inflation: A recent history of second stage pass-through*. Research Discussion Paper 9407, Reserve Bank of Australia.

Ghosh, A., & Rajan, R. S. (2007). *A selective survey of exchange rate pass-through in Asia: What does the literature tell us?* Available at SSRN 984063.

Goldhammer, B., Polina, A., & Christian, B. (2013). *Upstream carbon dioxide assessment at the product level. Efficiency and logistics* (Vol. 2013, pp. 163–174). Springer.

Greenaway, D., Hine, R., & Milner, C. (1994). Country-specific factors and the pattern of horizontal and vertical intra-industry trade in the UK. *Weltwirtschaftliches Archive, 130*(1), 77–100.

Greenaway, D., Hine, R., & Milner, C. (1995). Vertical and horizontal intra-industry trade: A cross-industry analysis for the United Kingdom. *The Economic Journal, 105*(433), 1505–1518.

Grubel, H. G., & Lloyd, P. J. (1971). The empirical measurement of intra-industry trade. *Economic Record, 47*(4), 494–517.

Han, J., & Shen, Y. (2016). Exchange rate pass-through to China's export price: A product-level investigation. *China & World Economy, 24*(2), 48–67.

Hong, P., & Zhang, F. (2016). Exchange rate pass-through into China's import prices: An empirical analysis based on ARDL model. *Open Journal of Social Sciences, 4*(4), 13–22.

Kim, W. J. (2007). Exchange rate pass-through on disaggregated Korean export prices: A structural VAR approach. *The Journal of the Korean Economy, 8*(2), 357–376.

Knetter, M. M. (1989). Price discrimination by U.S. and German exporters. *The American Economic Review, 79*(1), 198–210.

Krugman, P. (1991). Increasing returns and economic geography. *Journal of Political Economy, 99* (3), 483–499.

Krugman, P. R. (1986). *Pricing to market when the exchange rate changes.* NBER Working Paper Series.

Lutz, M. G., & Reilly, B. (1997). Incomplete exchange rate pass-through in the European Car Market: Evidence from hedonic price regressions. Discussion Paper 9715, Department of Economics, University of St. Gallen.

Marston, R. C. (1990). Pricing to market in Japanese manufacturing. *Journal of International Economics, 29*(3–4), 217–236.

Menon, J. (1996). *Exchange rates and prices: The case of Australian manufactured imports* (Lecture Notes in Economics and Management Systems, 433). Springer.

Nguyen, T., Tran, T., Tran, M., Hoang, V., Hoang, V., Nguyen, T., Hoang, X., Phan, H., Tran, K., & Tran, V. (2019). Impact efficiency of trade agreements on Vietnam's rice export. *Management Science Letters, 10*(5), 1085–1094.

Pollard, P. S., & Coughlin, C. C. (2004). *Size matters: Asymmetric exchange rate pass-through at the industry level.* University of Nottingham Research Paper, (2004/13).

Wickremasinghe, G. B., & Silvapull, P. (2004). Exchange rate pass-through to manufactured import prices: The case of Japan. International Trade 0406006, University Library of Munich. https://econwpa.ub.uni-muenchen.de/econ-wp/it/papers/0406/0406006.pdf

The manufacturer's authorised representative in the EU is Springer Nature Customer Service Centre GmbH, Europaplatz 3, 69115 Heidelberg, Germany. If you have any concerns regarding our products, please contact ProductSafety@springernature.com

Printed and bound by CPI Group (UK) Ltd, Croydon, CR0 4YY

30/09/2026

02225493-0002